Adulterous Alliances

Adulterous Alliances

Home, State, and History in
Early Modern European
Drama and Painting

Richard Helgerson

THE UNIVERSITY OF CHICAGO PRESS
Chicago and London

RICHARD HELGERSON is professor of English at the University of California, Santa Barbara. His last book, *Forms of Nationhood,* won the British Council Prize in the Humanities and the James Russell Lowell Prize of the Modern Language Association.

The University of Chicago Press, Chicago 60637
The University of Chicago Press, Ltd., London
© 2000 by The University of Chicago
All rights reserved. Published 2000
Printed in the United States of America
09 08 07 06 05 04 03 02 01 00   1 2 3 4 5
ISBN: 0-226-32624-1 (cloth)

Library of Congress Cataloging-in-Publication Data

Helgerson, Richard.
    Adulterous alliances : home, state, and history in early modern European drama and painting / Richard Helgerson.
        p. cm.
    Includes bibliographical references and index.
    ISBN 0-226-32624-1 (cloth : alk. paper)
    1. Middle class in art. 2. Working class in art. 3. Home in art. 4. Adultery in art. 5. Painting, Modern—17th–18th centuries—Netherlands.   I. Title.

NX650.M532 H45 2000
700'.455—dc21

                                                      00-023376

To the memory of my teachers
Don Cameron Allen
and
Jackson I. Cope

⟶⇻ CONTENTS ⇺⟵

"Freedom of thought, gravity, electricity, toleration, inoculation, quinine, the *Encyclopédie,* and *les drames.*"[1] These are the "follies" of his age the benighted Bartholo singles out for attack in Beaumarchais's *Barbier de Seville.* That *les drames*—the bourgeois domestic dramas that were then popular in theaters all over Europe—should find a place here is, if initially startling, remarkably apt. After all, Denis Diderot, the most prominent advocate of such drama, was also the chief compiler of the *Encyclopédie* and an Enlightenment champion of the other cultural and scientific departures that so bothered conservatives like Bartholo. Nor did Diderot's unsettling causes stop with the items on Bartholo's list. In his *Salons,* he also gave ardent support to the new genre painting that was just beginning to rival Italianate history painting in France. The bourgeois and domestic emphasis Diderot and many of his contemporaries favored in drama and painting was central to the great shift in cultural values Bartholo opposes, a shift that led eventually to the nineteenth-century European and American cult of domesticity and that, for the last two centuries, has continued to shape paintings, plays, novels, and a whole way of life.

This book concerns the prehistory of that movement. It began for me in the theater, at a performance of the anonymous *Arden of Faversham,* a play I knew then only by name. Almost from the first words, I was struck by a richness of social detail, a level of everyday particularity, wholly unlike what I was used to in other Elizabethan writing. Here in a story of adultery and murder—a story based, as I later discovered, on events that happened in a small town not all that far from the London theater where I was seeing them reenacted—the lives of ordinary people were presented with an immediacy foreign to both the elevation of tragedy and the ridicule of comedy, an immediacy that made those other forms themselves feel foreign, as indeed they were. Clearly, I had to learn more. Where had such a play come from? What could its extraordinary realism have meant in the England of 1591?

My initial impulse was to look for answers in the events themselves. I was just beginning another book when I first saw *Arden*, so I could not act on that impulse immediately. But the impulse kept at me and, as soon as I was free, I followed it to Faversham, to Arden's house, to the mayor's office and the town's Wardmote Book, to the county record office, to the library of Canterbury Cathedral, to the manuscript room of the British Library, and to the pages of Holinshed's *Chronicles*. What was needed, I thought, was a microhistory of Arden's murder and its reverberations through the remainder of the sixteenth century. But two things happened to change my plans. In the years I had spent working on that unrelated project, others, inspired by the historical turn literary criticism had taken in the 1980s and by a new feminist attention to marriage and the home, had found in *Arden of Faversham* and the Arden story a rich resource, and at least one of them, Lena Cowen Orlin, had wonderfully accomplished (though I did not yet know it when I made my trip to Faversham) the microhistory I only dreamed of writing.[2] And at the same time, my own interests had been moving in a new direction: out from *Arden* to the broader representational field to which it belonged and which it helped open.

What this broader field meant was at first little more than English domestic drama, a genre that had remained unnamed and perhaps unrecognized in Elizabethan and Jacobean England but that had been defined retrospectively by such nineteenth- and earlier twentieth-century scholars as John Payne Collier, Arthur Eustace Morgan, Henry H. Adams, and Andrew Clark, a genre that was also attracting the attention of more recent *Arden* enthusiasts like Orlin, Frances E. Dolan, Viviana Comensoli, and Frank Whigham.[3] But my thoughts soon began wandering outside the world of drama and beyond the English Channel. If what interested me was the realistic depiction of everyday domestic life, where better to look than at Dutch genre painting of the mid-seventeenth century, the painting of Gerard ter Borch, Johannes Vermeer, Pieter de Hooch, and their contemporaries? And from there, guided by the unexpected stereo-scopic image that emerged when I looked simultaneously at English do-mestic drama and Dutch genre painting, I moved back to England to pick up a couple of plays that do not usually figure in discussions of domestic drama, Thomas Heywood's two-part *Edward IV* and Shakespeare's *Merry Wives of Windsor*, then to early seventeenth-century Spain for a small col-lection of peasant dramas by Lope de Vega and Calderón de la Barca, then to mid-seventeenth-century France for a single play by Molière, his *Tartuffe*, and finally to late eighteenth-century France and those bour-geois dramas Beaumarchais and Diderot both wrote and Bartholo classed among the most dangerously upsetting innovations of his time.

So from a microhistory focused on a single event in a small provincial town and the play that staged it, I have ended with an episodic macrohis-tory that stretches over two centuries, four countries, and a large number of plays and paintings. My excuse for assembling such a heterogeneous set of materials is that together they reveal patterns that would otherwise be difficult to see, patterns that help in the understanding of each indi-vidual element. English domestic drama, Dutch genre painting, Spanish peasant drama, and Molière's one striking departure from his usual comic mode each emerged with no awareness of any of the others. Yet they share far more than one might suppose, as the eighteenth-century French discovered when they drew on all four in creating the bourgeois drama they thought no less revolutionary than the discovery of gravity or the campaign for freedom of thought.

Most obvious among these shared features is the serious attention all four give the nonaristocratic home and family. Where other, more familiar literary forms—fabliau, farce, commedia dell'arte, novella, and neoclassi-cal comedy—made the nonaristocratic home a scene of extravagant folly meant to provoke mirth, these new forms, whether of drama or painting, take the home seriously, invite viewers to identify with it and its inhabi-tants rather than laugh at them. Even *The Merry Wives of Windsor*, which remains firmly in the realm of farce and comic intrigue, plays against ex-pectation, and the others reverse it altogether. That something of this sort should have happened independently in four different countries at about the same time is itself worth remarking. But the similarities go further. Not only do these plays and paintings register a new interest in the non-aristocratic home. They also put that home into a significant and signi-fying narrative relation with the monarchic or potentially monarchic state. Again and again the home and the family on which it is based are disrupted by a sexually predatory intruder, an intruder who comes most often from the sphere of the state: a soldier, a courtier, a leading aristocrat, or even the king himself. And, almost as often, the state enters as a *deus ex machina* to resolve the problem it or its agents have themselves created. But whether disrupter or orderer (or both), the state is representationally and affectively outshone by the bourgeois or peasant home through which the state expresses its power. In these new genres, the nonaristocratic home thus emerges not simply as an adjunct of state power but as an alternative to it, a space that by the late eighteenth century would be making its own claim to both representational and political value as the affective base for a new revolutionary order.

My title, *Adulterous Alliances*, comes from the sexual predation that marks so many of these works. If in them the nonaristocratic home intersects with the state and if that intersection puts stories of the home in competition with the state and its history, the place of intersection is most often a woman's body. As the home is made to represent a whole range of values the state might either menace or uphold, so women's bodies are made to represent the home and its peculiar vulnerability. Why this association? Simple metonymy has much to do with it. Women represent the home because they were supposed to belong in it. Whatever the claims of early modern patriarchy, the domestic sphere is to a large degree theirs. But the association has a further dimension. In his famous celebration of unfallen sexuality, John Milton hails "wedded love" not only as the "true source / Of human offspring" but also as the "sole propriety / In Paradise of all things common else."[4] Wedded love is the basis and type of all property—Milton's "propriety"—and its violation is the violation of all property, including a man's ownership of his own identity. The story Milton tells, the story of the highly eroticized temptation of all mankind through the first woman, an episode in the no less highly politicized struggle for dominion between Satan and God, is itself presented as a domestic drama. For Milton, the first home was the first arena of sexual politics.

Western literature is full of such stories. Among those I will have occasion to mention in the course of this book are the biblical account of David and Bathsheba, the Roman legend of the rape of Lucretia, and, in a very different vein, the fabliau tales of Geoffrey Chaucer's Miller and Reeve. Even the story of Christ's incarnation, from which, in the words of Edward Said, "Western realistic literature as we know it emerges," can be imagined—as it is in a number of medieval mystery plays—as a domestic drama concerning the possession of a woman's body.[5] Old Joseph thinks his young wife has made him a cuckold. And if one wished to look in the other direction, beyond the eighteenth century, additional examples would not be hard to find. Sir Walter Scott's *Rob Roy*, Alessandro Manzoni's *Promessi sposi*, Pedro Antonio de Alarcón's *Sombrero de tres picos*, and (to shift from fiction to film) Mel Gibson's *Braveheart* were among those I noticed as I was working on this book. *Braveheart*, in particular, revives the mythical *droit du seigneur* adumbrated in Lope's peasant dramas and featured in Beaumarchais's *Mariage de Figaro*. But all four combine, in a way that closely recalls many early modern paintings and plays, sexual predation, difference of status between the predator and the object of his sexual attention, idealization of the lower-ranked home, and an active interpretive engagement with history. Stories like these explain how things came to be as they are or justify doing what is needed to change them. But the crucial point here is that, in the symbolic economy of such storytelling, rivalries between men are repeatedly made to center on a woman, with the result that women take on an importance the culture would otherwise have denied them. Nor is this importance only symbolic. Once made part of a narrative sequence, women act or resist in ways that have profound implications for the men who desire or possess them. What they do and what they suffer matters. In this, Eve and Mary, Bathsheba, Lucretia, and Chaucer's Alisoun lead the way for Alice Arden, Heywood's Jane Shore, Shakespeare's merry wives, Lope's Casilda and Laurencia, Calderón's Isabel, Molière's Elmire, and the many women featured in Dutch genre painting—as well as for the heroines of Scott, Manzoni, Alarcón, and Gibson. And though the eighteenth-century French would try to reverse this tendency and reclaim domesticity for men, in this region male power and possession depend inevitably on women.

But while this much broader range of stories, stretching from Creation to the day before yesterday, provides one context for understanding early modern domestic drama and painting, it does not explain the historical specificity of those works. Why then? And why there? Why were stories of the nonaristocratic home and its sexual disruption, stories that regard the home with an unaccustomed seriousness and sympathy, so frequently told at just this time and in just these places? An obvious answer would be the increasing influence among consumers of drama and painting of people like those portrayed: town-dwellers of middling status and significant means.[6] But this sociological explanation, appealing as it is, cannot be made to fit a good part of the evidence. Certainly all these works were the product of newly established or newly invigorated commercial sites for cultural production. In this, the greatly enlarged market for paintings in the Netherlands, a phenomenon that drew the startled attention of visitors from all over Europe, has its counterpart in the newly founded public theaters and newly organized acting companies in England, Spain, and France. Without these new sites neither the plays nor the paintings would exist. But the fit I was expecting is not to be found—at least not consistently. The new commercial patrons and the stories they paid to see only sporadically mirror one another. While it seems clear that a play like Heywood's *Edward IV* did respond in a very direct way to the interests of spectators who shared roughly the status of those whose home is disrupted in the play, nothing of that sort can explain the peasant dramas of seventeenth-century Spain. Peasants, even the rich peasants who figure most prominently in the work of Lope and Calderón, never had a large place in the theaters for which those dramatists wrote. Whatever audience demand helped produce Spanish peasant drama, it did not come from peasants themselves. And the evidence in the Netherlands and France is, at best, mixed. In Dutch genre painting, many of the images are ambiguous enough for a burgher purchaser to deny likeness, while in the French bourgeois drama of the eighteenth century, the very meaning of *bourgeois* loses most of its social specificity, to take on identification with enlightened and virtuous humanity at large.

If then this new theatrical and artistic attention to the nonaristocratic home cannot be broadly or consistently explained as simply another chapter in that well-known saga, the rise of the middle class, how can it be explained? The narrative intersection of home and state points to a more satisfying answer, one that speaks to both causality and meaning. Domestic drama and domestic painting emerged as a by-product of early modern state formation and defined themselves by their difference from the newly invented or newly revived genres of state: history painting, tragedy, historical drama, and history itself. Where those stately forms focus on the glory and the pathos of absolute power, these more homely ones give their attention to the subjects of such power. They reflect on the pressures monarchic consolidation put on older corporate structures, particularly on the chartered towns in which the homes the works represent are most often located. The private nonaristocratic home, as a focus for serious artistic attention, was thus brought into being not so much for itself as in response to a new organization of public power. Not merely an expression of the rise of the middle class—though certainly some sense of the increasing social, economic, and political significance of people of middling status does figure in all the episodes I consider—the new domestic genres register a still more broadly shared fear of subjugation and dispossession. And this is as much the case in republican Holland, recently successful in its eighty-year war against its Spanish overlord and concerned that a prince of Orange might claim the sovereignty the Spaniard had yielded, as in Tudor England, Habsburg Spain, or Bourbon France, where by the eighteenth century corporate nostalgia had given way to a more universalist conception of human rights. But whether the issue is municipal rights or the rights of man, the nonaristocratic home is made to figure as the privileged site of its representation, while the monarchic state is given a more dubious role as the external other from which, whether cooperatively or antagonistically, those rights must be won.

Thinking along these lines, we should not be surprised that each of the various moments at which these domestic forms first appeared has been retrospectively regarded as the "golden age" of its particular national culture. What, after all, makes a golden age golden? Greatness of accomplishment is of course essential. But scarcely less essential is a certain founding relation to the nation's idea of itself. These were the moments—the English Age of Elizabeth, the Dutch *Gouden Eeuw*, the Spanish *Siglo de Oro*, and the French *Siècle de Louis XIV*—in which for subsequent generations each of these countries was understood to have defined itself. Genres of state attempted to establish that self-definition in one direction. Genres of the home turned it in quite another. The competition between them determined the form the often marginal and subordinate genres of the home assumed, the stories they told, and the reception they received. To mention just the trait that struck me in *Arden of Faversham* and then drew my attention to Dutch genre painting: where the monarchic and seignorial state claimed the classically sanctioned territory of lofty artifice, the home made do (and eventually triumphed) by presenting itself as the refuge of the real. The everyday realism of a play like *Arden* or of paintings like those of Vermeer and de Hooch was thus not merely an aesthetic accomplishment; it was also an ideologically motivated act, whether or not its agents were always aware of its broader implications—an act in a contest where the very definition of the polity and the distribution of rights and privileges within it were at stake.

Having the French Revolution and the bourgeois republics of the last two centuries as the horizon toward which these works tend helps give such arguments greater plausibility. If *Tartuffe*, alone of all Molière's plays, was made a required school text in nineteenth-century France; if Vermeer and even de Hooch have emerged in the last two centuries as much-loved canonical painters; if Calderón's *Alcalde de Zalamea* in the eighteenth century and Lope's *Fuenteovejuna* in the nineteenth and twentieth have won large and sympathetic international audiences; and if even English domestic drama, a genre not known for its incontestable masterpieces, has been defined and repeatedly studied—if all this has happened, it is because these works, more than many others, mark out a path that leads up to us. Things *have* changed in ways domestic drama and painting seem to anticipate. Their values *have* spread, at the expense of the monarchic and aristocratic values with which they competed, over much of the Western world. But prior to the eighteenth century and the bourgeois drama it produced, the works did not themselves entertain any such futurist perspective. Instead of looking forward to a universal liberty yet unimagined, they looked back in an attempt to reclaim the more parochial liberties the communities from which they arose were in danger of losing. To adopt such a futurist perspective here, to the exclusion of the very different perspectives in whose terms the works were produced, would be to distort both those individual works and the specificities of the historical situations in which they arose.

Thus though this book has an inescapably progressive argument, an argument that supposes domestic drama and painting of the sixteenth and seventeenth centuries stand behind the more self-consciously militant bourgeois drama of the French eighteenth-century in something of the way that Copernicus and Galileo stand behind Newton and the theory of gravity, it also wants to resist that argument, to insist on its own episodic character. Differences between what happened in England, the Netherlands, Spain, and France are no less important than similarities, as are the differences between individual works. The identification of cuckold and crown in *Arden of Faversham,* the secular saintliness of Heywood's Jane Shore, the home's multivalence in Shakespeare's *Merry Wives,* the teasing ambiguity of Dutch genre painting, the violent agency in Spanish peasant drama, the controversial immediacy of Molière's *Tartuffe,* and the theoretical elaboration of eighteenth-century French bourgeois drama have no close counterpart in any of the others, and are each as much deserving of attention as anything the various works and forms have in common. The chapters that follow thus tell one story and many stories, describe one object and many objects. The news is twofold: both that these many objects are all part of one and that the individuality of each looks different when that commonality is understood. But for that news to have its effect, we need to get behind the headlines and immerse ourselves in the particular stories themselves. So, beginning with three quite sharply focused English examples and then moving to more broadly defined representational fields in the Netherlands, Spain, and France, let's see what place early modern playwrights and painters gave the nonaristocratic home. Along the way we can expect Bartholo's contempt to be frequently echoed. But we can also expect Beaumarchais's sense of great and daringly transgressive value to emerge with undeniable force. In the competition between those two responses, the cultural role of domestic drama and painting was crafted and made known.

On the Margins of History

Chapter One

━━━ ● ━━━

Murder in Faversham

HORRIBLENESS AT HOME

On February 15, 1551, Thomas Arden, a former mayor of the small town of Faversham in Kent and the town's largest landowner, was murdered by his wife, her lover, the lover's sister, two servants, three neighbors, and two hired killers. Forty years later, Arden's murder was made the subject of a play, *Arden of Faversham*. There is perhaps nothing very surprising about this appropriation of a sensational event by a sensation-craving and plot-hungry professional theater. But retrospectively *Arden* looks like a significant innovation. It is both the earliest true crime story in the English dramatic repertory and the earliest domestic drama—that is, the earliest play to concern itself in anything but a farcical way with the private or family life of English commoners, people of less than aristocratic status. And *Arden* has another distinction. It is also one of the earliest English plays to make a woman its most prominent and powerful character.

Without claiming any firsts and certainly without naming a new genre, the anonymous author of *Arden*—or whoever wrote the title page to the printed edition—advertises all three features: a true crime, a domestic setting, and a prominent woman. Like most sixteenth-century title pages, this one is lengthy. But it deserves reproduction in full for what it tells of how such a story was presented to its readers.

THE
LAMENTA-
BLE AND TRUE TRA-
GEDY OF M. AR-
DEN OF FAVERSHAM
IN KENT.

Who was most wickedly murdered, by
the means of his disloyal and wanton
wife, who for the love she bare to one
Mosby, hired two desperate ruf-
fians, Blackwill and Shakebag,
to kill him.

Wherein is shewed the great malice and dissimulation of a wicked woman, the unsatiable desire of filthy lust,
and the shameful end of all
murderers.

Imprinted at London for Edward
White, dwelling at the Little North
Door of Paul's Church at
the sign of the
Gun. 1592.

Even the bookseller's address at the bottom of this title page helps understand the play, for it supplies a preliminary intimation of the specificity
of place that is so much a part of both early modern culture and English
domestic drama. While listing its innovations, we should also remember
this: *Arden* is the earliest English play whose action can be closely followed
on a map. And, as it happens, the map of the play's action and the map
that would have led a sixteenth-century buyer to a printed copy of the play
overlap. In one of their many failed attempts to murder Arden, the two
hired killers, Blackwill and Shakebag, stand at a stall waiting for their victim,
who has come to London on business, to emerge from Paul's Walk on his
way to the Nag's Head in Cheapside. The sign of the Gun at the Little
North Door of St. Paul's Church is precisely on the way from Paul's Walk
to Cheapside. If the killers are not presumed to be standing there, they
can't be far off.[1] But this topographical conjunction of printed book and
represented action should remind us of the still more significant disjunction
between them. This is, after all, not *Arden of London* but *Arden of Faversham*—a play set for the most part in a small provincial town and brought
first to a specific London stage (though we no longer know which) and then

to a specific London bookshop by its exemplary horror: by the horror of crime, the horror of a wanton and disloyal wife, the horror of the everyday ordinariness of it all. This horrible crime happened in a place we can easily find on a map and visit, and it happened to people not so very much unlike the people who would have read it or watched it as a play.

"Horribleness" was already the term Raphael Holinshed used in his *Chronicles of England, Scotland, and Ireland* (1577) to justify his telling of the Arden story, a telling that served the playwright as source. "About this time," Holinshed wrote, "there was at Faversham in Kent a gentleman named Arden most cruelly murdered and slain by the procurement of his own wife, the which murder, for the horribleness thereof, although otherwise it may seem to be but a private matter and therefore, as it were, impertinent to this history, I have thought good to set it forth somewhat at large."[2] And set it forth at large he did, giving the story seven tightly printed columns of his large folio pages, nearly 5,000 words in all, considerably more than he gave many significant events of state and far more than he gave any other "private" crime. Most of the twenty-three murders listed in Holinshed's 1587 index get no more than a sentence or two. And Arden's nearest rival in length, the one-column account of the murder in 1573 of Master George Sanders by *his* wife and *her* lover, not only resembles the Arden story in its plot but also in its subsequent fortune: it too was turned into a play for the London stage, the anonymous *Warning for Fair Women* (1599). Horribleness is what made a particular and private matter—a matter of women, of commoners, of the home and the local community—fit for inclusion in either a national chronicle history or the repertory of a national acting company. Sensational crime endowed the ordinary with extraordinary significance.

Holinshed and the anonymous playwrights who wrote *Arden of Faversham* and *A Warning for Fair Women* were not the only ones to give currency to these stories. Even before Holinshed retold it, the Sanders murder had been the subject of a pamphlet—one of the earliest English crime pamphlets—by the puritan poet and translator Arthur Golding. The Sanders murder was also the lead piece in Anthony Munday's *View of Sundry Examples* (1580), while the Arden murder found a place in Thomas Beard's *Theater of God's Judgments* (1597), and both got listed in the "mass of murders" section of T. I.'s *World of Wonders* (1595). At the same time, both were appearing in successive editions of John Stow's *Chronicles* and *Annals* (1580 to 1631), and both appeared in Thomas Heywood's versified romp through English history, his *Troia Britanica* (1609).

THE LAMENTA-
BLE AND TRVE TRA-
GEDIE OF M. AR-
DEN OF FEVERSHAM
IN KENT.

Who was most wickedlye murdered, *by*
the meanes of his disloyall and wanton
wyfe, *who for the loue she bare to one*
Mosbie, hyred two desperat ruf-
fins Blackwill and Shakbag,
to kill him.

Wherin is shewed the great mal-
lice and dissimulation of a wicked woman, the vnsatiable desire of filthie lust
and the shamefull end of all
murderers.

Imprinted at London for Edward
White, dwelling at the lyttle North
dore of Paules Church at
the signe of the
Gun, 1592,
*

"Susan shall thou and I wait on them?"

Since then, the Sanders story has been less in view. But not only has the play *Arden of Faversham* been often revived—so often in Faversham itself that it has been called the town's "own passion play"—but the story has been retold in a variety of other forms: by the 1630s, as a broadside ballad; in the eighteenth century, as a new play by George Lillo, part of the general revival of domestic drama; as a puppet show; as a Sadler's Wells ballet; as an entry in the long-running and frequently updated *Newgate Calendar;* as a featured item in local histories of Faversham from the seventeenth century to the twentieth; and, in the last few decades, as an opera and a novel. It has even been reported that until quite recently Faversham children chanted a jingle that alludes to the story:

Mop, Molly, mop.
The more you mop,
The more you may.
Arden's blood will never decay.[3]

And, still more significant, the physical structure of Faversham has been made to remember the story. Arden's house, the scene of the murder, has been carefully preserved and marked. The Fleur-de-Lis, where Mosby lodged, is now the Faversham Heritage Center. And in 1992—the same year the play was produced (and not for the first time) in the garden behind Arden's house—the town's guildhall was taken over for a celebration of the fourth centenary of the play's publication, "Arden 400: An Exhibition of Life in Faversham over 400 Years Ago" (figure 1).

Figure 1   A page from the program for the 1986 production of *Arden of Faversham* at Arden's house. At the upper left is the title page from the 1592 quarto. At the upper right, two of the actors against the background of the house. And at the bottom, advertisements from local merchants. These advertisements serve nicely to suggest how the Arden story remains imbricated in the life of the community. The dispensing optician ties his product to *Arden* with two lines from the play—"Sweet Mosby is as gentle as a king / And I too blind to judge him otherwise"—as though Mistress Arden might have avoided all the fuss had she had a pair of glasses from Optima; the wedding designer advertises her services, with perhaps unconscious irony, in the program for a play about a spectacularly failed marriage, and associates marriage with the image of a house very much like Arden's; and finally, the two inns, one in Faversham and one in the neighboring town of Newnham, rest their claim not only on the local brew but also on their "home cooked" meals (another irony, since Alice tried to poison Arden with her home cooking) and on their location in fifteenth- and sixteenth-century buildings. As this page reminds us, England's homey self-image remains firmly associated with secular and domestic buildings of this period, the kind of building in which Arden was murdered.

EXILED FROM HISTORY

All this testifies powerfully to the Arden story's continuing hold on the imagination of successive generations, both in and out of Faversham. But, still, there is a striking blank in this list of reappropriations. Until the last few years, when historians and literary critics began reclaiming it under the aegis of such upstart genres as popular history, the history of crime, local history, women's history, domestic history or the history of private life, socioeconomic history, and anecdotal history, the Arden story has been hardest to find where it was once most prominent—in the national history of England. For more than half a century, from a first brief mention in the *Breviat Chronicle* of 1551 through the long and detailed account in Holinshed to the retellings in Stow and Heywood, Arden's murder was very much part of England's history. But then it left history to reappear in the motley gathering of genres well off the main line of English historical writing I have already mentioned—stage play, ballad, jingle, collection of wonders, calendar of crime, antiquarian treatise, puppet show, ballet, novel, opera—before finally being readmitted under the sponsorship of those newer subdisciplines that have opened in such profusion over the last few years.[4] Why this long exclusion? And what can it tell us about those interlocking concerns—crime, women, the local, the domestic, and the everyday—that first won the story the attention of Holinshed and the others? If horribleness promoted the Arden story, what demoted it?

The first thing to recognize is that the demotion was deliberate. Arden did not fade from history through passive neglect. It, along with much else, was forcibly ejected. The ejection was the work of those heroes of early modern English thought, Francis Bacon, William Camden, John Hayward, John Speed, Fulke Greville, Samuel Daniel, John Selden, and a large number of their lesser known followers, men who brought England the values and methods of politic and humanist historiography.[5] "Voluminous Holinshed," was the way they characterized the *Chronicles*, "full of confusion and commixture of unworthy relations"; "trivial household trash"; "vast, vulgar tomes . . . recovered from out of innumerable ruins."[6] From their point of view, English history had yet to be written. "Many great volumes carry among us the titles of histories," wrote Edmund Bolton in his *Hypercritica, or a Rule of Judgment for Writing and Reading our Histories* (1618), "but learned men . . . absolutely deny that any of ours discharge that office which the titles promise."[7] As history, chronicles simply did not count.

What would count was easily defined. "Histories," according to Thomas Blundeville, "be made of deeds done by a public weal or against a public weal, and such deeds be either deeds of war, of peace, or else sedition and conspiracy."[8] In short, war, politics, and the state were the only proper subjects for history. Blundeville's *True Order and Method of Writing and Reading Histories* was published in 1574, three years before the first edition of Holinshed's *Chronicles,* and reflects views then current in Italy and France, views that had made a brief English appearance decades earlier in the work of Thomas More and Polydore Virgil. But it was not for another quarter century that this newer view took over in England. A recent historian has suggested—plausibly, I think—that the specific impetus for this sharper focus on politics came from the Essex affair in the late 1590s and early years of the seventeenth century.[9] Many of those involved in the shift in historical practice were also involved with Essex. The intense, heady, and frightening experience of near proximity to revolt focused attention on the need for heightened political awareness, an awareness informed by the past. Already, in an Italy overrun by the French, Niccolò Machiavelli and Francesco Guicciardini had come to a similar conclusion, and their example showed what might be done. And, of course, for the Italians and the English alike, a still broader prompting came from the humanist recovery of classical antiquity and from the model of ancient historians like Polybius and Tacitus. Taken together, these various lines of influence pushed toward a sharply redefined historical practice, a practice that would limit itself, in the words of A. P.'s address to the reader of Sir John Hayward's *Life and Reign of King Henry IV* (1599), to "either the government of mighty states or the lives and acts of famous men."[10]

Making history more useful was a goal these men shared, but they had a quite different notion of what constituted appropriate use than had been common before. History had long been thought a repository of moral example and a revelation of divine providence. Holinshed certainly thought of it that way. The humanist historians redefined both the lesson and the audience. Instead of general moral and religious teaching, history now taught politics. And instead of a universal audience, it now addressed princes and other great men of state. With a sharpened focus came a distinct elevation in status. Bacon talked of a hierarchy "of books no less than of persons, for as nothing derogates from the dignity of a state more than confusion of ranks and degrees, so it not a little embases the authority of a history to intermingle matters of lighter moment . . . with matters of state," and Camden clearly agreed. "It standeth," he wrote in the preface to his *Annals* (1615), "with the law and dignity of history to run through business of highest weight and not to inquire after small matters." Similarly, Sir George Buck, in his *History of King Richard the Third* (1619), bragged that he had "omitted nothing of great matter or moment, nor anything else but some slight matters, and such as are to be seen in the common and vulgar chronicles and stories and which are in the hands of every idiot or mere foolish reader and to no purpose and for the most part not worth the reading." Nor was it any surprise if chroniclers wrote of base matters for a base audience, they themselves being, as Edmund Bolton charged, "of the dregs of the common people."[11] Low writers, low subjects, low readers. This was the degrading alliance humanist historians were trying to replace with a more elevating one, one made up of high writers, high subjects, and high readers. In this new configuration, a story like Arden's had no place.

But Arden's murder and stories like it were also squeezed out by a new insistence on narrative coherence, by what Lord Herbert of Cherbury called "an entire narration of public actions."[12] History was to contain the record of "things done"—the *res gestae*, whose "tyranny" over the early modern art of history has been frequently noticed—but not just any "thing" would do. History's "things" had to qualify for arrangement in a firm causal order. This is clearly what Bacon sought in the "one just and complete history" that he told Lord Ellesmere England and Scotland should have, and it is essential to his idea of "perfect" history.[13] But not only does such narrative coherence distinguish humanist history from its chronicling rival, it also underlies its politic didacticism. Only if actions are seen in relation to their causes and consequences can a statesman learn from them how to act in a similar situation. John Hayward makes just this point in a dedication to Charles I. History, Hayward writes, is "the fittest subject for your highness's reading, for by diligent perusing the acts of great men, by considering all the circumstances of them, by comparing counsels and means with events [i.e., outcomes], a man may seem to have lived in all ages."[14] Whatever did not qualify as the circumstance, counsel, means, or event of a great man's act was simply to be left out. It is thus with considerable pride that Camden, one of the most influential of the new historians, announces: "Digressions I have avoided."[15]

Avoiding digression was a prime objective of humanist historiography. But to avoid a digression, you had to be able to recognize one when you saw it coming. John Trussell, in his continuation of Daniel's *History of*

England (1636), supplies a helpful description, an elaboration of a list he borrowed from Bacon: "1. Matters of ceremony, as coronations, christenings, marriages, funerals, solemn feasts, and such like. 2. Matters of triumph, as tiltings, maskings, barriers, pageants, galley-foists, and the like. 3. Matters of novelty, as great inundations, sudden rising and falling of the price of corn, strange monsters, justice done on petty offenders, and such like executions, with which the *cacoethes* [bad habits] of the writers of those times have mingled matters of state."[16] All three exclusions merit attention, for all three name areas that recent historical study has retrieved. What the early modern ruled out, the postmodern is systematically readmitting. But, of course, it is Trussell's third category, "matters of novelty," that most interests us here. "Justice done on petty offenders, and such like executions" catches the Arden story directly. Alice Arden and two of the household servants were executed specifically for the crime of "petty" treason, the murder of a husband or master. But from the perspective of humanist and politic history, any common murderer, even one whose crime did not fall under the technical definition of petty treason, was a "petty offender" and, as such, had no place in a proper historical narrative.

And no less significant than the simple fact of exclusion is the company in which the excluded finds itself. Trussell classes "justice done on petty offenders" with such other "matters of novelty" as "great inundations, sudden rising and falling of the price of corn, [and] strange monsters." This, however odd it may seem to us, was not an idiosyncratic classification. What Trussell excluded from history as a related cluster reappeared as a related cluster in publications like *A World of Wonders*, where Arden's murder shares space with famine and dearth, with a tempest of venomous beasts, with a precipitous drop in the price of wheat, and with a fish shaped like a man. These "wonders," these violations of nature—Arden's murder as much as the others—are "signs, threats, tokens of God's wrath," acts of divine retribution and admonitions against further sin.[17] Beginning with horribleness and ending with a wondrous sign of God's vengeance, Holinshed's Arden story functions in much the same way. From this vantage point, the only fully coherent narrative would be the narrative of God's inscrutable will, and since God's will remains inscrutable it can be represented only in the fragmentary glimpses afforded by a "world of wonders" or a discontinuous chronicle.

The humanist historians were not ready to abandon all idea of divine providence working through time, nor were they immune to the lure of an occasional prodigy. But their primary aim was to explain human history—by which they meant the history of states and great men—in human terms. As a result, a gap opened between a world of state politics, of calculation and contingency, of human action and human effect, on the one hand, and a very different world of commoners and women, of crimes and prodigies, of the local, domestic, social, and economic, on the other. Only the former belonged to history. The latter had its place in poetry, religion, and similar old wives' tales—which is where the Arden story takes refuge. When Samuel Daniel identified "improvement of the sovereignty" as a prime accomplishment of the sixteenth century, he pointed toward the cause of his own historical discourse and that of his fellow politic humanists. "The better to fit their use," Daniel wrote, "I have made choice to deliver only those affairs of action that most concern the government."[18] History followed sovereignty. Its purpose was to serve and describe the state. Anything else was, as Daniel's successor put it, a "superfluous exuberance."[19]

An apparent exception to this exclusion, the mention of the Arden story as late as 1643 in Richard Baker's *Chronicle of the Kings of England,* is actually further evidence of it. Baker lumps Arden's murder with a burnt church, an episode of the sweating sickness, the birth of a child with "two perfect bodies from the navel upward," and the taking of nine dolphins— all in a section devoted to the "casualties" of King Edward's reign. Alluding to the humanist historians in his epistle to the reader, Baker remarks that "where many have written the reigns of some of our kings excellently in the way of *history,* yet I may say they have not done so well in the way of *chronicle,* for whilst they insist wholly upon matters of state, they wholly omit meaner accidents, which yet are materials as proper for a chronicle as the other." As a chronicler, Baker includes such meaner accidents, but as someone writing in the wake of the humanist historians, he confines them to a section separate from his political narrative—acknowledging, in effect, their removal from history.[20]

BOUNDARY-BREAKING FACTS

In admitting that his account of Arden's murder might be considered impertinent, Holinshed anticipates this split. Though for him horribleness—a near neighbor of wonder and novelty—can erase, as it couldn't for his humanist successors, the impertinence of a "private matter," he nevertheless recognizes that his most pressing obligation is to write public and political history. But, curiously, when we set Holinshed's account against the various surviving documents concerning Arden and his murder, the conceptual divisions on which both his sense of significant difference and the subsequent enterprise of humanist historiography depended—the division of elite from popular, of law-abiding (or law-making) from criminal, of public from private, of men from women, of national from local, of political from socioeconomic, of the truly historical from the merely anecdotal—all crumble. At every point, Holinshed's "private matter" turns out to have had significant public entanglements, and Holinshed himself is revealed as having helped create the impertinence for which he apologizes.

Consider, for example, these facts, most of them missing from Holinshed's account: Neither Arden nor his wife was a native of Faversham. They arrived just a decade before Arden's murder from London, where Arden had been clerk to Alice's stepfather, Edward North, and they came with a position and with property derived specifically from their official connections. North, soon to be Sir Edward North and eventually Baron North of Kirtling, was clerk of the parliament when Arden first appeared in his employ. From parliament, North moved quickly into the newly created Court of Augmentations, rising by 1546 to the post of its lord chancellor. It was Augmentations that administered land coming to the crown from dissolved monasteries, and it was abbey land in Faversham, acquired from its first lay holder, Sir Thomas Cheney, that enriched Arden. Either North or Cheney, who was lord warden of the Cinque Ports, must have secured Arden's appointment to the lucrative post of king's customs officer for the port of Faversham and later to the position of king's comptroller of the neighboring Sandwich port. Supported by this abundant flow of governmental largess, Arden lived in Faversham as the crown's officer and as the owner of much of what had been the crown's land there, a man with connections that reached all the way to the privy council, where his stepfather-in-law sat in his *ex officio* capacity as chancellor of the Court of Augmentations.[21] From the first, Arden was, in the words of Lena Cowen Orlin, who has described these relations in compelling detail, "a king's man in Faversham."[22]

Arden's Westminster connections may explain why he took a lead role in securing the town's royal reincorporation in 1544. And they may explain as well why the privy council showed such interest in his murder. The king's chief councillors sitting in official session ordered one suspect brought to London for questioning, arranged for the pursuit and arrest of two others, and determined the precise place and mode of execution for the first group to be apprehended and convicted: "Cicley Pounder, widow, and Thomas Mosby to be hanged in Smithfield in London; Alice Arden to be burned at Canterbury, and Bradshaw to be hanged there in chains; Michael Sanderson to be hanged, drawn, and quartered at Faversham, and Elizabeth Stafford to be burned there"[23]—a particularly eery decree if we notice that among the councillors who signed it was Alice Arden's stepfather, Lord North. For the humanist historians, these executions would rank among those digressive "matters of novelty," the sort of thing that should be left out of history. But clearly such acts of state, like the equally digressive matters of ceremony and triumph, figured significantly in a theater of power that the highest officers in the land thought it worth their while to stage. And, in this particular case, the victim of the crime whose perpetrators were being so spectacularly punished was (though it would be hard to guess it from Holinshed's account) himself a public man, a servant of the crown, a man whose participation in the royally dictated dissolution of church property and in nationally determined partisan and sectarian conflict may have helped bring on his death.

Everywhere one looks national actors and national actions impinge on this seemingly local and domestic event. Alice's lover, Thomas Mosby, was Sir Edward North's steward; John Greene, another of the conspirators, was Sir Anthony Aucher's man; and George Bradshaw, the goldsmith Holinshed thought innocent of the complicity for which he was executed, had served under Sir Richard Cavendish. It is hard to know just what weight to give these connections. North, Aucher, and Cavendish were all men of considerable political standing, and at least one of them has been thought party to the crime. "The murder of Arden of Faversham," writes Peter Clark, "may well have been related to a dispute between him and . . . Aucher." And Clark has also noted that "Arden's death was . . . interesting for another reason. . . . Sir Thomas Moyle and other Catholics sought to exploit the murder for their own ends, by trying to implicate an innocent man 'hating [him] for the gospel.'"[24] Nor were these the only public issues engaged in Arden's death. The hired killer, Blackwill, was a soldier from King Henry's French war, one of hundreds of marauders who terrorized the Kentish countryside in those years. And even Alice, if one accepts the arguments of Catherine Belsey, was prompted in her crime by a crisis in the institutional basis of marriage that derived from state action.[25] In this tangle of intersecting forces, who is to say where the public ends and the private begins? Surely, to consider Arden's murder as history—even as the kind of political history the humanists favored—would be no impertinence.

Yet impertinent (except, of course, for its horribleness) is precisely what Holinshed calls it, and either he or the reporters on whom he depended—those unnamed investigators who, as Holinshed tells us, "used some diligence to gather the true understanding of the circumstances"—made sure the story's political pertinence would remain invisible.[26] As it happens, the manuscript from which Holinshed worked is preserved in the Stow papers at the British Library. Comparison of it with the printed account shows already some tactful obscuring of possible public implications. Though Holinshed says that Mosby was "servant to the Lord North," he leaves out that Alice was "the Lord North's wife's daughter," that Mosby "was made one of the chiefest gentlemen about the Lord North," and that Arden winked at their adultery "in hope of attaining some benefits of the Lord North by means of this Mosby, who could do much with him."[27] But both accounts fail to note that Arden himself had also worked for North, that he had been jurat (that is, town councillor) and mayor of Faversham, that he was the king's customs agent for Faversham port, and that his extensive landholdings came from patronage ties to the upper reaches of the governing hierarchy.

What Holinshed omits, the anonymous playwright restores with a truth-telling fiction. "Arden, cheer up thy spirits and droop no more," says Arden's friend Franklin in the play's opening lines, "My gracious lord, the duke of Somerset"—then the lord protector of England—

> Hath freely given to thee and to thy heirs,
> By letters patents from his majesty,
> All the lands of the abbey of Faversham.
> Here are the deeds,
> Sealed and subscribed with his name and the king's.
> Read them, and leave this melancholy mood.[28]

No surviving document suggests that Arden received any part of the abbey lands as a direct grant from the lord protector or the king, but this speech does nevertheless give back to Arden's story a political dimension that Holinshed silently denies. And through the continuing presence of the fictional Franklin, who is identified as the lord protector's man, that dimension remains a dimly lit but clearly perceptible part of the play right up to the epilogue, which Franklin speaks and which once again alludes to the lord protector. But though *Arden of Faversham* pulls toward the national and thus toward history as both Holinshed and his humanist successors understood it, the play's very genre consigned it to the margins of Tudor historical writing, a place lacking the authority needed to establish a claim that would be recognized within the court of humanist historiography.

Why should the chronicler be so shy about the political implications of Arden's murder and the dramatist so bold? Both may have feared offending the surviving members of Alice Arden's stepfamily. Holinshed greatly diminishes the connection, and the playwright substitutes another name. But where Holinshed keeps the story local and domestic, the playwright gives it a new tie to the king's government. The answer lies, I think, in generic aims and anxieties. Despite Holinshed's fear of impertinence, he had in the story's exemplary quality—its beginning in horribleness and ending in wonder—adequate grounds for its inclusion. Of the three ends to which Holinshed thought "chronicles and histories ought chiefly to be written"—namely, "their native country's praise . . . , the encouragement of their worthy countrymen by elders' advancements, and the daunting of the vicious by sore penal examples"—Arden's murder and the spectacular executions that followed from it richly satisfy at least the third.[29] And for this purpose a local and domestic story does quite as well as a national one. Indeed, it may do better, since it belongs to a sphere where ordinary morality has more obvious and unequivocal application than it does in the highest affairs of state. But for a dramatist, wanting to give tragic stature to a domestic murder, some connection, however remote, to the crown was needed. After all, the usual understanding of tragedy—a genre that "meddled not with . . . base matters" but "set forth the doleful falls of infortunate and afflicted princes"—was as exclusive as the humanist notion of history.[30] A story like Arden's did not belong in either. But whatever the motivation, the effect of Holinshed's choice was to mark off a private space that might be labeled impertinent to the public matter of politic history, while the effect of the dramatist's choice was to keep alive, if only barely, a sense of the early modern interpenetration of the public and private.

Assembling all the surviving documents, we might conjecture that the murder itself was as much a "public" as a "private" event, that Arden died the victim of a crime whose treason was more than "petty." Alice and the others did not only kill an encumbering husband and master; they also killed a representative of the crown. Holinshed reports that "the fair"—which in Faversham opened annually on St. Valentine's Day, the eve of Arden's murder—"was wont to be kept partly in the town and partly in the abbey; but Arden, for his own private lucre and covetous gain, had this present year procured it to be wholly kept within the abbey ground, which he had purchased; and so reaping all the gains to himself and bereaving the town of that portion which was wont to come to the inhabitants, got many a bitter curse."[31] Once again, emphasis falls on the "private" character of Arden's action, but when we remember that Arden acquired this land through his official connections, as part of the largest royally dictated property transfer since the Norman Conquest, the story assumes a different appearance. The state and its privileged representative, a local courtier-monopolist, have taken the place of the church and its representatives.[32] Both oppress the local community, but the new oppression is even worse than the old.

Evidence of tension between Arden and the town is not hard to find. In an entry dated December 22, 1550, less than two months before Arden's murder, the Faversham Wardmote Book reports that "Thomas Arden, by cause he being jurat and sworn to maintain the franchises, liberties, and freedoms of the said town, hath contrary to his oath in that behalf gone about and labored by divers ways and means to the uttermost of his power to infringe and undo the said franchises, liberties, and freedoms, . . . shall be deposed from the bench, and no more to be jurat of the said town, but from henceforth to be utterly disfranchised forever."[33] The precise reasons for this disenfranchisement remain a matter of controversy, but it is clear that Arden's great connections and his willingness, as Holinshed puts it, to prefer "his private profit before common gain" made him an uncomfortable neighbor, one whose disappearance might have been welcomed. In keeping with his presentation of the story as a wonder, Holinshed credits divine intervention: "God heareth the tears of the oppressed and taketh vengeance: note an example in Arden."[34] But that vengeance had at least eight human instruments, who were no doubt encouraged by the general resentment Arden inspired. As Alice was reported to have said, Arden "was so evil beloved that no man would make inquiry after his death."[35]

But what then of Alice's own "unsatiable desire of filthy lust"? In effect, Arden's murder marks the juncture of two crimes: Arden's crime against the community and Alice's crime against Arden. Though in many ac-

counts only the second appears, both Holinshed and the play let us discover the double wrong. And the play, unlike the chronicle, makes it possible to imagine a royal invasion on *each* side. Not only is Arden backed
by the lord protector's grant of "all the lands" of Faversham Abbey, but
he fears that his rival Mosby might enjoy similar backing. Responding
to Franklin's question concerning Mosby—"Why, what is he?"—Arden
says,

> A botcher, and no better at the first,
> Who, by base brokage getting some small stock,
> Crept into the service of a nobleman,
> And by his servile flattery and fawning
> Is now become the steward of his house,
> And bravely jets it in his silken gown.
> FRANKLIN. No nobleman will countenance such a peasant.
> ARDEN.   Yes, the Lord Clifford, he that loves not me.
> But through his favor let him not grow proud;
> For, were he by the lord protector backed,
> He should not make me to be pointed at.[36]

Though Arden insists on his own difference from Mosby—"I am by
birth a gentleman of blood"—they were in fact surprisingly alike. Both
were new men. Both had "crept into the service of a nobleman." Both
were able to jet it bravely in a silken gown. And, as the playwright would
have known, the nobleman who countenanced one was also the nobleman
who countenanced the other. The historical "Lord Clifford," the man
Mosby served as steward, was, as we have seen, in fact Lord North, Alice
Arden's stepfather and Arden's patron. For Arden, only a few lines after
hearing of his own grant from the lord protector, to suppose, even in a
counterfactual subjunctive, that Mosby might also be "by the lord protector backed" reveals that likeness and gives it a powerfully political resonance. Arden and Mosby are rival twins in the service of the state and its
network of court-centered patronage.[37] Arden's appropriation of the abbey
lands in Faversham finds its counterpart in Mosby's appropriation of Alice
Arden's body.[38] Thus, in at least a metaphorical sense, the two crimes of
Arden of Faversham are one. Seen this way, adultery is no longer a purely
private crime, "impertinent" to the public matter of history. It is rather a
vehicle for thinking about history, for thinking, in particular, about that
"improvement in the sovereignty" that was responsible both for the emergence of politic history and for the dissolution of the English monasteries,
including Faversham Abbey.

Oeconomical History

The early modern invention of private life and of genres suitable to its representation was as much a function of the consolidation of state power as was the invention of politic history.[39] A sharpened sense of the *res publica* produced by difference a more clearly defined *res privata*. We have already seen something of that sorting out at work in the humanist rejection of the local and domestic as proper subjects for history. But in this earliest stage of that development, representations of the private in such newly invented genres as domestic drama turn back with remarkable frequency to reflect on the relation of the two newly severed domains. And often those reflections center on the issue of wifely chastity. The specificity of place that is so characteristic of domestic drama has its counterpart in this attention to female sexuality. The local and domestic space, whether it be the town or the house, is represented by the woman's body, and, when that body is invaded, the local and domestic are also violated. Already in the earlier genre of the medieval fabliau something of this sort had been the case. When witty clerks make love to the carpenter's wife in Chaucer's Miller's Tale or to the miller's wife and daughter in the Reeve's Tale the integrity of "Oxenford" or "Trumpyngtoun" is also compromised. But the cuckoldings in Chaucer are no tragedy. If stories like these express a widespread interest in the relation of the church and the local community, of clerks and commoners, the result is amusement rather than horror. Whatever the position of the particular fictional tellers, the genre sides with the clerks.

The very different early modern attitude is suggested by both *Arden of Faversham* and that other crime play anticipated by Holinshed, *A Warning for Fair Women*, whose Mosby-like adulterer and murderer, George Browne, is explicitly presented as a courtier, who returns to the court in a vain attempt to conceal his murder. And it emerges as well in the one historiographical treatise to make an explicit place for the kind of popular and domestic interests represented by the Arden story. In his odd "intermixed discourse upon historical and poetical relations," *The Scholar's Medley* (1614), Richard Brathwait both follows humanist teaching and departs from it. His preliminary definition could not be more orthodox or more exclusionary: "The true use and scope of all histories ought to tend to no other purpose than a true narration of what is done or hath been achieved either in foreign or domestic affairs." But then he goes on to introduce the strikingly anomalous category of what he calls "oeconomical histories, teaching private families how to be disposed." In this area it does not matter, he says, whether the "histories" are true or feigned. What does matter is that "order" be "attained by examples." "The best government in private proceeds from histories and the serious reading thereof, the virtuous matron squaring her course by that modestest of Roman dames, Lucretia, making her *colum* her *thorum*, her distaff her best companion in her bed when her husband was absent. No vicious mind can deprave her; she is fighting at home with her own passions, whilst Collatine, her husband, fights in the field against his country's enemy."[40]

A vicious mind might guess that Brathwait was indulging his irrepressibly salacious wit in this passage. The Roman Lucretia stayed up spinning with her maids; she didn't take her distaff dildolike to bed. But more significant is the equation Brathwait makes almost automatically and repeats again and again, not only in this book but also in his *Good Wife* (1618) and his *Ar't Asleep Husband? A Bolster Lecture* (1640): the equation of domestic order with female chastity. Retelling stories of chastity defended and violated constitutes for Brathwait "oeconomical history." But when one examines the particular "history" he offers as his prime example, the history of the Roman Lucretia, the difference between the "oeconomical" and the "political," between "private government" and "public," once again proves impossible to maintain. Not only is there a likeness between Lucretia's fight at home and Collatine's fight in the field, but Lucretia's fight ends by remaking the state. As a result of her rape by the younger Tarquin, the son of the Roman monarch, "the state government changed," as Shakespeare puts it in the dedication of his *Rape of Lucrece* (1594), "from kings to consuls."[41] Outraged by the prince's tyrannical act, Lucretia's husband and the other nobles drove the Tarquins from Rome and established a republic. The Roman republic was thus founded on Lucretia's domestic virtue.[42]

No comparable claim can be made for Alice Arden's domestic vice. The only thing that seems to have been founded on it is the genre of the true crime story. Yet, like Lucretia's, Alice Arden's is an "oeconomical history" that has refused to stay at home. First brought to the London stage at the same time as the earliest "chronicle history" plays, Alice's murder of Arden has continued to stand for an alternative history of England, a history focused not on the court and the battlefield, as were those other plays, but on the household and the local community. This alternative history is not, however, indifferent to the court and the great affairs of state. On the contrary, it engages them at every point. The state was lived in Arden's life and death, and the state is known when his story is retold. The dissolution of the monasteries, the establishment of a state religion, the growth in royal sovereignty, the networks of national patronage and affiliation, the laws of marriage and divorce—all these are implicated in this local story of adultery and murder. To know Arden's story is to know these public events more concretely and more fully, to know not only what was done by the state but also how its doings were experienced and resisted. To know Arden's story is, in short, to know a significant bit of politic history—though official historiography has not always let that fact be known.

Chapter Two

Weeping for Jane Shore

To those who know Jane Shore, if at all, only as the "Shore's wife" mentioned a few times in Shakespeare's *Richard III,* the title of this chapter may seem puzzling. Shakespeare's "Mistress Shore," as she is also called, is a figure of fun: King Edward's whore, Lord Hastings's whore, just about anyone's whore, to judge from what Richard says about her. Why should we weep for her? To get a preliminary intimation of a very different Jane Shore and a very different affective claim, let me fast-forward from the 1590s, when Shakespeare's play was first produced, to the 1780s. "We then, indeed, knew all the luxury of grief." That, according to a contemporary witness, was the experience the great Sarah Siddons offered London theatergoers in the title role of Nicholas Rowe's *Tragedy of Jane Shore* (figure 2). Women sobbed and shrieked, and men, after struggling to suppress their tears, "at length grew proud of indulging" them. Before the intense appeal of Rowe's play and Mrs. Siddons's acting, "the nerves of many a gentle being gave way . . . and fainting fits long and frequently alarmed the decorum of the house."[1] Sobbing, shrieking, and even fainting over a royal concubine? What's going on here?

Whatever the answer, it is not specific to either Rowe's play or Mrs. Siddons's acting. We do not have to wait for the notoriously lachrymose sensibility of the eighteenth century to find audiences moved by the plight of Mistress Shore. Since its first appearance more than half a century before Shakespeare wrote, her story—the story of a London wife seduced

Figure 2   William Hamilton, *Sarah Siddons as Jane Shore* (1791). Watercolor on paper, 24.2 × 15.9 cm. Victoria and Albert Museum, London. Photo: V&A Picture Library.

by one king, Edward IV, and harshly punished by another, Richard III—had been calling forth an emotional response that is not easily rivaled in either intensity or persistence.[2] But, more than that, through the shaping power of its extraordinary emotional appeal, the Jane Shore story was already, centuries before Mrs. Siddons played the part, remaking the generic map of English literature—pushing against the affective limits of old genres and helping to forge new ones, including most obviously the kind of domestic tragedy Rowe wrote.

This is a big claim, and it is going to get bigger as the chapter goes on. If the whole of our modern, middle-class world does not arise from the story of Jane Shore—and it surely doesn't—a fair part of its literary self-representation does. To a far greater extent than the murder of Arden of Faversham, this story puts the intersection of home and state at the very center of attention. No one could retell the story without it. If that intersection, that adulterous alliance, is, as I am arguing, essential to the emergence of the domestic and bourgeois drama and painting that, since the late eighteenth century, has occupied a dominant position in Western literature and art, the story of Jane Shore comes as close as we are likely to get to providing a paradigmatic, perhaps even a founding, case. But, even at this point, I have to acknowledge the unlikeliness of such a claim. How can a story that most people, even people who work in the field of early modern English studies, either do not remember or remember only as a sneering joke be supposed to have grabbed hold of the literary system and given it a transforming shake? How, for that matter, can such remarkable agency be attributed to any story, when, after all, stories exist only in their various tellings—tellings that in this case transformed the story almost beyond recognition? That transformation points to a quite different way of locating agency: not in the story that needed to get told, but rather in the culture that, because of its changing social and political configuration, needed to do the telling—needed, in particular, a story like what it made of this one. Though I will sometimes be formulating things one way and sometimes another, it seems to me that both the push and the pull are going on all the time. Yes, the story was summoned forth by tensions within the culture that craved a medium through which to express themselves. But, at the same time, the story worked to define those tensions and bring them to conscious realization. Even more than most significantly resonant stories, the story of Jane Shore helped remake the world by which it was made.

But however we characterize this process, Shakespeare resisted it—resistance no less significant than the affective power it would have denied. Focus, as Shakespeare does, on King Richard to the exclusion of Mistress Shore—she never gets on stage in *Richard III*—and you have one image of English history and the English nation. Focus, as both Nicholas Rowe and many of Shakespeare's contemporaries do, on Jane Shore to the near exclusion of both her royal lover and her royal tormenter, and you have quite another. To laugh at Shore's wife in a chronicle-history play like Shakespeare's or to weep for her in a domestic tragedy like Rowe's means (even though Rowe bragged that he was writing in the manner of Shakespeare) choosing one or the other of two, competing ideological positions, each of which bears clear and mutually contradictory class and gender implications. But the playing field on which these competitors meet is by no means even. It wasn't then, and it isn't now. That the story of an adulterous middle-class woman would dare aspire to the aristocratic and largely masculine realms of history and tragedy has always been felt (whatever the story's popular success) as profoundly transgressive. Richard may be a monster, but he is also a nobleman and a king. History and tragedy belong to him by right. Mistress Shore's claim is of another sort altogether, one based on sexual waywardness, on suffering, and, paradoxically enough, on her very unfitness for the social, political, and literary domains to which adultery raised her.

OUT OF HISTORY

Resistance is anticipated from the first. In his *History of King Richard III*, the earliest and most influential account of Shore's wife, one that continued to appear in every sizeable chronicle history of England for the next century, that was repeatedly reissued in chapbook form for another century and more, and that provided Shakespeare with his main source for *Richard III*, Sir Thomas More admits that readers may fairly object that this middle-class woman is "too slight a thing to be written of and set among the remembrances of great matters."[3] But why then did More, unlike Shakespeare, risk violating the decorum of history to include her?

One can imagine many explanations. Shore's wife was among the few living links to the story More was writing. In 1513 or 1514, the most likely dates for More's composition of the *History*, she was still in London, and he would seem to have known her. Her "pleasant behavior" may also have appealed to the famously witty More. And she, like More, was a Londoner and thus helped support the *History*'s clear London perspective. But More's own explanation points rather to the emotion she inspired. "Me seemeth the chance," he writes,

> so much the more worthy to be remembered, in how much she is now in the more beggarly condition, unfriended and worn out of acquaintance, after good substance, after as great favor with the prince, after as great suit and seeking to with all those that those days had business to speed, as many other men were in their times, which be now famous only by the infamy of their ill deeds. Her doings were not much less, albeit they be much less remembered because they were not so evil. For men use, if they have an evil turn, to write it in marble, and whoso doth us a good turn, we write it in dust; which is not worst proved by her, for at this day she beggeth of many at this day living, that at this day had begged if she had not been.[4]

Here a woman who once enjoyed position, wealth, and influence has been reduced to beggary; a woman who used her power for the benefit of many has been abandoned even by those she aided; a woman notable for her goodness has been forgotten, while the fame of evildoers lives on. The pathos of her situation is, in short, what gives More his excuse.

Such pathos is not, however, a gratuitously isolated effect in a chronicle-like compilation. On the contrary, it is obviously meant to serve a broader rhetorical purpose. More's *Richard III* is a polemical history, a book intended to blacken the reputation of its principal subject. To that end, More sets up a series of contrasts: first between Richard and his brother Edward IV, then between Richard and his hapless victims. Shore's wife has a place in both. As the most conspicuous of Edward's many mistresses, Shore's wife, sympathetically portrayed, helps undermine the charge that Edward's philandering polluted the throne and the royal lineage. And when, as the mistress of Lord Hastings, who took her over after Edward's death, she is caught in Hastings's sudden fall and subjected to public humiliation after his execution, it adds to the revelation of Richard's brutality and hypocrisy.

Shore's wife is by no means Richard's only victim, nor is her suffering as great as that of many others. Indeed, she is one of the few who survive, a defect later writers would correct. But the unexpected sympathy that gathers around this obviously sinful woman—together with her merriness, her goodness in power, her dignity in suffering, and her bourgeois nearness to More's London audience—makes her stand out even in the heart-rending company of the little princes in the Tower, their distraught mother, the queen's other children and brothers, and Richard's own cast-off followers, including Hastings and Buckingham. Other than Richard himself, no figure in More's *History* has proved more memorable than Shore's wife, and she, unlike Richard, has accomplished that feat without the magnifying effect of Shakespeare's brilliant appropriation. Indeed, she has done it despite Shakespeare's laughing scorn.

Elizabethan readers thought More's *History of Richard III* the best writing in all the chronicles, and a twentieth-century critic calls the three pages devoted to Shore's wife "surely the most charming piece of prose that had yet been written in England." But others have objected that the "pathetic tribute to Jane Shore" mars the *History*'s unity.[5] In formalist and thematic terms, the objection is easily answered. The description of Shore's wife not only fits More's overall plan: it has an essential place in it. Yet despite this demonstrably tight fit, the sense of affective excess remains. Shore's wife is an integral part of More's *History*, yet stands apart from it. In choosing this bourgeois wife and adulteress as a foil to his villainous Richard, More sets history against itself. It is precisely her unfitness for history that gives Shore's wife her pathetic appeal, an appeal that not even the little princes can match. They at least were born to power and its perils. She wasn't. Buckingham is made to play on the incongruity of her role at court in his Edward-bashing speech to the citizens of London. And

More plays on it as well. In power, Shore's wife is a more just and less self-interested mediator than the great ones who surround her, and, in her unmerited fall, she equals the grace and courage of the best of them.

Instead of remaining a submissive figure in a well-wrought rhetorical design, Shore's wife emerges to claim an unexpectedly large share of our interest and concern. Without her leaving the bourgeois and domestic sphere from which Edward seduced her, no such claim would have been possible, for she would then have had no place in a history like More's, not even as a rhetorical foil. But having been seduced into history, she nevertheless retains a certain detachment from it—and on that detachment the special pathos of More's account depends. However high she mounts or however far she falls, she is always "Shore's wife," the wife of a London citizen of good substance. Nor does the pathos belong to her alone. It is shared with the common, everyday urban world from which she comes, the world from which both More and the editors and readers of the chronicle histories in which his *Richard III* was repeatedly included also came. Shore's wife is a representative figure whose troubling encounter with history suggests the possibility that tragic emotion may not be the exclusive province of the great, that something like what would later be called "bourgeois" or "domestic" tragedy is not simply a ridiculous misnomer. And not only does More's account of Shore's wife look forward to a literary genre yet unborn. It also embodies in the midst of this, the first humanist history to emerge from the English Renaissance—which is as much as to say the first modern political history in English—what might be thought of as the first "antipolitical history," a commoners' history to set against the royal history of Richard III.

INTO VERSE

Between More's *History* and the emergence in the late 1590s of a Shore-centered domestic tragedy, the story of Shore's wife provided the impetus for still another new genre, the so-called female complaint. The intense, though short-lived, taste for this new kind belongs especially to the early 1590s, when so many generic innovations were changing the face of English poetry. But the poem that served as its inspiration and model first appeared thirty years earlier. In 1563, Thomas Churchyard's *Shore's Wife* was published as part of the much expanded second edition of the *Mirror for Magistrates*. The *Mirror* itself, a collection of "tragedies" in the tradition of Boccaccio's *De casibus virorum illustrium* and John Lydgate's *Fall of Princes,* "ran," in the words of one literary historian, "a career perhaps more complex and influential than that of any other Elizabethan book."[6] But no poem in the *Mirror* was more influential than *Shore's Wife.* Already in 1563 William Baldwin's prose endlink included the report that the poem "was so well liked that all together exhorted me instantly to procure Master Churchyard to undertake and to pen as many more of the remainder as might by any means be attainted at his hands"; and in the 1590s Thomas Nashe was still hailing Churchyard's accomplishment: "*Shore's Wife* is young, though he be stepped in years."[7]

In calling Churchyard's muse "grandmother to our grandeloquentest poets at this present," Nashe knew what he was talking about. Earlier that same year—1592—Samuel Daniel, in obvious imitation of *Shore's Wife,* had found another tragic royal mistress and given expression to her woes in *The Complaint of Rosamond.* The next year, Thomas Lodge found still another—Elstred, the abandoned mistress of the legendary British king Locrine—and Michael Drayton followed in 1594 with Piers Gaveston, the male lover of Edward II, and Matilda, the chaste victim of King John's frustrated lust, whose lament was soon repeated in Richard Barnfield's *Complaint of Chastity.* That year also saw the publication of *Willobie His Avisa,* the story of an innkeeper's wife who triumphantly resists the adulterous advances of a whole string of would-be lovers, and of Shakespeare's *Rape of Lucrece,* a classical reappropriation of the complaint that would be reaffirmed by John Trussell's *Raptus I Helenae: The First Rape of Fair Helen* (1595), Peter Colse's *Penelope's Complaint* (1596), and Thomas Middleton's *Ghost of Lucrece* (1600).[8]

As one might expect from her initiating role, Shore's wife often figures in these poems. Daniel's Rosamond objects that

> Shore's wife is graced and passes for a saint.
> Her legend justifies her foul attaint.
>> Her well-told tale did such compassion find,
>> That she is passed, and I am left behind.

Drayton's Matilda is similarly jealous: "Shore's wife is in her wanton humor soothed, / And modern poets still applaud her praise." And Willoughby's Avisa reinforces her virtue with memories of the "ghastly end" suffered by "Shore's wife" and "fair Rosamond."[9] But the story of Shore's wife did not depend for its continued currency on these recollections in poems about other women. In 1593, Anthony Chute published *Beauty Dishonored, Written under the Title of Shore's Wife;* Thomas Deloney opened his *Garland of Good Will* with ballads on Rosamond and Shore's wife; and even old Churchyard, not wanting to slip out of the fashion he had set, issued a much-augmented version of his own *Shore's Wife* from the *Mirror for Magistrates*. And in 1597, Drayton featured letters between Shore's wife and King Edward, along with others linking a dozen pairs of royal and noble lovers, including Rosamond and Henry and Matilda and John, in *England's Heroical Epistles*.

Any common characterization of these Shore's-wife and Shore's-wife-inspired poems would be contradicted by at least one of them and often by more than one. With Drayton's *Piers Gaveston* on the list, even gender specificity gets blurred. These "female complaints" are neither all female nor all complaints. But all do inhabit a significant part of the territory opened by More's *History of Richard III* and by Churchyard's *Shore's Wife*, a territory marked by passionate sensuality and often abject suffering. The extraordinary beauty of Shore's wife, foregrounded in Chute's *Beauty Dishonored*, is shared by Rosamond, Elstred, Matilda, Avisa, Lucrece, and the others; just as Edward's licentious desire finds counterparts in the passion of Henry, Locrine, John, Tarquin, and Avisa's numerous suitors. And, most often, as in the story of Mistress Shore, beauty and desire result in the tragic ruin of desire's object. Rosamond and Matilda are poisoned, Elstred is drowned, Lucrece stabs herself, and Piers Gaveston is beheaded.

The appeal of these poems, and particularly their claim to a truly tragic pathos, did not, however, go uncontested. As early as 1593, and with specific reference to Shore's wife, the elder Giles Fletcher, assuming the voice of Mistress Shore's great antagonist, Richard III, smiled

> to see the poets of this age,
> Like silly boats in shallow rivers tossed,
> Losing their pains and lacking still their wage,
> To write of women, and of women's falls,
> Who are too light for to be Fortune's balls.[10]

The obvious answer to Fletcher's charge is that these women, Shore's wife most conspicuous among them, attain tragic weight by association with male figures who, like Richard himself, more properly command the attention of history and Fortune. That association is what justifies Drayton in calling his amorous epistles "heroical," and he confirms the claim by following each set of letters with annotations from "chronicle history." Chronicle history is equally the matrix from which the *Mirror for Magistrates*, including Churchyard's *Shore's Wife*, emerged, and it would remain the obvious and elevating source of Daniel's *Rosamond*, Lodge's *Elstred*, and Drayton's *Piers Gaveston* and *Matilda*. At a time when English poetry was just beginning to find a place for itself, and when the places it had found in love lyric and pastoral were considered morally and socially suspect, it is no wonder that a hybrid form, coupling passion and history, would have seemed so attractive. If these poems have obvious affinities to the protracted longing of Petrarchan sonnet sequences and to the ornamented sensuality of Ovidian epyllia, both genres that were making their first English appearance at about this time, they also share the engagement with history, especially with England's own history, that was producing the English history play and poems like Daniel's *Civil Wars* (1595) and Drayton's *Mortimeriados* (1596). All that was most dangerously pleasurable in poetry, as the Elizabethans knew it, here met all that was most instructively useful.

The point of intersection could, however, claim a troubling identity of its own. Shakespeare's *Lucrece* is a third-person narrative, and Drayton's *Piers Gaveston* is spoken by a man, but the voices we hear in these poems are otherwise those of women. Unlike sonnet, epyllion, or history poem, the Elizabethan complaint is a transvestite genre. The poets are men, the speakers women. Shore's wife was the first woman, after an unbroken string of twenty-five men, to be heard in the *Mirror for Magistrates*. Clearly, that gender distinction contributed to her extraordinary success. At once desired object and suffering subject, she obviously engaged her readers, including her male readers, more powerfully than did the fallen princes who surround her, even when she mouthed the same platitudes about fickle Fortune as they. And that heightened appeal suggested new ways of writing. Poets in drag could do things they couldn't do straight. They could inhabit the body of desire, give voice to suffering beauty, add greater pathos to history. Churchyard, finding this when he read Daniel's *Rosamond*, rushed to crowd more of the new sentiment into his old poem—"not," he claimed, "in any kind of emulation, but to make the world know my device in age is as ripe and ready, as my disposition and knowledge was in youth."[11]

Owning these women's voices and winning credit for whatever fame they attained continued to be matters of significant concern. Men dress as women to rival other men and to join with those other men in a shared literary enterprise.[12] They bond, compete, and aspire over the suffering body of a beautiful woman. Yet their ownership is never complete. Unlike the desiring "I" in a sonnet sequence or even the narrative "I" in an epyllion, the "I" of these poems is never the poet's. He is not she. And though the poet supplies the words, he uses them to tell a story that is not his, a story whose otherness is enhanced by both gender difference and historical distance. The events his poem recounts, or something like them, are supposed to have actually happened—and to someone quite unlike the poet. A reality thus underlies the repeated fiction of the poet being solicited by the ghost of the woman whose story he tells, of his being chosen "since others fail."[13] The story does seek out the men who tell it, just as the men's ambitions summon up the story. Looking back over the brief history of the Elizabethan female complaint, one sees shaping forces converging from many directions: a sharpened sense of national identity and national lack that puts new stress on English history and English poetry; a growing awareness of ancient genres that still had no English exemplars; the particular success of *Mirror*-style tragedies; the demands of an expanding market; the ambitions and rivalries of individual poets and groups of poets. But high on the list would also have to be the special attractions of a woman's voice, the energy released by the transgressive encounter of home and state, and the distinctive emotional range revealed in the story of Shore's wife.

If forces like these came together in the early 1590s to produce the female complaint, the resulting poems, even those that center on Shore's wife, nevertheless split off from one another, sometimes sharply. Shore's wife has many voices. In Churchyard's poem she proposes that her story serve as a looking glass to "maid and wife":

> A mirror make of my great overthrow:
> Defy the world and all his wanton ways,
> Beware of me that spent so ill her days.[14]

But along the way she says much that contradicts this moral reading. She talks of the chaste modesty of her youth and tells how her modesty was abused by those who should have protected it, the parents who forced her to marry too young and the king whose power seduced her away from her husband. In familiar *Mirror* fashion, high place itself brings danger ("The quiet life is in the dale below"), and evil Richard turns danger to disaster. Deloney's version has no such excuses: the rebellious daughter of a "wealthy merchant man," she "straight obeyed" the king's lustful command. The pathos of her story comes from the depth of her well-deserved fall: "How strange a thing that the love of a king / Should come to die under a stall."[15] Pathos is more richly and more variously expressed, along with a passionate outpouring of often syntactically incoherent hyperbole, by the "mortal deity" who is Shore's wife in Chute's *Beauty Dishonored,* but it disappears altogether, except perhaps as a shadow of what we know will happen, in Drayton's epistle. Where Chute has Shore's wife speaking to posterity as a ghost returned to her deathbed, Drayton's "Mistress Shore" writes to King Edward even before she has fallen. Chute's heroine belongs in a heaven of beauty and suffering; Drayton's would be more at home in the worldly-wise pages of Ovid's *Art of Love,* a book she cites and whose lessons she has thoroughly mastered.

What unites Churchyard's good girl, Deloney's bad girl, Chute's transcendent beauty, and Drayton's sophisticated flirt is their shared brush with history—that and a social status that should have put them far from history's reach. The first, the brush with history, they have in common with Rosamond, Elstred, Matilda, Piers Gaveston, Penelope, and Lucrece. The second, the low status, only with Avisa. Joining the two makes Shore's wife unique even in this literary field that her story did so much to open. Individual Shore's-wife poems make much of the clash between status and history. Churchyard and Chute both advertise their speaker's low birth; Deloney gives her a specific London address, "at the Flower-de-Luce in Cheapside / Was my dwelling"; and Drayton builds both the action (a disguised visit by the king to her husband's shop) and the witty conceits of his epistles on the contrast between city and court. But, as a whole, the genre neglects and even disdains the status transgression that figures so importantly in its founding story. Striving to elevate poetry as they strove to elevate themselves, Elizabethan poets were careful to find erring, abused, or heroically resistant women of better birth than a mere citizen's wife. And the one obvious exception, Willoughby's *Avisa,* includes no king or other historically significant man among its heroine's wooers. But what the female complaint neglected proved central to the continuing generative power of the Shore's-wife story. Of all the unhappy royal concubines celebrated in the Elizabethan female complaint, only Shore's wife went on to be made the subject of plays that redrew the generic map of European drama even more remarkably than her story had redrawn the generic map of Elizabethan poetry—a distinction she owes as much to her bourgeois origin as to her encounter with two English kings.

ON STAGE

"Jane Shore"—as opposed to "Mistress Shore" or "Shore's wife"—is the invention of the Elizabethan stage. But that theatrical emergence into homely first-name accessibility was not immediate. It was, on the contrary, as vigorously resisted as were her appearances in history and poetry. In Shakespeare's *Richard III*, the future "Jane" not only fails to win a first name; she also loses the presence, the voice, and the very pathos that were hers from More, through Churchyard, to Chute, Deloney, and Drayton and that would continue to be hers for centuries to come. In *Richard III*, Shore's wife is often spoken of, but she is never allowed to speak, nor is she ever seen. And the way she is spoken of leaves her, as I have already remarked, as little more than a degraded and degrading figure of off-color fun.

Given that Shakespeare's play was based on More's *History* and was first produced just as the poetic fad initiated by Churchyard's *Shore's Wife* was taking hold, this must be regarded as a deliberate debasement and exclusion.[16] Although Shakespeare was as intent as More on demonizing Richard, he obviously did not want a bourgeois heroine in his play, did not want to shift his gaze or ours from the center of political power, did not want to detract from his monster king by giving expression to the affective power associated with Shore's wife. So instead of featuring Mistress Shore, Shakespeare disfigured her and relied for pathetic affect on Richard's more safely royal and noble victims: Queen Margaret, Queen Elizabeth, Queen Anne, Prince Edward and Prince Richard, Clarence, Rivers, Dorset, Grey, Hastings, and Buckingham.

As if in direct answer to Shakespeare, Thomas Heywood did exactly the opposite in the work that, after More's *History*, has contributed most to the legend of Shore's wife, his two-part *King Edward IV* (1599). Where Shakespeare suppressed Shore's wife, Heywood built her up at the expense of King Edward, King Richard, and all the others as well. This move may have been part of a larger difference between Shakespeare's vision of English history and that of playwrights like Heywood who worked for the theaters controlled by Philip Henslowe. Whereas Shakespeare, in his English history plays, focused almost exclusively on the succession, maintenance, and expression of royal power, the Henslowe dramatists were more interested in figures who mediate between king and people, figures who are themselves often the victims of kingly tyranny.[17] But of all these mediating figures—and there are many of them—none achieved the show-stealing emotional impact of Shore's wife in Heywood's *Edward IV*, the play in which she first acquired the endearingly familiar name of "Jane."

But a first name was not all Jane Shore acquired in Heywood's two plays. She also got a brave and loving husband. From More's "honest citizen, young, and goodly, and of good substance" to the "doting old and cold and foolishly jealous" husband of Chute's *Beauty Dishonored,* Master Shore had assumed almost as many guises as his wife.[18] But he was never a prominent figure in her story, nor was their relationship ever one of mutual affection. Whoever told the story, Mistress Shore was married too early and had too little say in the choice of her husband ever to love him. In *Edward IV* all this changes. Heywood's Jane and Matthew Shore—he gets a first name too—are bound to one another by an intense love, a love that survives her infidelity and his jealous anger. This love makes Heywood's *Edward IV* a "domestic" tragedy in a way that no other version of the story could have been. The home violated by King Edward's lust is, for Heywood, a place of great value, as powerful a representation of what we retrospectively recognize as a bourgeois ideal as the Elizabethan stage can furnish. Only the loyalty a subject owes his sovereign can rival it.

Edward IV pits these values against one another, consciously and insistently opposing the bond between husband and wife to the bond between subject and sovereign.[19] In submitting, however reluctantly, to the king's lecherous command, Jane chooses the latter bond, and Matthew does much the same when, about to flee into self-imposed exile, he refuses to reclaim his wife.

> Thou go with me, Jane? Oh, God forbid
> That I should be a traitor to my king!
> . . . .
> No, my dear Jane, I say it may not be.
> Oh, what have subjects that is not their king's?
> I'll not examine his prerogative.[20]

Heywood's play endorses this unconditional loyalty. But the play also makes clear that the kings who command it—first Edward, then Richard—are unworthy the high office each has usurped. Though the bourgeois home can finally offer no effective or legitimate resistance to either Edward's self-indulgent desire or Richard's tyrannous persecution, it does nevertheless emerge as a far more compelling locus of affective attachment, both for the characters and for the audience, than does the court of either king. We are made to care about Jane and Matthew in a way that we never care about Edward or Richard. Jane and Matthew's happiness and suffering simply matter more than the success or failure of their kings.

The asymmetry between state and home, with the state commanding absolute obedience and the home claiming the larger share of affective attachment, is essential to the tragedy of Jane Shore, and perhaps to the emergence of domestic tragedy more generally. If we think of the two parts of Heywood's *Edward IV* not only as being in competition with Shakespeare's *Richard III* and his other English history plays, but also helping to initiate a new tragic genre that would compete with the royal and noble tragedies Shakespeare began writing about the time *Edward IV* first appeared, what makes such competition possible is the antagonistic separation of home from state and the emotional preeminence granted the home. Antagonism with the state keeps the home in the elevated company to which tragedy properly belongs but makes it a distinguishable protagonist in that company, while the home's emotional preeminence shifts spectator identification in its direction. It may not be what Aristotle recommended, but in *Edward IV* it works.

Heywood shows the crucial split between home and state happening. At the opening of *1 Edward IV* the two are closely allied, as the citizens of London—Matthew Shore prominent among them—heroically resist Lord Falconbridge and the rebellion Falconbridge leads. "Tell me," Jane asks Matthew, "why you fought so desperately?" His answer provides a neat summary of his loyalties.

> First, to maintain King Edward's royalty;
> Next, to defend the city's liberty;
> But chiefly, Jane, to keep thee from the soil
> Of him that to my face did vow thy spoil.[21]

Falconbridge had vowed to overthrow King Edward, to sack London, and to sleep with Shore's wife. To oppose him, as Matthew does, is at once to protect all three and to affirm an identity based on all three. But when Edward, in obvious but unconscious imitation of Falconbridge, turns, as he says himself, "rebel" to his royal duty and seeks to carry off Matthew's wife, the happy union of home, city, and state breaks down, opening the way to Matthew Shore's self-division and to the new genre of domestic tragedy.[22]

The insertion of the city's liberties between King Edward and Jane in Matthew's list of loyalties marks another of Heywood's innovations.[23] The Shores are always Londoners, but in no previous telling does the city's corporate identity—its liberty—figure so conspicuously in their story. Matthew fights specifically as a citizen of London, under the command of the lord mayor, the recorder, and the aldermen. The political and commercial organization of London is thus converted into a military organization, with "whole companies / Of mercers, grocers, drapers, and the rest, / . . . drawn together for their best defense"; "from every hall / . . . at least two hundred men in arms."[24] Nor is this the first time London has gone to war. As both the lord mayor and Matthew Shore recall, citizens of London led the defeat a century earlier of Jack Straw's rebellion, an event commemorated in the city's arms and in the chronicles of England. Like their forebears, these Londoners aspire to a place in history. Matthew Shore's defense of his wife and city against the rebel Falconbridge thus inscribes itself in a broad tradition of civic action in which Londoners— merchants, craftsmen, and apprentices—have, in the words of Heywood's lord mayor, "bestirred [them] like good citizens, / And shown [them]- selves true subjects to [their] king."[25]

Given the strong identification of the Shores as Londoners, the violation of their home by the state involves the simultaneous violation of the city and its liberties. Not only is the king described as a Falconbridge- like rebel, but the "violent siege" he lays at the walls of Jane's "plighted faith" echoes Falconbridge's siege of London.[26] Furthermore, Edward's first sight of Jane comes at a banquet given in his honor by the lord mayor, a widower for whom Jane fills the part of "lady mayoress," and the king's subsequent visits (borrowed from Drayton) to the Shore's goldsmith shop, "muffled like a common servingman," are at the same time surreptitious visits to the city.[27] Now, these are not the only visits the disguised king pays to a commoner home. He also graces the home of Hobs the tanner of Tamworth, in whose pretty daughter he takes a momentary interest. But if that interest never turns to destructive passion and if the tanner's home never escapes the comic register, the difference comes in large part from the greater stature and dignity Heywood grants London and its citizens. For all their protestations of humility—including Matthew's refusal of a knighthood for his defense of London and Jane's applause of that refusal—these are figures whose civic standing makes them worthy of both history and tragedy. Heywood contests Shakespeare's version of history and tragedy not in the name of all English subjects, but specifically in the name of London and its citizens.

But not only does Heywood give London a new prominence, he also makes the king's act more obviously and complexly transgressive than does any earlier account and makes Jane's response more unambiguously peni- tential, changes that profoundly transform the story's political and cultural significance. Many of Heywood's additions heighten the king's guilt. Prominent among them are the loving bond between Jane and Matthew, the attention given the king's own marriage to the widow Grey, the obligation the king owes Matthew and his fellow Londoners for the defeat of Falconbridge, the likeness drawn between the rebels and the king, Jane's marked disinclination to yield to the king's advances, the absolute command to which the king finally resorts, and the dramatic parallel between the king's forcible appropriation of Jane Shore and the "benevolence" he requests in support of his dynastic war in France. For at the very time when Edward is transgressing all the familial, communal, and national bonds and obligations that should have prevented his seizure of Jane Shore, his subjects, including the wronged citizens of London, are giving willingly of their substance to aid his royal ambitions. This benevolence, absent from all other accounts of Shore's wife, turns the king's act of sexual appropriation into an illegitimate and forced taxation, a tyrannical abuse of his subjects' property.

Still more remarkable is the change in Jane's response to her adultery. Unlike the Shore's wife of More's *History* or the female complaints, Heywood's Jane Shore never glories in her social elevation, taking no apparent pleasure in the prince's love or the "world's pomp."[28] Instead, she wears her courtly attire like a robe of shame and performs acts of mercy as though they were acts of penance. If Daniel's Rosamond had already complained that "Shore's wife is graced and passes for a saint," Heywood carries the process of canonization much further. Through transgression, repentance, and the acts that spring from both, Jane's very powerlessness is transformed into a beneficent, wonder-working power, and Jane herself is transformed from a passive possession of her husband and Edward—a token of male power passed back and forth from one to the other—into an active intercessor between suffering subjects and their inattentive king. Neither More, whose assertion of the "comfort and relief" Shore's wife afforded many suitors forms the basis of this saint's "legend," nor the succeeding poets, who elaborated the legend, gave her deeds any concrete particularity or a motivation that includes contrition.[29] Heywood's Jane Shore acts primarily out of contrition, and the beneficiaries of her mediating grace are made prominent characters in the play.

Of these, easily the most significant is Matthew himself. He first observes his wife's goodness to others with bitterness as he prepares to leave England, robbed of name, home, and country by the shame of her infidelity. But on his return and without her recognizing him, he is twice saved from death by her intervention. On the first occasion, Jane wins him a pardon from King Edward; on the second, she applies "a precious balm . . . King Edward used himself" to a wound Matthew has received defending the little princes in the Tower.[30] In both instances, the saving power comes from the king; but, in both, it is used to undo a royal wrong. Herself the victim of just such a wrong—a victim who takes on herself the full guilt of the wrong that has been done her—Jane uses the king's power to relieve the suffering of others. As both penitent and mediator, she acts as a secular saint in a universe where the king holds the place of a willfully self-indulgent or a brutally tyrannical god.

The death Heywood gives Jane completes her legend. She dies, somewhat improbably, with Matthew as the result of King Richard's hypocritically vindictive proclamation,

> On pain of death, that none shall harbor you,
> Or give you food, or clothes to keep you warm;
> But having first done shameful penance here,
> You shall be then thrust forth the city gates
> Into the naked, cold, forsaken field.[31]

"Thrust forth the city gates," this saint of London—this "comfort-ministering, kind physician, / That once a week in her own person [had visited] / The prisons and the poor in hospitals / In London or near London every way"—cries out to London itself: "Farewell to thee, where I was first enticed, / That scandalized thy dignity with shame."[32] Her sin has wronged the city as much as it has wronged her husband and marriage. But in exile and suffering, she is reunited with her husband, and in death she and Matthew are together made objects of veneration: "The people, from the love they bear to her / And her kind husband, pitying his wrongs, / Forever after mean to call the ditch"—that is, the ditch where with a kiss Jane and Matthew die—"Shore's Ditch, as in the memory of them."[33] Shoreditch, to the north of London, was one of those areas outside the city walls where, in Heywood's own time, the public theaters were located. Heywood's fanciful etymology thus associates the spectacle of Jane Shore's death with its theatrical reenactment in his play. Watching that play, weeping over Jane Shore, Londoners in 1599 were made one with the beneficiaries of her merciful acts, who, in defiance of King Richard's command, attempt to relieve her suffering.

Edward IV does not preach rebellion. On the contrary, it preaches loyalty and submission in the face of all but the most abusive royal transgression. The citizens of London are right to risk their lives in defense of King Edward's shaky title, and they are right again to contribute to Edward's benevolence. But in defying Richard's command and succoring Jane, they are also right, as she was wrong to put Edward's command above her duty to Matthew and to London. Thirteen years later, in his *Apology for Actors* (1612), Heywood recalls only her error. "Women . . . that are chaste," he says in defense of the theater's role as a moral teacher, "are by us extolled and encouraged in their virtues, being instanced by Diana, Belphoebe, Matilda, Lucrece, and the countess of Salisbury. The unchaste are by us showed their errors, in the persons of Phrine, Lais, Thais, Flora, and, amongst us, Rosamond and Mistress Shore."[34] Jane takes a similar view of her story: "Whoso knew me and doth see me now, / May shun by me the breach of wedlock's vow." But if she was wrong, so in still greater measure was the "king [who] did cause her blame."[35] *Edward IV* divides its audience's loyalties and suggests, through the strong affective preference its grants Jane and Matthew, that, if supreme power resides with the state, ultimate value belongs rather to the home and the local community.

By her "breach of wedlock's vow," her association with royal power, her long repentance, her acts of merciful mediation, and her exemplary death, Heywood's Jane Shore became the representational conduit of both power and value, a figure through whom London audiences could feel themselves at once touched by the desires of state and superior to those desires. Jane Shore was as much a mediator for them as for any character in the play. The emotions her "saintliness" aroused fed an emerging bourgeois cult of home and community, a cult that defined itself in conflicted relation to the competing cult of monarchy.

Or so we may guess from our own reading of Heywood's play and from the evident signs, even in the sparse records of the period, of the play's success. In 1603, four years after the first production of *Edward IV*, Philip Henslowe paid Henry Chettle and John Day an advance on "the book of Shore," still another play "wherein Shore's wife is written."[36] This second Jane Shore play has not survived, but two ballads from about the same time, "The Woeful Lamentation of Mistress Jane Shore" and "A Most Sorrowful Song of Banister," do survive to testify to the impact of Heywood's invention. Both retell the story with Heywood's additions, the "Song of Banister" going so far as to express gratitude for the mediatory suffering Heywood had so powerfully represented: "Cease then from mourning, lovely Jane, / For thousands thank thee for thy pain."[37] And further testimony comes from the ghost of Jane's persecutor, Richard III, in a 1614 poem by Christopher Brooke:

> And what a piece of justice did I show
>   On Mistress Shore, when with a feigned hate
> To unchaste life I forced her to go,
>   Barefoot, on penance, with dejected state?
> But now her fame by a vile play doth grow,
>   Whose fate, the women so commiserate,
>   That who, to see my justice on that sinner,
>   Drinks not her tears, and makes her fast, their dinner?[38]

Jane's tears have become nourishment for London audiences, particularly for the women in them. Through her, the urban and domestic world with which both she and they were identified has been lifted to the eminence of history and tragedy, a position from which, at least in Heywood's rendition, it outshines even the threatening glory of kings.

RICHARD AND JANE

"Too slight a thing to be written of and set among the remembrance of great matters," Shore's wife found a place in More's *History* as a foil to King Richard. In Heywood, she is still a foil to Richard, though less to Heywood's own Richard, a relatively pale and marginal figure, than to Shakespeare's. In the interest of the monarch-centered history he was making his own, Shakespeare suppressed Shore's wife. In the interest of a very different, subject-centered history, Heywood brought her back and made her a more prominent character than either of the kings who oppressed her. But long before Heywood wrote, the rivalry implicit in More's *History* between Richard and Shore's wife and between their respective literary claims had taken hold, and that rivalry continued well after. Recall, for example, that in 1593 it was in Richard's voice that Giles Fletcher labeled women as "too light" for tragic narrative and that twenty years later it is still Richard, now in Christopher Brooke's poem, who complains of the success "a vile play" has had in making Mistress Shore a more compelling figure than even he. And much earlier, in the 1563 edition of the *Mirror for Magistrates,* Shore's wife already appears as a stylistic antidote to Richard, whose "tragedy" immediately precedes hers. "To supply that which is lacking in him," says the editor, "here I have Shore's wife, an eloquent wench, which shall furnish out both meter and matter, that which could not comelily be said in his person."[39]

The sense that not everything could "comelily" be said in Richard's person, that the tragic and historic doings of kings needed to be complemented by a representation of the suffering of subjects, persisted, as did the more specific complementarity of Richard and Jane Shore. In 1714, in the first performances of Rowe's *Tragedy of Jane Shore*, the part of Richard was taken by Colley Cibber, who had already claimed the role in his own frequently staged adaptation of Shakespeare's *Richard III.* As if to enforce the connection, Cibber wore the same costume in the two plays.[40] The effect must have been like what we now experience in seeing *Hamlet* and Tom Stoppard's *Rosencrantz and Guildenstern are Dead* performed by the same company. One play is the negative image of the other. Something of the same effect would have been repeated later in the eighteenth century when John Philip Kemble was playing Shakespeare's Richard as his sister, Sarah Siddons, was moving audiences to those resonant sobs and shrieks in Rowe's *Jane Shore.* And it would have been repeated yet again in the 1820s when English actors took *Richard III* and *Jane Shore* to Paris, where a French playwright, Népomucène Lemercier, had already combined elements of the two plays in his *Richard III et Jane Shore* (1824).[41] Richard III and Jane Shore, royal tyranny and bourgeois suffering, politic history and domestic tragedy—these antagonistic pairs remained in a mutually dependent relation for centuries.

But, as we have repeatedly noticed, that relation has always been felt to be transgressive. A London wife simply does not belong in the company, whether literal or literary, of an English king. The first transgression, the literal one, was Edward's in taking Shore's wife as his mistress, an act that opened her way into his story and Richard's. The second transgression, the literary one, belongs to the writers who, unlike Shakespeare, insisted on keeping her in their retellings of those stories, especially those who, like Heywood and Rowe, went so far as to make the story more hers than that of either Edward or Richard. "Too slight a thing" for More's imagined critics, "too light" for Fletcher's Richard, Jane Shore assumes a place that literary decorum in humanist and monarchic England would have strenuously denied her. Nowhere is that denial expressed with greater vehemence than by Charles Gildon in *A New Rehearsal* (1714). "Jane Shore is," Gildon insists, "no tragical character. . . . Her station of life was too low. A shopkeeper's wife of the city never can rise above the sock"—that is, above comedy—"and her having lain with the king and two or three lords will never be thought ennobling enough to fit her for the buskin [of tragedy], since that very crime renders her incapable of it."[42] Though this may seem merely an extreme expression of neoclassical prejudice, more recent prejudice with regard to the status of Heywood's version of the Jane Shore story as history is scarcely less rigid. In Irving Ribner's Shakespeare-oriented view, "the amount of history in *Edward IV* is so negligible that it is lost under the weight of sentimental romance," and even Kathleen McLuskie, a feminist scholar, writing in a book devoted to Heywood and Thomas Dekker, can say that "in *Edward IV*, Heywood used the role of Jane Shore to transform history into domestic melodrama."[43]

"History," as the word is used by these critics, has nothing to do with fidelity to the facts of the past. Shakespeare's liberties in that regard are hardly less large than Heywood's. No, *history*, like *tragedy*, names a generic category rather than a relation of representation to fact, a category to which Jane Shore and the emotion she arouses are refused entry. Call her story "comedy," as Gildon does. Or call it "sentimental romance" or "domestic melodrama" with Ribner or McLuskie. But do not call it "history" or "tragedy." Those genres are reserved for protagonists of another social status and, most often, of another gender. After all, even Nicholas Rowe thought that the kind of play he wrote needed a name of its own. In the epilogue to *Jane Shore*, he calls it "she-tragedy." If, as he wryly remarks, its example is followed, "The poets frequently might move compassion, / And with she-tragedies o'errun the nation."[44] Moving compassion, as Jane Shore does, is the stuff of she-tragedy, of sentimental romance, of domestic melodrama, of what the eighteenth century would enjoy and condemn as weeping comedy. And overrunning the nation is more than a threat that bad art will drive out good. It is a threat that the nation will be taken over by the values of a newly promoted class and a newly promoted gender.

Central to those values are the bourgeois home and marriage that earn plays of this sort the designation *domestic*. But if we think of the *domus* in a slightly different way, neither Shakespearean tragedy and history nor the Greek tragedy on which neoclassical understanding of the genre relied are any less domestic than Heywood's *Edward IV* or Rowe's *Jane Shore*. Indeed, they could be considered more domestic. In a great many instances, if not in all, the action of those Greek and Shakespearean plays is centered on conflicts within a particular family or "house." This is obviously true of the Sophoclean plays on which Aristotle's definitions were based, and it is also true of Shakespeare's two tetralogies of English history plays and of such paradigmatic Shakespearean tragedies as *Hamlet* or *Lear*. In these plays, brothers war on brothers, sisters on sister, children on parents, nieces and nephews on uncles. Tragic and historical action remains locked in the royal or aristocratic family. *Richard III*, with its litany of murdered and murderous Plantagenets—Edwards, Richards, and Harrys—is just such a play.

Edward IV and *Jane Shore* belong to another kind altogether. In them, the bourgeois *domus*—now more a place and a marital bond than a lineage or an extended family—suffers disruption from without, not from within. As a subject for tragic or historical (as opposed to farcical) representation, the bourgeois house comes into existence only in relation to the more usual protagonists of those lofty genres, protagonists who enter its space with destructive effect. As Matthew Shore puts it,

> A king had all my joy, that her enjoyed,
> And by a king again she was destroyed.
> All ages of my kingly woes shall tell.[45]

Matthew and Jane Shore deserve to have their woes told by "all ages" not because of who they are but because of who caused those woes. Where Greek and Shakespearean history and tragedy are fundamentally endogamous, even on occasion incestuous, the new kind of historical tragedy represented by *Edward IV* and *Jane Shore* is exogamous. Its action, particularly its sexual action, crosses status lines, not lines of forbidden consanguinity. Marx, not Freud, thus provides the appropriate language for discussing tragedy of this sort. Instead of Oedipal intrigue, it represents class conflict.

This is not an altogether new claim. In his influential study of eighteenth-century bourgeois drama—territory to which we will return in a later chapter—Peter Szondi takes up the arguments of George Lukács and Arnold Hauser that, in Szondi's words, "bourgeois drama was the first theatrical form to take social conflict for its subject and thus to place itself openly in the service of class struggle."[46] In apparent opposition to these arguments, Szondi points out that none of the plays by George Lillo, Gotthold Ephraim Lessing, and Denis Diderot that got this genre going in eighteenth-century England, Germany, and France presents a conflict between burghers and nobles and that the main characters of the Lessing and Diderot plays are not even of bourgeois status, belonging rather to the nobility. But then, in a subtle and largely convincing reading of these plays, Szondi shows that, whatever the status of their leading characters, the plays' values are bourgeois and that the seemingly excessive emotional response they call forth was precisely the product of the bourgeoisie's position under the ancien régime. "As long," Szondi writes, "as the urban middle-class did not rise up against [royal] absolutism and claim power for itself, it would necessarily live a life of sensibility and weep powerlessly in the theater over the misery imposed on it," even when that absolutist imposition was not directly represented.[47] Had Szondi taken the Jane Shore story as his paradigmatic example, as its extraordinary influence might well have justified his doing, the subtle indirection of his argument would not have been needed, for here both the protagonist's middle-class status—specifically and insistently urban and mercantile—and the confrontation between the burgher household and the absolutist state are explicit. Indeed, in Heywood, both are emphasized in every way possible.

The ultimate transgression of the Jane Shore story, one that even the "bourgeois" dramas of Diderot and Lessing would avoid, was to make readers and theatergoers feel the tragic emotions of fear and pity, woe and wonder, for a mere "shopkeeper's wife of the city." Such transgression has not been readily forgiven, as nearly five centuries of denigrating remarks amply attest. Old systems of authority do not easily give way to new ones, particularly not in the conservative field of literary representation. And make no mistake: to weep for Jane Shore is to grant her and others like her an authority that had previously been reserved for kings and saints. No wonder then that both ancient forms of charisma, the kingly and the saintly, are deployed in the elevation of this bourgeois wife to tragic and historic stature. But, remarkably, the Jane Shore we weep for in most retellings of her story is less the king's mistress or the saint than the bourgeois wife. We do, of course, weep for the saintly victim of royal power but also and especially for the loss of the middle-class home and the urban community for which Jane Shore stands. And in weeping for their loss, we affirm their value, just as we affirm the value of inherited, patriarchal monarchy when we experience the cathartic fear and pity induced by the fall of kings.

That the forms of these new representational and ideological configurations—the female complaint and the she-tragedy—should be so indelibly gender marked derives from the way in which gender and class can be read as versions of one another, both alternatives to the patrilineal and monarchic construction of reality that underlies Greek and Shakespearean history and tragedy. The very adulterous exogamy that gives Jane Shore her story and provides the basis for the claim she makes on our emotions doubles the terms of difference, putting a royal man in illicit relation to a bourgeois woman. It thus prepares the way for that feminizing of culture, which is also a bourgeoisifying of culture, that critics have both celebrated and lamented.[48] As we have seen, such mixed reaction has greeted the Jane Shore story ever since its first telling. Invading the exclusively ruling-class and masculine domains of humanist history, *de casibus* lament, national history play, and classical tragedy, that story has provoked repeated hostility. But it has also remade those generic domains in its own image and, in so doing, has helped remake the culture from which they arose. The tears that were shed over Jane Shore prepared the way for a world in which urban merchants, like the Londoners Jane came from, would take the place of kings, a world in which the middle class would have other luxuries than the luxury of grief.

Chapter Three

———=≼ • ≽=——

The Buck Basket, the Witch, and the Queen of Fairies

In 1607, just four years after his accession to the English throne, James I commissioned John Norden to produce a survey of "the honor of Windsor," the royal domain that included Windsor Castle and the surrounding forests. What we see in Norden's beautifully drawn and colored maps is the visual equivalent of a country house poem: an estate wholly amenable to the pleasure and possession of its proprietor. The most detailed of the maps is a perspective view of the royal manor house, Windsor Castle itself (figure 3). The other sixteen maps show large or small parcels of the park and forest lands, all carefully delineating what most interested this sports-minded king: the opportunities the land afforded for hunting. The general map lists kinds of deer that can be found in each part of the domain, and other maps, like the map of Little Park (figure 4), show some of those deer along with an occasional hunting dog. Seeing images like these, one might think of Gamage Copse in Ben Jonson's poem "To Penshurst," "That never fails to serve the seasoned deer," or of "the loud stag" in another of Jonson's country house poems, "oft rousèd for [King James's] sport."[1] In the closely related genres of estate survey and country house poem, the land and all its features belong to the lords who own it, both to the individual landlords and to their liege lord, the king—who was, of course, himself the direct owner under God of the honor of Windsor.

But look again at Norden's maps of Windsor Castle and Little Park. Over at the far right-hand side of each, crowded around the west end of

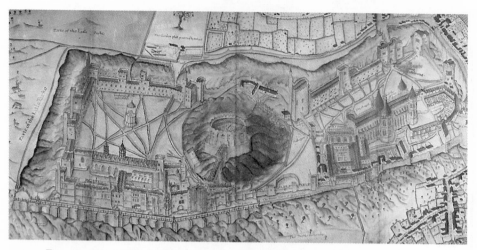

Figure 3   View of Windsor Castle from John Norden's "Description of the Honor of Windsor" (1607). Harleian MS 3749. By permission of the British Library.

the castle close, is a space that belongs neither to the king in the way that the rest of what we see on the map does nor to a genre like the estate survey or country house poem. Flaring out from the castle walls, dwarfed by castle and park, are the few house-and-shop-lined streets of the town of Windsor—a borough town since 1277, with its own courts and responsibility for its own affairs, a town whose charter, and thus whose relative autonomy, had been renewed by King James in the first year of his reign. If Windsor Castle and Windsor Forest might suit a country house poem, the town of Windsor is a more likely subject for a play in the classical tradition of "new comedy," a play about the doings of urban dwellers of middling status. And, of course, there exists just such a play: Shakespeare's *Merry Wives of Windsor.*

Though it may seem a large jump from an estate survey like Norden's to a comedy like Shakespeare's, the first provides a surprisingly apt introduction to the second. Indeed, regarded more schematically, Norden's maps might serve almost as well to introduce the plays featured in the last two chapters: *Arden of Faversham* and *Edward IV*. As Windsor Castle is to the town of Windsor, so the royal abbey of Faversham is to the town of Faversham, and so the royal court of Westminster is to the neighboring city of London. Windsor, Faversham, and London are each located in close proximity to a major royal emplacement, and this shared proximity deeply informs all three plays. Without the royally mandated dissolution

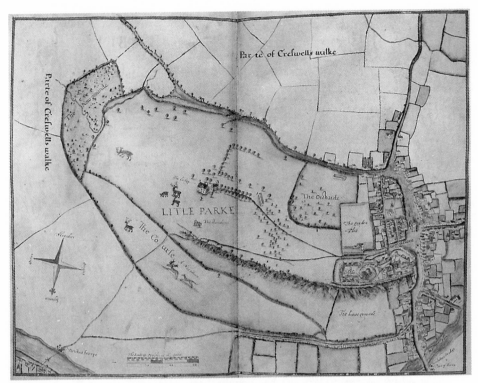

Figure 4   Little Park and the castle and town of Windsor from Norden's "Description of the Honor of Windsor" (1607). Harleian MS 3749. By permission of the British Library.

of Faversham Abbey, an abbey established four centuries earlier by royal donation, the action of *Arden of Faversham* could not have happened. And the actions of *Edward IV* and *Merry Wives* are equally unthinkable without the proximity in the first of Westminster and the royal court and in the second of Windsor Castle. Norden's survey thus provides a useful gloss on all three plays. Like *Arden of Faversham* and *Edward IV*, *The Merry Wives of Windsor* is about the relation between town and crown, between the burgher household and the royal state. In all three, the marginality we see on Norden's maps gets played out in the experience of characters who inhabit that marginal space.

Nor are the relations only social and political. They are also discursive. Inasmuch as history—that is, the kind of writing that claimed the name of history—was coming to be identified as the exclusive province of state actors and state actions, the Arden story, the story of Jane and Matthew

Shore, and Shakespeare's Windsor story are all defined by their marginal relation to it. Though far more conventional in its treatment of middle-class domesticity than either *Arden* or *Edward IV*, *Merry Wives* locates itself, as both the Arden and Shore stories are located, on (or even beyond) the margins of history. For each, history is the off-stage "other" from which its own values and transgressions take their particular meanings. And for each, the principal actors in this meaning-laden exchange are women. As Alice Arden kills the king's man in Faversham and as Jane Shore suffers and triumphs from her adulterous relation with the king, so the Windsor wives humiliate a mock king and courtier. But this final set of actions takes off in new directions, adding new dimensions to our understanding of the early modern home. Though Shakespeare wrote no domestic tragedy—certainly not if one takes *domestic* to mean both "not foreign" and "pertaining to the private, nonaristocratic home"—and though he scrupulously kept Shore's wife out of his *Richard III*, he did nevertheless produce in *Merry Wives* a comedy focused, as both *Arden* and *Edward IV* are, on the intersection of home, state, and history, a comedy in which the home's marginality is both questioned and reaffirmed.[2]

HISTORY AND SHAKESPEARE'S *MERRY WIVES*

The Merry Wives of Windsor has usually been read in terms of another, though closely connected, marginality: its marginal relation to Shakespeare's great sequence of chronicle history plays. Why this should be so is suggested by the title page of its first edition, the "bad" quarto of 1602: *A Most Pleasant and Excellent Conceited Comedy of Sir John Falstaff and the Merry Wives of Windsor*. Sir John Falstaff, as any Elizabethan playgoer would have known, was the famously dissolute companion of Prince Hal in Shakespeare's *Henry IV*. To bring him into a domestic comedy was to put that comedy and the world it represents in relation—however uncertain the nature of the relation—with the history plays and the world they represent. But if we take that world of history to be what both Shakespeare and the humanist historians took it to be—namely, the world of high politics, war, and monarchic government—the Windsor of Shakespeare's *Merry Wives* has still other relations to it. The play's first speech mentions Star Chamber; the privy council comes up a few speeches later; and it is not long before we are hearing about the king and parliament. Nor is this casual intimacy with the leading institutions and persons of state power only a matter of the play's characters and setting. After telling us that this "pleasant and excellent conceited comedy" was written "by William Shakespeare," the title page continues: "As it hath been divers times acted by the right honorable my lord chamberlain's servants, before her majesty, and elsewhere." On at least one occasion, the court was just off-stage. The queen was a member of the audience.

What brought this comic tale of jealousy, wit, and attempted seduction to the royal presence? Legend has it that Elizabeth was herself responsible. According to Nicholas Rowe, writing in 1709, more than a century after the play's first production, the queen "was so well pleased with that admirable character of Falstaff in the two parts of *Henry the Fourth* that she commanded [Shakespeare] to continue it for one play more, and to show him in love."[3] More recently, and with considerably better evidence, another royal occasion has been proposed, the 1597 ceremony at which Lord Hunsdon, the lord chamberlain and patron of Shakespeare's company, was initiated into the Order of the Garter. Windsor was not only the "supremest place of the great English kings," but also "the Garter's royal seat."[4] The Chapel Royal at Windsor Castle was then, as it still is today, the chief gathering place of the order, the place where the Garter knights post their arms and have their stalls. A play set in Windsor, one whose final scene includes a blessing on Windsor Castle and "the several chairs of order," was thus neatly fitted for a Garter feast.[5]

Or was it? What, after all, were the queen, the court, and the Garter knights invited to see at their solemn banquet? Not a heroic history of knightly triumph, some piece of England's crusading and conquering past, but rather a comic tale of knightly defeat: the story of Sir John Falstaff's frustrated attempt to seduce two merry wives of Windsor and get his hands on their husbands' wealth. Was this in any sense the courtly audience's own defeat, as a history of knightly triumph would certainly have been felt to be their triumph? Probably not. Fat Jack Falstaff was hardly a figure with whom monarch or court or Garter knights would have identified. Yet, in an odd way, such identification would not have been far wrong. Carnival king and lord of misrule in part 1 of *Henry IV*, drinking companion and surrogate father to the Prince of Wales, Falstaff does represent the apex of royal power, even if only negatively. He stands for the king. No wonder that the *Merry Wives'* Host of the Garter Inn should call him "an emperor—Caesar, Keiser, and Pheazar" or that he should liken himself to Jove metamorphosed for love.[6] Falstaff *is* an emperor of sorts, a mock god descended from a mock heaven. When he comes to Windsor, history comes with him.

Falstaff is not the only outsider in Shakespeare's Windsor. With him, he brings his page, Robin, and his followers, Bardolph, Pistol, and Nym. There too are Justice Shallow, his cousin Slender, and Slender's man Simple, all from the county of Gloucester; the Welsh parson, Hugh Evans; the French physician, Doctor Caius; some unnamed Germans, who never get on stage but who do steal the Host's horses; and Fenton, a gentleman and companion of "the wild Prince and Poins."[7] Though Windsor is as firmly and concretely realized as any dramatic setting Shakespeare ever created, as much a real and mappable place as the setting of *Arden of Faversham, Edward IV,* or any other English domestic drama, it is nevertheless a place invaded by strangers. *Merry Wives* is about that invasion, about the relation between Windsor and its "others."[8] Here, as in both *Arden of Faversham* and *Edward IV,* the local and domestic are not only staged for the entertainment of a national audience, an audience that in the case of the *Merry Wives* included the queen and the court, they are also engaged in a series of actions that involve a much broader national and even international community. And here, as in *Arden,* that involvement has a double target: property and women's bodies. Falstaff pursues the wives and wealth of Windsor, while Slender, Caius, and Fenton compete for the love and fortune of one of Windsor's daughters. Look at the first of these plots and you see the local and domestic successfully repelling the invader. Look at the second and you see the invader—or at least one of the invaders—carrying off his desired prize. The Windsor wives, Mistress Ford and Mistress Page, utterly defeat the carnival king who seeks to woo them, but the Windsor daughter, Anne Page, happily gives herself to another courtly marauder.

Both actions are essential to Shakespeare's construction of English domesticity and English localism. If the local-*cum*-domestic can overcome the adulterous incursion of the outside world, its future will nevertheless be determined by marriage with an outsider. "Stand not amazed," says a Windsor neighbor to the parents whose own schemes for their daughter's wedding have been so thoroughly frustrated.

> Here is no remedy.
> In love the heavens themselves do guide the state.
> Money buys lands, and wives are sold by fate.[9]

The union of young Fenton and Mistress Anne Page is a wonder. Government and commerce may be ruled by reason; "wives are sold by fate." Here the same logic—or rather the same escape from logic—that removed Arden's murder from history and made it a thing of wonder turns Fenton's triumph into an incontestable act of God. Though Anne's father protests that "the gentleman is of no having," that "he kept company with the wild Prince and Poins," that "he is of too high a region," that "he knows too much," and insists that "he shall not knit a knot in his fortunes with the finger of my substance," his protests and insistences are of no avail. "What cannot be eschewed must be embraced."[10] Thus the play mystifies marriage and, with it, the transfer of Windsor wealth into courtier coffers. Fate and Shakespeare are on Fenton's side.

But they are not on Falstaff's—unless one reads Fenton and Falstaff as types of one another, as Falstaff himself seems to do when he finds consolation for his own defeat in Fenton's victory: "I am glad, though you have ta'en a special stand to strike at me, that [in the case of Fenton] your arrow hath glanced." Even more obviously than Arden and Mosby, Falstaff and Fenton are mismatched twins—both companions of "the wild Prince and Poins," both prodigals who have wasted their substance in riotous living, both intent on repairing their decayed fortune with the wealth of Windsor, both convinced that the way to Windsor's wealth passes through the affections of its women. Fenton "smells April and May"; Falstaff more nearly resembles "a hodge-pudding . . . old, cold, withered, and of intolerable entrails."[11] But if these obvious differences lead to very different outcomes, Falstaff's story and Fenton's nevertheless remain contrasting versions of the same story, a story of the relation between the local community and the court, between the middle-class household and the aristocratic state, between Windsor and history.

Watching this twice-told tale, different segments of Shakespeare's audience might have found different reasons for satisfaction. The court would have applauded Fenton's victory; the town, Falstaff's defeat. But given the way Shakespeare sets things up, both would in fact have applauded both. Falstaff is such a preposterous lover, Fenton such an obviously attractive one, that any outcome other than the one Shakespeare provides would have been shocking. Yet the very characteristics that determine our response reveal the play's ideology most starkly. When the deck is so obviously stacked, we have a pretty good idea where the playwright's sympathies lie—in this case with the prodigal courtier.

More interesting because less clearly predetermined is the way the two stories are told. The end of each may be obvious even from the beginning, but the middle isn't. The pursuit of Anne Page spins off plot, subplot, counterplot, by-plot at a vertiginous rate. Here we need not follow them all, but it is worth pointing out how they sharpen the sense of Englishness, of the "domestic" in the most common Elizabethan usage—that is, in the second of the meanings I mentioned above: the "home-grown," the "not foreign." Though Slender and Caius are the rival candidates for Anne Page's dowry and love, Shakespeare manages to substitute Evans for Slender in the mock duel with Caius, thus pitting the play's two prime abusers of "the King's English"—"*our* English"—against one another.[12] Among Shakespeare's comedies, *The Merry Wives* is not only uniquely English as a simple fact of its setting; it also works at its Englishness, insists on it, makes it fundamental to the definition of a domestic space that court and town can share. That commonality underlies the easy acceptance by both audience and characters of Fenton's eventual triumph: Anne Page is an English woman; Fenton, an English man. Their union confirms the union of classes and conditions in a harmonious national state, while the noisy and aggressive confusion that fills the middle of their story shows what that union is not.

But what then of the other story, the merry wives' rejection and humiliation of Falstaff? If he too represents, though in a comically distorted way, the king and the court, how is he undone? This, it seems to me, is where things get most interesting. In the Fenton/Anne Page plot, the principals are largely kept off stage and out of view. All the attention is given to the futile and misdirected efforts of the losers. In the end, the lovers turn to their own uses an occasion that others have prepared. But in the Falstaff plot the merry wives control the action. They don't simply reject Falstaff. They punish him for his presumption. And they do it with a series of devices that define them and their world with extraordinary resonance, complexity, and precision.

In their response to Falstaff, the Windsor wives seize opportunistically on what comes to hand. And so does their author. First a buck basket, then an old woman's hat and gown, and finally a local legend. Each of these devices marks the intersection of the women's world of household and town and the playwright's world of literary kind and convention. And each suggests its own, quite different relation to court, state, and history. As is so often the case—the contrasting fates of Falstaff and Fenton have already supplied an example—Shakespeare teases his audience with ideological multiplicity. But that very multiplicity can suggest better than a more decided narrowing of options the full shape of a contested territory.

Early modern domesticity is just such a territory, and the three humiliations of Falstaff have surprisingly much to say about it.

THE BUCK BASKET

Consider the episode of the buck basket. No sooner has Falstaff appeared at Mistress Ford's house in response to her invitation than Mistress Page breaks in to announce that Master Ford, "with all the officers in Windsor," is on his way home "to search for a gentleman that he says is now in the house." Feigning concern for Falstaff's safety, the two women cram him into a buck basket (a kind of laundry basket), cover him with foul linen, and direct two of Mistress Ford's men to carry him "among the whitsters in Datchet Mead," where by prearrangement the men are to toss him into "the muddy ditch close by the Thames side."[13]

But why a buck basket? In this tale of attempted cuckolding, the name itself has a punning potential Shakespeare is quick to exploit. "Buck!" shouts the jealous Master Ford when he hears of the buck-washing. "I would I could wash myself in the buck! Buck, buck, buck! Ay, buck! I warrant you, buck—and of the season too, it shall appear." But still more resonant than Ford's mistaken identification of himself as a bucklike horned beast is the physical fact of the basket—the physical fact and the material practices associated with it. There is of course the obvious utility of the buck basket as a container that is large enough to hold Falstaff and that can be plausibly carried out of the house. There is also the foul linen: "stinking clothes that fretted in their own grease." A few lines earlier Falstaff had been bragging how his love—a knight's love—proved Mistress Ford "an absolute courtier," worthy to appear "in a semicircled farthingale."[14] The buck basket reverses that redressing. Stuffed in the basket with clothes dirty enough for buck-washing—that is, washing in a boiling alkaline lye—the court intruder himself gets redefined as filth in need of harsh cleansing.[15] And finally there is the gender and status specificity of buck-washing and other laundry work. The buck basket evokes a world of domestic labor, labor presided over by bourgeois wives and performed by servants, like the ones who carry Falstaff off to Datchet Mead, and by the lower-class women who could be found at places like Datchet Mead working as laundresses and whitsters.

But the buck basket also evokes a world of story. Stories like this—stories of an adulterous lover interrupted by a jealous husband and hidden in some odd place—abound in those earlier genres of the domestic: the French fabliau and the Italian novella. Closest to this is the second story in Ser Giovanni's *Il Pecorone* (1558), where the wife hides her lover under a pile of damp laundry. But in *Il Pecorone*, after the husband has completed his futile search and gone off, the wife locks the door, takes the lover from under the wet clothes, dries him by the fire, prepares him a lavish meal, and then leads him to the bedroom, where they spend the night "giving one another that pleasure each desired."[16] What a difference between this lover's fate and Falstaff's, between that night of pleasure and a hot, cramped, greasy, and frightening ride that ends in a muddy ditch!

Shakespeare's Windsor belongs in the company of the fabliau and novella, in a narrative tradition of elaborate and amusing sexual intrigue, but it reforms that tradition, playing deliberately against its most familiar expectations. Both Falstaff and Master Ford think they are in a story like *Il Pecorone*'s. The Windsor wives intend to show them their mistake. "We'll leave a proof, by that which we will do, / Wives may be merry, and yet honest too." But they defend their honesty with much the same domestic prop that served the novella wife to conceal her vice. "This 'tis to be married!" exclaims the still deluded Ford when he learns how Falstaff evaded his search. "This 'tis to have linen and buck-baskets!"[17] A man's house may be his castle, as the familiar sixteenth-century saying had it; it was nevertheless a castle, like the "castle" of his wife's virtue, that she knew better than he and could better use to serve her own purposes.

At the furthest remove from the "public" realm of history and state power is the "private" domain of the domestic interior. And that domain belonged by fact, if not by right, to women. As Mistress Ford says to her husband, "Why, what have you to do . . . with buck-washing?"[18] If a woman chose to open her house, her buck basket, or her body to an outsider, there was little her husband could do to prevent her. "How many women," wrote Boccaccio in the work that followed his cuckold-filled *Decameron*, "have already dared, and dare day in and day out, to hide their lovers from their husbands' eyes under baskets or in chests? How many have had them make their entrance silently, in the very same bed as their husbands lie in? . . . And, an even greater insult, there is an infinite number who dare to have their pleasure while their husbands are watching."[19]

So runs the paranoid male fantasy that governs fabliau, novella, and domestic drama alike. The genres that deal most concretely—some would say, most realistically—with the house and the local community are also the genres most obsessed with the crafty manipulation of domestic space by the women who inhabit it. What then are we to make of a play that uses the same female control of domestic space to correct this male fantasy in both its paranoid and its wishful versions? It may seem a long stretch to summon John Milton for an answer, but I cannot help thinking of the famous sentence from *Eikonoklastes:* They in whom true virtue "dwell[s] eminently need not kings to make them happy but are architects of their own happiness and whether to themselves or others are not less than kings."[20] The merry wives' "honesty" provides the basis for just such an autonomy, an autonomy that is able not only to expel a licentious mock king like Falstaff but also to cure the culturally induced jealousy of a domestic patriarch like Ford. "Pardon me, wife," says the chastened Ford, when much later he discovers the truth of the events he has so badly misunderstood. "Henceforth do what thou wilt."[21] "Do what thou wilt"— which was, not so incidentally, the motto of Rabelais's utopian Abbey of Thélème—might also be the motto of the republican bourgeois household, with of course the unspoken proviso that you must keep your virtue intact.[22]

But before we get to the patriarch's abdication, there is a second episode that significantly complicates this untroubled image of domestic virtue. And that episode is followed in turn by one that calls into question not the virtue of the female-dominated household, but rather its autonomy from royal government.

THE WITCH

Just as they played on anxieties concerning women's control of domestic space in their first punishment of Falstaff, so in their second Mistress Ford and Mistress Page play on the no less virulent fear of female society, the fear of what women do together. Again Falstaff is lured into the Ford house and again Mistress Page bursts in to announce the imminent and angry arrival of Master Ford. But this time, instead of being hidden in the buck basket, Falstaff is disguised as Mother Prat, Mistress Ford's maid's aunt, "the witch of Brainford."[23]

Again we may ask: Why this particular device? Like the buck basket, it has a double purpose. It gets Falstaff out of the house, but at the same time gets him punished. As the wives know it will, the appearance of Mother Prat provokes Ford's wrath, prompting him to beat Falstaff. Already Ford had expressed concern about the secret intimacy of his wife and Page's: "I think, if your husbands were dead, you two would marry."

And he feared their intimacy would prove his undoing: "Our revolted wives share damnation together." Now the very mention of the old woman brings on another misogynistic tirade:

> A witch, a quean, an old cozening quean! Have I not forbid her my house? She comes of errands, does she? We are simple men; we do not know what's brought to pass under the profession of fortune-telling. She works by charms, by spells, by th' figure; and such daubery as this is beyond our element—we know nothing. Come down, you witch, you hag, you. Come down, I say![24]

What Ford dreads is a world of concerted and secret female power beyond the ken of men. And since, despite Mistress Ford's appeal, none of the other men standing by intervenes to stop his beating of the old woman, it seems likely they share at least enough of his fear to think his action appropriate.[25]

Fears of this sort were endemic to Elizabethan culture. Shakespeare's Richard directs them at Mistress Shore, whose alleged "witchcraft" he blames for his withered arm.[26] And they seep into *A Warning for Fair Women*, that *Arden*-like play of adultery and murder Shakespeare's company staged a couple years after *The Merry Wives of Windsor*. Though pamphlet and chronicle accounts had presented the wife's gossip merely as an accessory to the murder, the play transforms her into a witch—a "cunning woman" expert in physic and fortune-telling—and makes her the murder's chief mover. *A Warning for Fair Women* thus does to the Sanders story what Ford's overexcited imagination would do to his own household and what Richard's cynical accusation would do to his kingdom: make it appear a scene of rebellious female enchantment.[27] Nor, unlike Richard's, are Ford's fears wholly misplaced. Falstaff's disguise does, after all, put Mistress Ford and Mistress Page into relation with a figure of occult female power. If they did not actually know the witch of Brainford, if she was not part of their circle of female acquaintance, why would her hat and gown be hanging in Mistress Ford's chamber and why would Ford have had to forbid her his house? In the same way that the buck basket evokes a world of domestic labor in which the Windsor wives are presumed to be actually engaged, the hat and gown evoke a world of witchcraft in which they are no less concretely involved.[28]

That Shakespeare should have linked witchcraft to small-town domestic life seems to me highly suggestive, for nowhere in Elizabethan England, with the obvious exception of religious observance, was state intervention in local and domestic affairs more intensely marked than in the prosecution of witchcraft. The royal government may not itself have been active in initiating such prosecutions, but without laws enacted early in Elizabeth's reign and strengthened early in James's, witchcraft would not have even been punishable in the royal courts.[29] The state established the framework within which witches could be treated as criminals. And, no less important, the witch became, for at least a few decades in the late sixteenth and early seventeenth centuries, one of the state's defining others—a signifying alterity that was put to dramatic use in two plays based on actual cases of witchcraft, as *Arden of Faversham* and *A Warning for Fair Women* were based on actual murders: Dekker, Rowley, and Ford's *Witch of Edmonton* (1621) and Heywood and Brome's *Late Lancashire Witches* (1634).[30]

In *The Witch of Edmonton*, suspicion of witchcraft, mounting in the minds of her neighbors to a certainty, fastens on the "poor, deformed, and ignorant" Mother Sawyer. Just as a band of these neighbors is about to attack and hang her, an unnamed justice intervenes. "Go, go," he says,

> pray vex her not. She is a subject,
> And you must not be judges of the law
> To strike her as you please.[31]

"She is a subject." Here the witch is snatched from the hands of her unruly neighbors, saved from a purely local judgment, by a representative of the crown, who eventually judges her himself and sends her to execution. And in *The Late Lancashire Witches*, at a comparable moment a gentlemen turns to the newly arrested witches and asks, "Have you known so many of the devil's tricks and can be ignorant of that common feat of the old juggler; that is, to leave you all to the law, when you are once seized on by the talons of authority? I'll undertake," he continues, pointing to the officer standing by, "this little demigorgon constable, with these commonwealth characters upon his staff here, is able in spite of all your bug's-words to stave off the grand devil for doing any of you good till you come to his kingdom to him."[32] Not only does the state make witches subject, it also takes from them whatever autonomous strength and authority they may once have exercised. Through the witch, the state demonizes the local and domestic other, only to prove the demystifying power of its own "commonwealth characters."

But what would happen in a domestic world without the state? That is what Heywood imagines in still another of his domestic dramas, *The Wise Woman of Hogsdon* (1604). In the 1590s the prominent puritan divine

William Perkins had preached that so-called "good" witches, those wise men and women who used their powers to heal and restore, were still more deserving of death than "bad" witches, for where the latter only destroyed the body the former enslaved the soul.[33] And in 1604, the year of the play itself, parliament had increased the penalty for a second conviction of the practices most commonly associated with "cunning folk" from life imprisonment to death. Heywood's play takes a very different line. His wise woman is, to be sure, a fraud. The power of demystifying national drama is sufficient to see through this local charade. But, despite her transparent falsity and her well-documented lawlessness, the wise woman nevertheless presides over the comic resolution of the play's various domestic conflicts. The denouement takes place in her house, where all the characters have assembled, and under her supervision. And in the play's last words, she is invited as the "chief guest" to the triple nuptial feast which her actions have made possible. The wise woman—"the witch, the beldam, the hag of Hogsdon," as she is called—thus functions as an alternative to the state. Think, for comparison, of Dekker's *Shoemaker's Holiday*, where it is the king himself who appears in the last scene to resolve all problems and who is invited as chief guest to the shoemakers' feast; or think of those plays of domestic crime and witchcraft—*Arden of Faversham*, *A Warning for Fair Women*, *The Witch of Edmonton*, or *The Late Lancashire Witches*—where a representative of the king's justice comes on in the fifth act to bring resolution and to mark closure. In the absence of such state action, the witch fills the void by supplying her own comic remedy.

How much of all this can we suppose to have been evoked by the disguise the Windsor wives choose for Falstaff? Certainly, the issues themselves—the fear of witchcraft and the use of state power in its suppression—were as pressing in the mid-1590s as they were in later decades when the Dekker and Heywood plays were produced.[34] But, still, this disguise seems like little more than a characteristic piece of theatrical opportunism on Shakespeare's part. Dressing Falstaff as the witch of Brainford, he could, as we have noticed, both get him out of the house and get him beaten, thus embarrassing the jealous Ford, humiliating the rapacious Falstaff, vindicating the witty wives, and maintaining the situation itself for a third and final round. Why should we insist on attaching broad cultural significance to what can be so satisfactorily explained as a brilliantly effective dramatic device? Because it is precisely in choices like these—choices of what works and what doesn't—that the richest meanings inhere. We have already seen how the equally opportunistic buck basket can serve as a powerful synecdoche for a whole range of domestic relations. In a similar way, Falstaff's disguise connects Mistress Ford, Mistress Page, and the female community to which they belong to the illicit and mysterious world of wise women and witches, a world inscribed in both literature and social practice.

In Ford's beating of Falstaff, two actions are performed simultaneously: a man beats a woman, and two women secure the beating of a man. Ford beats (or at least thinks he beats) the witch of Brainford, and Mistresses Ford and Page secure the beating of Falstaff. In the fiction of the play, only the second "really" happens. But both are represented, and both tie up to the broader cultural and political concerns that we have seen associated with witchcraft. The domestic patriarch, worried about the "petty treason" threatened by his and Page's "revolted wives," exercises his authority on the body of the forbidden witch. Where he earlier imagined himself the cuckolded victim in a fabliau or novella, Ford here mistakes himself for a prototype of Master Generous, the deluded husband in *The Late Lancashire Witches*, whose wife and female friends have been consorting with devils. And Falstaff fears that his disguise will bring down on him not only Ford's beating but also the kind of state action that seized on Master Generous's wife: "But that my admirable dexterity of wit . . . delivered me, the knave constable had set me i' th' stocks, i' th' common stocks, for a witch."[35] But the "real" plot of *The Merry Wives of Windsor* is more like that of *The Wise Woman of Hogsdon*.[36] In both, women conspire to expose and reform wayward men. Though Mistress Ford and Mistress Page use no actual magic—the wise woman of Hogsdon uses none either—they do use the appearance of magic, or at least the appearance of a connection to a world of cunning folk and witches, a world, as Ford defines it, of fortune-telling, charms, spells, and occult figures. And because the men who get corrected in *The Merry Wives of Windsor* are a carnival king, the comic representative of the court, and a domestic king, the patriarchal governor of the family, we can see shadowed in the women's successful action a reversal of the usual prosecution of local disorderliness by an ordering state. Here the local and the domestic, in the persons of Windsor's merry wives, take control.

THE QUEEN OF FAIRIES

And the women keep control—at least of the Falstaff plot—in the third and last of these episodes. But this episode takes a very different turn. After the success of their first and second schemes, the scheme of the buck basket and the scheme of the witch, Mistress Ford and Mistress Page decide to let their husbands in on what has been happening and to make Falstaff's third punishment a public shaming, for, as Mistress Ford puts it, "Methinks there would be no period to the jest, should he not be publicly shamed." This impulse is deeply rooted in premodern English folk practices, in traditional rites of social control like the skimmington that is staged in Heywood and Brome's *Late Lancashire Witches*. And this particular punishment has a still more specific local resonance, based, as it is, on the "old tale" of "Herne the Hunter, / Sometime a keeper here in Windsor Forest."[37] But as the performance develops, it takes on a generic aura well removed from local practices and particularities. As numerous critics have remarked, the play of Herne the Hunter is a masque, a complementary entertainment of just the sort that courtly poets were accustomed to staging for the queen. Suddenly, the world of fabliau, farce, and domestic drama is transformed into a royal pageant.

The switch is signaled by a change in place, from the town of Windsor to Windsor Park, from the burgher corporation to the royal domain. But there is also a change in style from prose (*The Merry Wives* has a higher proportion of prose than any other Shakespeare play) to verse. So abrupt is this change that some scholars have thought that in his rush to satisfy a royal command Shakespeare simply stuck an earlier masque onto an ill-suited play. This seems an unlikely and unnecessary supposition, but it does point to the marked change in direction represented by the final scene. Even the time of the play seems to change. On the strength of Falstaff's presence and Fenton's supposed association with "the wild Prince and Poins," we imagine that *The Merry Wives of Windsor* takes place in the early fifteenth-century reign of Henry IV. Yet the masque seems clearly to address Queen Elizabeth and thus suddenly brings the play into the present—where, of course, it has in fact always been.

But, more than addressing the queen, the masque of Herne the Hunter puts her on stage, makes her the instrument of its reforming action. Presiding over these forest solemnities is the "Queen of Fairies," incongruously played by Mistress Quickly, the merry wives' gossip and fellow conspirator. In the years following the publication of Spenser's *Faerie Queene*, it would have been difficult to evoke the Fairy Queen without at least a suspicion that Elizabeth might be meant. And when Pistol, in the role of Hobgoblin, says, "Our radiant Queen hates sluts and sluttery," the onstage queen of fairies and the off-stage queen of England seem equally implicated. As a result, the Fairy Queen's punishment of Falstaff, her command that the fairies "Pinch him, and burn him, and turn him about" and the song she sings as they do it—"Fie on sinful fantasy! / Fie on lust and luxury!"—is made to come as much from the royal spectator of this play as from the fictional wives who are presumed to have written the script.[38] The local and the domestic are thus subsumed into the national, and women who just a few scenes ago were associated with the witch of Brainford have suddenly acquired a quite different ally.

That Queen Elizabeth was herself not always free from the taint of witchcraft has been shown by Leah Marcus and Louis Montrose, among others.[39] Opposites are always in danger of collapsing into one another, particularly in a case like this where the outlaw rebel and the lawgiving supreme magistrate are both women. A fairy queen has, moreover, a relation to the occult that is at least comparable to that of the wise woman or witch. But here difference seems more significant than similarity. In *The Merry Wives of Windsor,* the local and the domestic, represented most tellingly by Mistress Ford and Mistress Page, are successively linked to contrary poles in the hierarchy of power, to the witch and the queen. Both work to defeat the intruding Falstaff. The witch draws patriarchal fury down on him; the queen exposes his mock kingship, his assumption of the lustful prerogatives of Jove, to the force of her more potent monarchy. But there is a large difference between being defeated by women in league with a neighboring wise woman and being defeated by women in league, if only metonymically, with the reigning monarch. In one case, the deeply and irremediably local expels the court-based outsider; in the other, the court itself overcomes a wayward pretender.

In moving from one to the other, Shakespeare takes his representation of local domesticity in a direction made familiar by his own comedies, so many of which end in a scene of recognition or reconciliation presided over by the ruler of whatever kingdom or dukedom the characters happen to find themselves in. But here an ending of this sort may come as a surprise. After all, this play—Shakespeare's only English comedy—has no onstage ruler, no king or duke, to dominate its final scene. But Shakespeare makes up for this lack by having the off-stage queen of England play that role. Perhaps this is what we should have expected from the play's setting in Windsor or from Shallow's opening threat to "make a Star-Chamber matter" of Falstaff's riots. Though Shallow's grievance quickly disappears from the play, the merry wives put his threat into effect for their own reasons and in their own way by haling Falstaff before the court of the Fairy Queen. Once again, as in the domestic dramas of mur-

der and witchcraft, the national claims jurisdiction over the local. Like
the witch of Edmonton, Falstaff is a subject and must submit to a royal
judgment, a judgment that would come in another and still harsher form
at the end of *Henry IV, Part 2*, where the newly crowned King Henry V
brutally casts off the misleader of his youth. But in *The Merry Wives of
Windsor* the wives themselves remain, as they insist, "the ministers" of
Falstaff's correction.[40] That fact gives a double aspect to even this final
scene. The Fairy Queen's punishment of Falstaff is *both* the queen of England's correction of an errant knight, one who would have troubled the
domestic peace of her common subjects, *and* the commons' rebuke of a
mock king and courtier. And in that second aspect, the domestic buck
basket and the local witch are complemented rather than displaced by this
midnight shaming ritual.

The last time we were offered a double impression of this sort, in the
episode of the witch of Brainford, it was easy enough to see that the wives'
chastisement of Falstaff really happened, while Ford's beating of the old
woman only seemed to happen. Here things are less clear. What may,
however, tip the hermeneutic scales in the direction of a reading that sees
the court as the chief ideological beneficiary of the fairy masque is the
way in which it is made the occasion not only of Falstaff's final defeat
but also of Fenton's ultimate victory. It is during the masque that Fenton's
rivals and their Windsor sponsors, including one of the merry wives, are
frustrated in their marriage plans for "sweet Anne Page" and that Fenton
himself is rewarded. And if we take—as I think there is good reason for
doing—Falstaff and Fenton as versions of one another, we can see the
defeat, in which both the local community and the queen participate, of
the one as cover for the far more significant victory of the other. After
wondering whether the "class dynamic" of *Merry Wives of Windsor* should
be represented "as the victory of a bourgeois solidarity over the aristocratic
court, as the reconciliation of the best of both bourgeois and aristocratic
worlds, or as the consolidation of aristocratic power through a populist
approach," Peter Erickson concluded that the third provides the most accurate account. "The play resolves class tension in a way that favors aristocratic interests."[41] I think he is right.

I also think Erickson is right in stressing the many connections between
Merry Wives and Shakespeare's English history plays—not just the sharing of a handful of characters but also (and perhaps more important) the
sharing of an emerging nationalist ideology of Englishness.[42] Shakespeare's English comedy is history by other means. Its "private" world of

the domestic household and the small-town community is made to serve the purposes of a very "public" theatrical discourse. In this sense, Shakespeare and his audience, both the courtly audience and the public theater audience, may seem the ultimate intruders in domestic Windsor. But domestic Windsor was created to be invaded. Its women and its wealth, its very privacy, were produced for appropriation—Fenton's appropriation and ours. But along the way to that preordained culmination some odd things happen with a buck basket and an old woman's hat and gown, things that threaten to undermine and reverse the court's otherwise easy victory. As Queen Elizabeth watched *The Merry Wives of Windsor*, she was seeing an expression not only of the royal power she represented—power that both disrupts and orders the local and domestic—but also of an alternative to such power, the expression of a local and domestic and female authority that stood for a significantly different England than the one based on patriarchy and royal dynastic succession over which she, as a woman, so incongruously ruled.

꙳

As we leave England and drama for the Netherlands and genre painting, we should keep in mind this double perspective, as well as the multiple perspectives afforded by the Arden story and the story of Jane Shore. Though Dutch paintings were informed by theatrical conventions shared with English drama and often look as though they could serve as illustrations for plays like the ones we have been reading, they come to us without a script. They invite a narrative response but leave us to guess at the story. Having a repertory of actual stories should help in this task. That these English stories do in fact coincide so well with what we see there may, however, provoke some surprise and even skepticism. In the decades that will be at the center of our attention, the Netherlands was, after all, a republic—and a loosely united republic at that. Surely, concerns like those we have encountered in monarchic and consolidating England should have no place there. Yet for all the Netherlands' republican independence and bourgeois government, this new polity lived surrounded by ambitious and potentially encroaching kings. Thinking back to the schematic version of Norden's maps, we can see that even the Low Countries fit. As Windsor Castle is to the town of Windsor, so monarchic Europe is to republican Holland. And when we add that the Netherlands had in the princes of Orange home-grown pretenders to royal sovereignty, the foreign threat becomes domestic: a Mosby in Faversham, an Edward in London, or a Falstaff in Windsor. Nor is the role of women in this Dutch domestic setting any less decisive than in the English plays we have studied. But what course will those Dutch women take? Will they act like the murderously adulterous Alice Arden, the reluctantly and repentantly adulterous Jane Shore, or the virtuously resistant merry wives? Or will they behave in a way all their own? Given the tantalizing mystery of silent, freeze-frame painting, we may often not be able to answer these questions even when we have the paintings before us. But that very uncertainty gives new urgency to the spectator's part, to the problem of interpretation itself. It is to that problem and its specifically Dutch expression that we now turn.

At Home in the
Dutch Republic

Chapter Four

——◁ • ▷——

Soldiers and Enigmatic Girls

THE LESSONS OF A MISREADING

Among the entertainments they devise to pass the dull winter days, the aristocratic protagonists of Goethe's *Elective Affinities* (1809) stage some famous paintings. First on the program are history paintings by van Dyck and Poussin. But for their third *tableau vivant*, Goethe's characters switch from history to genre, from van Dyck and Poussin to Gerard ter Borch's *Paternal Admonition* (figure 5). Here is how Goethe describes this third *tableau:*

> One foot thrown over the other, sits a noble knightly-looking father; his daughter stands before him, to whose conscience he seems to be addressing himself. She, a fine striking figure, in a folding drapery of white satin, is only to be seen from behind, but her whole bearing appears to signify that she is collecting herself. That the admonition is not too severe, that she is not being utterly put to shame, is to be gathered from the air and attitude of the father, while the mother seems as if she were trying to conceal some slight embarrassment—she is looking into a glass of wine, which she is on the point of drinking.[1]

Of all the misreadings of a Dutch genre painting, this is the best known. Getting from Goethe's *Paternal Admonition*—a title that was attached to the painting long before Goethe described it and that has remained in place ever since—to the very different scene we now suppose the painting to represent seems to have required focusing on what is *not* there, but

Figure 5   Gerard ter Borch, *Paternal Admonition* (c. 1654–55). Oil on canvas, 70 × 60 cm. Gemäldegalerie, Staatliche Museen, Preussischer Kulturbesitz, Berlin. Photo: Jörg P. Anders.

may once have been: a coin between the upraised thumb and forefinger of the "noble knightly-looking father." On that invisible fulcrum, the whole sense of the painting tips. This is no father, nor are the women his daughter and wife. This is a customer offering payment for the sexual favors of the young woman, a transaction witnessed by the young woman's bawd.

That not only Goethe but generations of viewers should so badly have misread this scene tells much of how Dutch genre painting was received in the centuries immediately following its production—of how, for that matter, we are still inclined to receive it. Wherever possible, we have wanted to find in these paintings images of a powerfully comforting domestic intimacy, images of family life at its most warmly engaging. Nor, despite the best efforts of a generation of iconographic reinterpreters, are we always disappointed. A great many Dutch genre paintings remain, even now, the quietly convincing celebrations of everyday life we have always supposed them to be.[2] Dutch genre painting does, of course, also offer many obvious, rollicking, comic scenes of sexual licence, scenes where there is little chance of mistaking the house for a home. But what continues to make a painting like ter Borch's *Paternal Admonition* so disturbing is the way it moves from one category to the other without ever quite settling in either. Though we may feel sure the seated man is no father, can we be equally sure that the standing lady, who turns so bashfully away from both him and us, is not a modest daughter or wife?

Similar questions arise even with paintings that could never have been mistaken for virtuous domestic scenes. Consider, for example, ter Borch's ironically titled *Gallant Officer* (figure 6). Here the coins are at last clearly visible and their purpose easily guessed. We hardly need the iconographers' solemn reminder that fruit, wine, bed, and money could all have erotic implications to recognize that mercenary love is here in question. But no number of proverbial sayings of the *Der pennings reden klinkt best* (Money talks) sort can erase the uncertainty that radiates out from the woman's expression to encompass the whole painting. This money may be talking, but it is far from clear that its message is either welcome or persuasive. And from that uncertainty come others: Is this woman a prostitute or an innocent (and startled) maiden or wife? And is the space she inhabits a bawdy house or a middle-class home? Nothing in the setting itself or the woman's elegant dress would make the second possibility unlikely. Fruit, wine, and bed can imply the erotic, but each could also be part of a quite ordinary domestic scene. And if such uncertainty haunts so explicit a scene of mercenary love, what do we make of ter Borch's far more understated *Lute Player and an Officer* (figure 7)? Harmonious wooing and polite gallantry seem here to have taken the place of mercenary love. But musical instruments, particularly the lute, and maps, like the indistinct map that hangs on the wall behind the soldier, were frequent emblems of sexual licence and worldliness in Dutch genre painting. Is

Figure 6   Gerard ter Borch, *The Gallant Officer* (c. 1662–63). Oil on canvas, 68 × 52.2 cm. Musée du Louvre, Paris. Photo: © RMN.

this then another whore in another brothel? Or is this rather another maiden or wife in her own home, straying from the path of virtue, urged on by music—music she herself plays—rather than money? Are *The Gallant Officer* and *The Lute Player* to be read as scenes of the same sort or as scenes of radically different sorts? How do we tell a bawdy house from a middle-class home?

The home in at least one of these paintings may in fact have been ter Borch's own, for the model who sat for the woman in *The Gallant Officer* would appear to have been his sister Gesina. But this coincidence of real-life sister and fictional débauchée (if that's what she is) points to a more general interpretive situation. Any substantial Dutch burgher might have seen his own sister, wife, or daughter in these women, might have seen his own house in the rooms that surround them. The seemingly accidental substitution at work in the misreading and rereading of ter Borch's *Paternal Admonition* has a cultural significance that is not accidental at all. In that painting and the other two as well, the intruding soldier stands in for the missing brother, husband, or father. It is the soldier's presence

Figure 7   Gerard ter Borch, *Lute Player and an Officer* (1658). Oil on panel, 36.8 × 32.4 cm. The Metropolitan Museum of Art, New York. Bequest of Benjamin Altman, 1913 (14.40.617). Photo: All rights reserved, The Metropolitan Museum of Art.

coupled with the householder's absence that threatens to transform an otherwise respectable woman into a whore and to make a brothel of a bourgeois home.

Both sides of this substitution deserve attention. The absent house-holder helps us identify the primary consumer of these images, while the present soldier serves as an index to what may have been among the most acute personal and political anxieties of such householders: the fear that their own preeminence and authority in the affairs of the Dutch Repub-lic—their political home—would be supplanted by a military-based mo-narchic regime. Dates are important here. These paintings belong to the 1650s and 1660s, decades distinguished by the new kind of genre painting pioneered by ter Borch and practiced by many others, including Johannes Vermeer, Pieter de Hooch, Nicolaes Maes, Gabriel Metsu, Jacob Ochter-velt, Frans van Mieris, and Quirijn van Brekelenkam. But the 1650s and 1660s were also marked by a unique set of political circumstances. This is the period of what the Dutch themselves called the "True Freedom," the period in which the United Provinces were for the first time free from their Habsburg monarch, the king of Spain, who, after eighty years of war, had in the 1648 Peace of Westphalia finally renounced all claim on the northern Netherlands, and free too from their local quasi-king, the princes of Orange, the latest of whom, William II, died suddenly in 1650 in the midst of a bitter political conflict with the merchant oligarchs of Holland. Not until the crisis of 1672 and the collapse of the "True Free-dom" would Holland again be dominated by a stadholder of the House of Orange. As one might expect, much of the political energy of the in-tervening two decades was spent articulating and defending that newfound but clearly precarious republican autonomy. Whatever self-representations the Dutch produced during these decades—and genre paintings like the ones ter Borch and the others painted are among the most telling of those self-representations—it seems likely that they responded, however obliquely, to this novel situation.

In making this suggestion, I do not mean to turn the paintings into deliberate political allegories. I do not pretend to have found either ter Borch's intentions or the decoding mechanism his first viewers applied to these paintings. Ter Borch's choice of subjects, like the choice of subjects of his genre-painting contemporaries, was richly overdetermined, and the ways in which those paintings were received were no doubt equally varied. But the facts remain that he and his contemporaries did choose such sub-jects and that the subjects found viewers. In the 1650s and 1660s, the

Dutch produced a great many paintings of women, almost always without a male householder, engaged in activities of often morally ambiguous significance in domestic or domestic-like interiors. And in a considerable number of these paintings the domestic space is shared by a soldier or other young man of soldierlike appearance. From these observations a number of questions arise, ranging from the seemingly simple "Why all those women?" and "Why all those soldiers?" to the apparently more complex, but not unrelated, question of the broad cultural meaning of Dutch domestic realism, the Dutch taste for painted representations of the everyday and its violation.[3]

To anticipate a little, I will be arguing that the "True Freedom" itself, the nature and survival of Dutch republican government, is at stake in these domestic scenes of sexual negotiation. Realism's defining "other," the kind of elevated and text-centered painting the seventeenth-century called "history," is, I will suggest, just offstage in much the way that monarchic government—the government that provided the strongest seventeenth-century support for history painting—was just off the stage of Dutch politics. In their apparent avoidance of politics, these paintings were at their most actively political. They not only represent an implicit competition for power between men like those who appear in them and those who don't—a competition in which women play a more than merely symbolic role—they also participate in that competition by simultaneously inviting and discouraging a response that would turn "genre" into "history," republican freedom into monarchic usurpation. For the Dutch burghers who collected them, genre paintings of this sort thus provided, among their many other pleasures, an occasion to experience and, oddly, even to enjoy the moral and constitutional uncertainties of the polity they collectively possessed.[4]

BURGHER HOUSEHOLDERS AND THE DUTCH ARMY

The virtual absence of more substantial male householders, whether husbands, brothers, or fathers, from mid-seventeenth-century Dutch genre paintings is among the most curious, if least remarked, features of these works. Male householders are easy to find in peasant or craftsman interiors, but as the status of the household goes up, adult men belonging to the house—or, more accurately, adult men to whom the house belongs—disappear. Not only is Goethe's "noble knightly-looking father" not to be found in ter Borch's *Paternal Admonition;* he is not to be found in other

Dutch genre paintings either. With the exception of an occasional shadowy figure silhouetted in a distant room, there are scarcely any men at home in these paintings. And when a householder does appear in a genrelike setting, the painting itself is likely to shift categories from genre to portrait.[5] With the householder there, dramatic and typical action of a morally ambiguous sort is transformed into static, respectable, and individualized being. On their own, women, children, servants, peasants, craftsmen, and interloping male suitors act. Upper-class male householders and the people who surround them simply are.

I have no evidence that anyone involved in the production or consumption of seventeenth-century Dutch genre painting was consciously aware of this pattern. As a category, genre painting was defined only retrospectively, and its various subtypes received little explicit discussion. Choices about what got in seem to have been governed by an unwritten and perhaps unspoken sense of decorum. Genre painters simply understood that well-to-do male householders did not belong in such scenes. But if he is shut out of the represented scene, the male householder nevertheless served as its primary spectator. He, after all, was the person for whom the paintings were made, the person by whom they were most often bought and hung.[6] In the genre paintings of the 1650s and 1660s, men were invited to see their own homes and, by metaphoric extension, their own homeland from the outside. They were peering into an intimate setting that belonged to them but from which they had been at least temporarily excluded.

But why would soldiers appear so often in their place?[7] To understand that substitution we need to remember the peculiar role of the military in the Low Countries. Unlike the other most powerful countries of Western Europe, the Dutch had neither a strong military tradition nor a large aristocratic class devoted to arms. Yet if their revolt against the Spanish king was to succeed, they clearly had to fight. And the reverses of the first two decades of the revolt, the loss of the ten southern provinces, including the commercial and political centers of Flanders and Brabant where the revolt had begun, and the invasion of the north, showed that the Dutch needed something more than heroic burghers fighting for freedom and their faith. They needed a real army. So they bought one. Relying on the extraordinary—almost miraculous—prosperity of the northern Netherlands, prosperity to which a flood of refugees from the south had contributed enormously, the Dutch hired troops and officers from all over Europe, supplied them with arms that had been standardized to a degree previously unheard of, trained them in tactics that were equally novel, organized them in unconventionally small fighting units with an unusually large officer corps, and paid them on time—an innovation no less striking than any of the others. The result has been called a "military revolution," the "creation of the first modern professional army," an army "held together not by its sense of honor and its loyalty to its sovereign but by the terms of its contracts."[8] This was the army for a commercially oriented state, for a state ruled by an urban, nonaristocratic, merchant oligarchy.[9]

The system erected by the Dutch in the 1590s and the first decade of the seventeenth century "sought to create," as one military historian has put it, "an effective army for a middle-class republic without distorting the constitutional framework or the social composition of the setting where it operated."[10] This was the ideal. The burgher regents, the municipal councillors of Amsterdam and the other leading cities of Holland, supported by their allies in the mercantile, financial, professional, and guild communities throughout the United Provinces, gave the orders, and the army, including its commander, the captain-general, stadholder, prince of Orange, followed them. But the ideal often banged up against resistant reality. So long as the war with Spain continued, the system worked smoothly enough. The army fought; the towns prospered and ruled. But whenever peace threatened to replace war, tensions grew. Those tensions, never far from the surface of Dutch politics, erupted in crisis three times in the seventeenth century: in 1618, 1650, and 1672. And each time, peace and war, military preparedness and the role of the army and its commander, were at issue.

The first crisis occurred during the Twelve Years Truce with Spain (1609–21). This truce, negotiated by the States Party leader and "Advocate" of Holland, Johan Oldenbarnevelt, was opposed by Prince Maurits, the man most responsible for developing the new professional army, and by the Orangist Party: the army, the Calvinist ministers, and much of the populace. In 1618, Orangist frustration turned to action. Maurits arrested Oldenbarnevelt, tried him on trumped-up charges, had him executed, and replaced many of the States Party regents with men loyal to the House of Orange. The second crisis, the crisis of 1650, followed a similar pattern. Again the regents negotiated peace with Spain—this time the Peace of Westphalia—and again the stadholder, the army, the Calvinists, and the common people went along only grudgingly. And when, following the peace, the regents ordered sharp reductions in the size of the standing army, the stadholder—now Prince William II—rebelled. He arrested six of Holland's deputies to the States General and laid siege to Amsterdam. Only William's sudden death from smallpox saved the regents from utter defeat and the establishment of a quasi-monarchical regime.

Returned providentially to power and remembering both 1618 and 1650, the States Party resolved never again to combine the offices of stadholder and captain-general and never again to allow military command to become a dynastic privilege—resolutions that were upset only by the third crisis, when in 1672, under the pressure of a simultaneous invasion by France, England, Münster, and Cologne, the Netherlands' weakened defenses collapsed. In this moment of national peril, a new prince of Orange, William III, the posthumous son of William II, regained his father's offices, and an outraged mob tore the leaders of the States Party, the Grand Pensionary Johan de Witt and his brother Cornelis, limb from limb, thus ending the "True Freedom" of the previous twenty-two years in an orgy of blood.

The burghers who in the 1650s and 1660s bought the genre paintings of ter Borch, de Hooch, Ochtervelt, Maes, Metsu, and Vermeer could not know what was coming in 1672. But they did know about the fall of Oldenbarnevelt and the stadholder's attack on Amsterdam, and they had good reason to fear—or perhaps in some cases to hope for—a new military coup d'etat. Such fears fill the political pamphlets of the period and dominate the more theoretical defenses of the stadholderless "True Freedom," books like Johan de Witt's own *Deduction* (1654) and *The True Interest of Holland* (1662), often attributed to de Witt but actually written by his admirer Pieter de la Court.[11] As de la Court insists, "the welfare of Holland is founded upon manufactures, fishery, trade, and navigation." For these to prosper, Holland had to remain an open and religiously tolerant republic, a state without a monarch. Whatever Holland called itself, to appoint another stadholder and captain-general would be to establish "a monarchy in practice and in fact." It would be "to return to Egypt out of that free land of promise, and there obstinately to pull down upon our own heads a heavy yoke, under which our forefathers were constrained to groan and from which we by the mercy and blessing of God were wonderfully delivered." It would, in short, be to ruin everyone "but courtiers and soldiers."[12]

From this, it is easy to guess who might want such a change: "officers, courtiers, idle gentry, and soldiery" and "all those who would be such."[13] No wonder then the burgher householders of Holland mistrusted soldiers and the courtly hangers-on who affected soldierlike garb and manners.

And no wonder those burghers admired regents like de Witt "by [whose] prudence and good direction a good part of the supernumerary and useless land forces, and especially of the foreign soldiery, [were] reduced and discharged."[14] For its success, the Dutch revolt needed hired soldiers. But once peace had been won, soldiers became a threat to the very freedom for which they had been paid to fight. Where safety had formerly depended on maintaining soldiers, it now depended on getting rid of them. But, as the events of 1650 proved, soldiers did not go easily. And there remained always the fear—a fear that motivates de la Court's book, as it motivated de Witt's policies—that with the return of a prince of Orange to the offices of stadholder and captain-general, the soldiers would be back in force.

When Goethe saw "a noble knightly-looking father" (ein edler, ritterlicher Vater) in ter Borch's *Paternal Admonition,* he was mixing categories that in seventeenth-century Holland were purposely kept separate. Respectable fathers were not noble and knightly-looking, and knights—or rather their officer descendants in a mercenary army—were not respectable fathers.[15] Merchants and soldiers, burgher fathers and knightly officers, belonged to opposing kinds, each defined by its differences from the other. "The soldier thinks of a short life and a merry," begins Sir William Temple's list of antithetical qualities in his *Observations upon the United Provinces* (1673); "the trader reckons upon a long and a painful. One intends to make his fortunes suddenly by his courage, by victory, and spoil; the t'other slower but surer by craft, treaty, and by industry"—and so on through a full paragraph that doesn't end until it has found place for an assertion of the inevitable political differences that divide soldiers from merchants. Where the merchant "love[s] to live under staunch orders and laws," the soldier "would have all depend upon arbitrary power and will." Merchants are natural republicans; soldiers, natural monarchists. And indeed, as Temple remarks, the gentlemen and officers of the Dutch armies are "all . . . generally desirous to see a court in their country."[16] As a result, "the whole tenor of the republican regime, after 1650, was," in the words of a recent historian, "to play down military values, and the role of the army, in the life of the state."[17]

But what about the life of the household? Substituting soldiers for merchant householders, as the genre painters of the 1650s and 1660s do, was tantamount to replacing one form of government with another. These were not the heroic images of military glory the regents avoided. Images of that sort belonged to the elevated realm of history painting. But the genre paintings were, in their own way, no less insidious. Where merchants had ruled, soldiers were now taking their pleasure. Nor could such apprehension be dismissed as mere paranoid fantasy. The experiences of 1618 and 1650, as well as the kingly pretensions of Frederik Hendrik, the prince of Orange who held the offices of stadholder and captain-general for much of the time between those two moments of crisis, had taught the ruling burghers how tenuous their hold really was. Living on a low-lying republican island in the midst of a troubled monarchic sea, they were in constant danger of being washed away. Such calamity had already overtaken the ten provinces of the southern Netherlands, provinces the fathers and grandfathers of many of those burghers had fled. Clearly, it could also overtake the north. After an eighty-year struggle to free themselves from the tyrannical rule of the king of Spain, the merchant oligarchs of Holland could easily imagine another monarch—a monarch from the House of Orange—imposing equally oppressive rule in Spain's place. Is it any surprise that such imagining found expression in the paintings they bought?

SOLDIERS AT HOME

"It is very sad," wrote a former Dutch officer, "that the soldiers who serve on our side in the greater part live a godless life. They spend most of their free time swearing, cursing, playing cards and dice, drinking, and whoring, which is found among the chief officers as well as the base soldiers."[18] Hundreds of paintings from the middle decades of the seventeenth century could be used to illustrate this charge. If we cannot hear the swearing and cursing, we can certainly see the card games and dice games, the drinking and whoring. But the remarkable thing is not so much that these activities should have been painted—though that in itself, given the number of the paintings, is remarkable enough—as that their painted representations should have shifted ground. Sometime early in the 1650s, carousing soldiers, who for decades had most often been seen in barracks and guardrooms, began appearing in settings that belonged more to their female companions than to them: in brothels, inns, and private domestic interiors—settings that, as we have already noticed, are not easily distinguished from one another.

This seems to me a momentous change. Figures whose otherness had been their most distinctive feature, figures who, whatever the licentiousness of their behavior, could be kept at a safe distance from respectable Dutch society, soldiers were gradually coming home. They were finding their way into dwellings like those owned and inhabited by the prosperous burghers who bought most of these paintings. And though there remained always the possibility of asserting difference and distance—"That's a brothel or inn, not a respectable burgher home!" "That's a servingwoman or whore, not a burgher daughter or wife!"—the signs of difference became increasingly difficult to read. And as well-to-do homes melded into brothels and virtuous women into whores, soldiers themselves became increasingly difficult to distinguish from nonmilitary gallants. While many men in armor, men wearing a cuirass or shirt of mail, still appear in these paintings, many other figures that contemporaries and subsequent commentators have agreed in calling soldiers are distinguishable by little more than a sash, a sword, and a general extravagance of dress and manner. Were all these men meant to be seen as soldiers? Who can say? But that uncertainty, like the uncertainty about the interior spaces and the women who belong to them, is precisely the issue.

What opponents of a monarchic regime feared was just this blurring of categories. As the Remonstrant historian Gerard Brandt put it, foreign soldiers, the mercenaries who filled the Dutch army, "brought the splendid and magnificent clothing of the cities they lived in, seducing the natives to misuse the same vanity; [they also brought] an excess of meals and delicacies, here to a land where such things were formerly unknown and unwanted."[19] Foreign manners were the mark of the foreign monarchic regime some hoped and many more feared to see planted in Holland, a regime that already had a fast-growing seedling in the stadholder's court. "In The Hague, God bless us, it is not much different from the way things are in France: fornication and adultery are common there, with which the House of Nassau"—the stadholder's house—"is very much infected."[20] Remember that it was not only officers and soldiery Pieter de la Court warned against, but also courtiers, idle gentry, and "all those who would be such." Even in the stadholderless decades of the "True Freedom," the contagion of foreign, aristocratic, and courtly manners threatened burgher virtue and burgher rule. The realization of that threat, the melding of categories that a burgher republic depended on keeping distinct, is what we see in the genre paintings of the 1650s and 1660s. Sober merchant householders, remarkable in genre painting mainly for their absence, could still be told from soldiers and soldierlike gallants, but the homes and the women of those householders were being progressively "soldierized."[21]

Nicolaes Maes's *Naughty Drummer*, where the offending "soldier" is a

Figure 8   Nicolaes Maes, *The Naughty Drummer* (c. 1654). Oil on canvas, 62 × 66 cm. © Museo Thyssen-Bornemisza, Madrid.

small child, provides an apparently whimsical example of such soldierizing (figure 8). We do not need to adopt the allegorical reading proposed by one art historian—the sleeping baby is the nascent Dutch Republic (or, more particularly, Maes's native town of Dordrecht); the naughty drummer, the Orangist Party, unhappy at the prince's exclusion from the stadholdership; and the mother, the States Party, led by another Dordrecht native, Johan de Witt—to sense that the map, based on a Visscher map of the Seventeen Provinces, and the military drum signal some broader political concern.[22] Not only the peace of this private household, but also the peace of the Netherlands is at stake in this painting. That such peace is so easily established, that domestic virtue is so firmly in control, may owe something to the fact that, quite exceptionally, the male householder is *not* absent from the scene. Reflected in the mirror over the mother's head is the face of her husband, Nicolaes Maes himself, the painter at work at his easel producing this very picture. Hovering between family portrait and genre painting, between political testament and everyday domestic vignette, *The Naughty Drummer* provides in a strikingly unusual way what is nevertheless characteristic of virtually all these paintings: an intimation of a threat that, while it comes much closer to home than it ever did in the guardroom scenes of previous decades, remains always at a cautious remove.

In his Dordrecht *Eavesdropper,* Maes marks that remove in still another way (figure 9). As in other paintings in his eavesdropper series, Maes puts the wooing soldier on a different level both socially and physically from the middle-class owner of the house the soldier invades. The soldier is downstairs with the kitchen maid; the householder, upstairs with his soberly dressed guests. Between them and between their sartorial signs—

Figure 9   Nicolaes Maes, *The Eavesdropper* (1657). Oil on canvas, 92.5 × 122 cm. Rijksdienst Beeldende Kunst, The Hague (on loan to the Dordrechts Museum, Dordrecht) (NK 2560). Photo: RBK, The Hague, Tim Koster.

the soldier's sword and red cape under the map in the lower right-hand corner and the householder's black coat hanging in the shadows to the left of the staircase—is the eavesdropping wife. As critics have often noticed, her role as amused observer and her pose looking out at the audience with her finger up to her lips put her in the company of the licensed fools who similarly note vice in many earlier paintings and plays.[23] But wife and fool have fundamentally different relations to the scenes they observe. The fool's detachment comes from his condition and trade. He is a professional outsider who happily shows us that all the world shares his folly. When a wife, the mistress of the house, is made to appear similarly detached, we can only suppose that she is complicit in the action she overhears. Though not she but her maid is consorting with the soldier, she shows no inclination to intervene and no marked disapproval. From whom, after all, is this secret being kept? From no one but her husband, who stands at the table upstairs, across from her empty chair, complacently toasting his guests. Her inbetweenness—between upstairs and down, between black coat and red, between husband and soldier, between domesticity and worldliness—is the painting's subject. And when we spot the bust of Juno, the goddess of marriage, high on the partition against which the wife leans, we may feel confirmed in our sense that more than the kitchen maid's virtue is in jeopardy here.

The bright red of the military cape in Maes's *Eavesdropper* and the light that falls on it make sure that, whatever the visual appeal of the more distant action, we will not fail to read this sign of a soldier's presence. In his hauntingly beautiful *Interior with a Woman at a Clavichord* (figure 10), Emanuel de Witte does just the opposite. Only after we have delighted in the perspective that takes us through doorway after doorway and finally through a half-open window to the garden beyond do we notice the faint glimmer of a sword leaning on the chair in the left foreground, the broad brim of a dark hat, the lighter tones of a linen shirt, the reflection of a swordsman's sash, and, if we keep looking hard enough, the deeply shadowed face of the officer himself, peering out from between the bed curtains. Even this wonderfully tranquil domestic scene, where light and space seem to mean so much more than story, has its military interloper. And, like the Maes *Eavesdropper*, it too sets up an implicit competition between domesticity, represented here by the woman dutifully sweeping in the far room, and worldliness, evidenced by the woman in the foreground's abandonment of herself to the sensual pleasures of music and love. With

Figure 10   Emanuel de Witte, *Interior with a Woman at a Clavichord* (c. 1665). Oil on canvas, 77.5 × 104.5 cm. Rijksdienst Beeldende Kunst, The Hague (on loan to the Museum Boymans-van Beuningen, Rotterdam) (NK 2685). Photo: RBK, The Hague, Tim Koster.

the greater part of the picture's width separating the woman at the clavichord from her soldier lover, we may still doubt the soldier's ultimate success. But the threat—or the promise—is clear.

Seeing paintings like these, laughing at the tricks they play with visual and narrative convention, buying them, hanging them, sharing them with friends, Dutch householders entertained and were entertained by the representation of an invasion that few of them would have welcomed, the invasion of their homes by the very mercenary soldiers they had hired to protect themselves and their independent state. Through the use of such images, they were, in effect, gaining cognitive and emotional control over the very threat the paintings so artfully evoke. Given the chance to experience danger as a joke, they were able to evade, even as they unconsciously acknowledged, the seriousness of that danger.

LADY WORLD OR DAME HOLLANDIA?

The seriousness is at once lessened and heightened by another shift in the Dutch genre painting of the 1650s and 1660s, one no less momentous than the shift of scene to intimate domestic (or domestic-like) interiors: the shift in attention from men or large mixed groups of people to women, often to just one woman. Whether the new interior spaces are clearly private homes, as in *The Naughty Drummer, The Eavesdropper,* and the *Interior with a Woman at a Clavichord,* or are places of more ambiguous character, as in the three ter Borch paintings with which we began or— to add still other examples from a very large store—Gabriel Metsu's *Music Party* (figure 11) or Pieter de Hooch's *Interior Scene* (figure 12), women have a proprietary relation to them. Where in the guardroom scenes, women had been little more than signs of the soldiers' wantonness, signs on a par with cards, dice, drink, and tobacco, in the genre paintings of the 1650s and 1660s they become a powerful locus of energy and mystery. What they do matters. Instead of appearing as camp followers, dependent on the soldiers whose barracks they visit, they become essential decision makers, figures whose bodies, beds, and homes will be yielded or not, as they choose, to the military and courtly invaders. The paintings are at least as much about them as they are about their would-be seducers.

I say seriousness is "lessened and heightened" because, while the new emphasis on women keeps genre painting safely in a domain where comedy and farce are the norm, it also attributes to those women and the paintings that depict them a novel symbolic status. Women—and I am thinking here not only of women entertaining soldiers but also of those we see busy with needlework, childcare, cooking, cleaning, and other household tasks in hundreds of other works by these same painters—come to stand, by the force of sheer repetition, for home and homeland. But these women are not passive symbols. As actors and agents in the narrative vignettes that are Dutch genre paintings, they exercise an extraordinary power to maintain or subvert the home they represent. On their virtue or vice depends the fate of the nation.

That potential for good or ill is enhanced and confirmed by a detail that may easily go unremarked: the maps that hang on the walls of so many of these rooms. I have already noticed the maps in ter Borch's *Lute Player* and Maes's *Naughty Drummer,* but there are many others, including the world map on a side wall in Maes's *Eavesdropper,* the barely perceptible

Figure 11   Gabriel Metsu, *Music Party* (1659). Oil on canvas, 61.6 × 54.3 cm. The Metropolitan Museum of Art, New York. Marquand Collection, Gift of Henry G. Marquand, 1890 (91.26.11). Photo: All rights reserved, The Metropolitan Museum of Art.

map in the second room of de Witte's *Interior*, and the readily decipherable maps in Metsu's *Music Party* and de Hooch's *Interior Scene*. Why so many maps? An obvious reason is that maps did in fact hang in many Dutch homes. In the seventeenth century, the Dutch produced more maps than anyone else, and they bought more. But, as a generation of iconographic interpreters has taught us to recognize, the details in Dutch genre paintings are rarely so innocent. Like the painting of the education of the

Figure 12   Pieter de Hooch, *Interior Scene* (c. 1658). Oil on canvas, 73.7 × 64.6 cm. © National Gallery, London.

Virgin hanging ironically over the fireplace in de Hooch's *Interior Scene*, the maps have a meaning in relation to the foreground action. But what is that meaning?

The answer is that maps stood both for the worldliness I have mentioned already *and* for a strongly positive national self-consciousness. Each of these views has had influential advocates in recent scholarship. The first has been argued by the leading iconographic interpreter of Dutch genre painting, Eddy de Jongh, and has been repeatedly seconded by his host of followers.[24] For the iconographers, the map functions as though it were a flashing neon sign that says, "Watch out! Worldliness!" The second can be found in Simon Schama's enormously successful book on seventeenth-century Dutch culture, *The Embarrassment of Riches,* and has been much elaborated by Bärbel Hedinger in the only monograph devoted wholly to the maps in Dutch paintings, her *Karten in Bildern.*[25] For these writers, the maps in Dutch paintings are more like a national flag hanging at the back of the painting, interpellating the viewer and forcing him to read the foreground action in relation to this undeniable sign of patriotic value. This is of course particularly true of maps of Holland, like the one in Metsu's *Music Party,* or maps of the Seventeen Provinces, like the one in de Hooch's *Interior Scene,* but even maps that do not show the Netherlands, maps of the world or maps of other regions, could be taken as positive reminders of Dutch success in science, trade, and manufacture and thus serve as incitements to national pride. On both sides the inclination has been to ignore or actively deny the opposing interpretation, but the arguments for both are strong and their simultaneous availability tells far more about the significance of these paintings than either would alone—and tells more, as well, of the women they depict, for in each case the map can be read as an iconic attribute of the women. For the iconographers, map and woman are together fused into the traditional emblem of Lady World—*Vrouw Wereld,* as the Dutch called her—the arch-misleader of men, while for the cultural historians, the two are more likely to be read as Dame Hollandia, the allegorical figuration of Holland itself.

In any particular instance, we may be inclined to think one reading more plausible than the other. Sometimes we may think either far-fetched. But both were part of the interpretive field in which these paintings functioned. Both were available and could easily be triggered. As an extreme test case, consider Nicolaes Maes's *Young Girl Sewing* (figure 13). If there was ever an image of Dutch domestic virtue, this soldierless scene is it. Needlework, according to the dictates of numerous sixteenth- and seventeenth-century household manuals, ranked right up with chastity, silence, and obedience as the mark of a virtuous woman. Wholly absorbed in her worthy task, this girl is, as one critic has put it, "a model of diligence

Figure 13   Nicolaes Maes, *Young Girl Sewing* (1657). Oil on panel, 40 × 31 cm. Private collection.

and proper training."[26] And the map, with the same prominent and patriotic Leo Belgicus cartouche that appears on the map in *The Naughty Drummer,* seems as unequivocally positive a symbol of Dutch national identity as one could hope to find. Unsurprisingly, Bärbel Hedinger sees this painting—map and girl together—as the perfect expression of the

"True Freedom" in action. But, even here, can we really be sure that no viewer could read the map as the penetration of a menacing worldliness into this claustrophobically virtuous setting? Maes himself often used maps in iconographically suggestive ways. Indeed, two of his paintings appear as examples in de Jongh's seminal article on the disguises of Lady World. Does no residue of moral apprehension carry over to this very different painting? And what of the girl herself? One art historian has remembered that the Dutch verb *naaien* meant (and still means) both "to sew" and "to make love."[27] Suddenly, our fresh-faced Dame Hollandia gives signs of becoming a sexually transgressive Lady World, threatens to lay her needlework aside, as the women in many Dutch genre paintings do, and give herself over to the delights and torments of an illicit romance.[28] As unlikely as this transformation might seem, it could readily be imagined. In the eyes of a Dutch burgher of the 1650s and 1660s, a burgher who looked at these paintings but could enter them only at the cost of freezing action into the static respectability of a portrait, the virtuous lacemaker, the very embodiment of Holland's homely republican identity, might always seem on the verge of becoming a soldier's whore. That is what it meant to invest women and their chastity with the symbolic power of national representation.

Nowhere is this focus on a woman sharper or more troubling than in Vermeer's *Soldier and the Laughing Girl* (figure 14). This extraordinary painting—one of the twenty or so by Vermeer that later inventories suggest were in the collection of his wealthy Remonstrant patron, Pieter van Ruijven—pares away everything but the two figures and a few essential props and thrusts those remaining elements so close to the picture plane that they seem almost ready to break through. The effect is to build tension and deepen meaning, even as the sources of the tension and the intent behind the meaning are made more elusive. No interpretation of this painting can ignore its bold formal features: the sharp contrast between the dark looming soldier and the much smaller but brilliantly illuminated woman, the oddly insistent perspective, the enormous and sharply detailed map, the strong lines that link map, window, and soldier and that box the smiling woman in a radiant pool of light, the squarely facing chairs with their forward-leaning lion's-head finials, the bright intervening table top, the emotionally charged but ambiguous posture and expression of the figures themselves, the still glass of wine—all this shot through with narrative and emblematic conventions that would seem ready to fix meaning, yet never quite succeed in doing so. In this, *The Soldier and the Laugh-*

Figure 14 Johannes Vermeer, *The Soldier and the Laughing Girl* (mid-1650s). Oil on canvas, 50.5 × 46 cm. © The Frick Collection, New York.

ing Girl does not so much differ from the other paintings we have been looking at as raise their uncertainties to a higher power.

"To a contemporary," John Nash assures us, "Vermeer's image would not be unfamiliar. It recalls the theme of mercenary love."[29] Lawrence Gowing expands on the point:

> The incident . . . is drawn from the common stock; in the early fifties it was a typical subject of De Hooch. It is a legacy of the wars, the entertainment of foraging soldiery in a house that is more or less of a tavern, a scene in which the extent of the hospitality that will be exacted of the agreeable hostess is rarely open to doubt. . . . This subject with its delicate hint of erotic *force majeur* is a translation into the domestic idiom of the formal theme of venal love.[30]

In this context, the map plays a no less conventional role. It lets us know, as a de Jongh disciple puts it, that this woman is "a personification of worldly vice—in effect, a contemporary Vrouw Wereld."[31] But what then of the more positive and patriotic reading of the map? Focus on it and the whole sense of the painting can change—as it does in Bärbel Hedinger's book. Denying that this is a tavern scene or that mercenary love is the painting's subject, Hedinger reads woman and map together as an ideal figuration of the province of Holland: *Hic est Hollandia.* Both the woman and the soldier are, Hedinger tells us, described in the legend of the actual map from which Vermeer's is copied—the same 1620s Berkenrode-Blaeu map of Holland and West Friesland that Metsu used in his *Music Party*—where Dutch men are praised for their courage and Dutch women for their domestic virtue. What Hedinger sees and what she claims Vermeer's contemporaries would have seen is thus a quite unthreatening exchange between virtuous Hollandia and one of that province's brave defenders.[32]

How can such diametrically opposed readings be reconciled? Or how can one be chosen over the other? I don't think that either reconciliation or reliable interpretive choice is possible. On the contrary, the very force of Vermeer's painting derives from its undecidability.[33] And that undecidability carries over to the painting's tone. The theme of mercenary love invites a comic response. The glass of wine, with its recollection of hundreds of Dutch "merry companies," points the same way. Even the soldier's jutting elbow and knuckles on hip bring comic reminders. *Il Capitano*, the braggart soldier Dutch farce inherited from the commedia dell'arte, held himself in just this way, a pose that shows up in works as various as Jacob Duck's *Soldiers and Prostitutes in a Guardroom*, Rembrandt's theater sketches, and the title illustration to G. A. Bredero's satirical farce *The Spanish Brabanter*.[34] Yet the soldier's dark monumentality, the brilliant light illuminating the woman, and the huge, insistently detailed map cut off our laughter and give the painting instead the epiphanic intensity of a secular annunciation. However trivial and even farcical the scene, something important is going on. This ordinary and anonymous smiling woman, whether virtuous maiden or profligate whore, is made a vessel of destiny, a Dame Hollandia who could also be Lady World. With donor Pieter van Ruijven looking on, as it were, invisibly from the missing left-hand panel and husband "Joseph" busy with mercantile matters in the equally missing right-hand panel, her reception of military power in the person of a red-coated officer is symbolically deciding Holland's political future.[35]

EXHIBITS FROM HISTORY

Paintings like ter Borch's *Paternal Admonition*, de Witte's *Interior*, and Vermeer's *Soldier and the Laughing Girl* come from a moment of intense political uncertainty. The "True Freedom" lasted twenty-two years, but its republican, States Party solution to the problem of how an independent Netherlands should be governed remained under constant pressure, pressure that repeatedly verged on irretrievable crisis. Polemical books like Johan de Witt's *Deduction* and Pieter de la Court's *True Interest* represent one response to that pressure. The genre paintings of these decades represent another. In both, the prosperous Dutch home is in danger of succumbing to the blandishments of a seductive military intruder. But the conventions of genre painting complicate the response. Not only is there the sense of serious and immediate peril that de Witt and de la Court are at such pains to define. As we have repeatedly noticed, there is also a comic distancing, a lessening of the danger, making it more like the averted threat of 1650, a threat that could now be laughed at in retrospect, than a present menace. And there is even an element of sympathetic participation, the titillating promise of a sexual consummation to be secretly, if vicariously, enjoyed. But however complex and self-contradictory the response, the issue of power at home and in the Dutch homeland would have remained active for most contemporary viewers.

Certainly the association of sex with power had a well-established place in Dutch political discourse. Here, for example, is how one pamphleteer

describes the reconciliation of Holland and Zeeland after the death of
Prince William II:

> Now I already see the Zeelanders, who were the first to condemn Holland
> and support the prince, embracing Holland. I hear them say with great mod-
> esty and humility, "You are our oldest and truest allies." I hear Zeeland say
> to Holland, "You are the husband and I am the wife. Let us never part."
> Now I see the wife fall at her husband's feet—now that the servant, with
> whom she committed adultery and for whose sake she left and despised her
> husband, is gone. And now I see the married couple living happily together.[36]

How easily the language of politics slides over into the language of sexual
rivalry and adultery! Zeeland is the erring wife; the prince of Orange, the
servant and lover; Holland, the cuckolded husband and master. And how
familiar the story is: a standard plot from domestic farce called up to expose the hypocrisy of a sudden switch of alliance.

As the last three chapters should already have suggested, the Dutch
were not alone in thinking of politics in sexual terms, nor were such stories
always told in a comic vein. Those stories were, on the contrary, as much
a part of European history painting and historical narrative in the high
heroic forms of epic and tragedy as of genre painting, comedy, and farce.
Three exhibits will help fill out this claim and return us to the genre paintings of the 1650s and 1660s with a sharpened sense not only of their own
historical potential but also of their unique resistance to history. One of
these exhibits comes from historical drama; two, from history painting.
Of the stories that inform them, two concern the abuse of home and
marriage by the intrusion of state power; one, the virtuous refusal to engage in such intrusion. Though the specific items I will be putting on
display are all Dutch, two of the informing stories are European in their
diffusion. One finds its source in ancient Roman history; one, in biblical
history. The third story comes from Dutch chronicles, but it too has well-
known European counterparts. But all three—and this is the important
point here—had a particular application to Dutch politics in the seventeenth century and thus have a particular relevance to a reading of genre
painting as similarly engaged in political rivalry, ambition, and fear.

Exhibit A. The Continence of Scipio. In many parts of early modern Europe, virtuous moderation in the exercise of supreme power was represented by the refusal of the Roman general Scipio Africanus to keep another man's fiancée for his own use. The story, as told by Livy, Polybius,
Plutarch, Valerius Maximus, Florus, and Aulus Gellius and retold by doz-

Figure 15   Gerbrandt van den Eeckhout, *The Continence of Scipio* (1650s). Oil on canvas, 138.1 × 161.5 cm. The Toledo Museum of Art, Toledo, Ohio. Gift of Arthur J. Secor.

ens of later European poets, playwrights, and painters, is that young Scipio, fresh from his conquest of the Iberian town of New Carthage, was given a beautiful maiden, the daughter of a wealthy New Carthage family and the intended bride of the Iberian leader, as one of the spoils of victory. When her parents and fiancé offer a rich ransom for her release, Scipio magnanimously frees her, turns back the ransom, and asks only that they pledge friendship to Rome.

Among the many Dutch paintings of this scene is one now in the Toledo Museum of Art by Gerbrandt van den Eeckhout (figure 15). Any version of *The Continence of Scipio,* as this scene is often called, would be of interest, for here power distinguishes itself by its specifically sexual restraint. Unlike the stadholder captain-general, who in the pamphlet runs off with Holland's wife, Scipio refrains from that ultimate abuse. But for at least two reasons van den Eeckhout's version has a still more particular interest in the context of this argument: first, because this history painting is also a family portrait, and second, because Scipio seems here to stand, as he did in many polemical texts, for the House of Orange.[37] Van den Eeckhout's Toledo *Continence of Scipio* is both an affirmation and a denial of States Party fears concerning Orangist ambitions. Yes, this Scipio is a figure of unquestionable power. He and his forces have just overthrown New Carthage in much the way that William II and his army had threatened to overthrow Amsterdam. To that extent, republican fears are justified. But this Scipio is a magnanimous ruler, one who leaves his subjects' women and property untouched. Fears of universal ruin should a new prince of Orange reclaim his father's offices are thus grossly misplaced. Or at least that is what the wealthy Amsterdammers who commissioned this painting and who posed as the four suppliant citizens of New Carthage seem to have hoped. We can no longer identify this family of Dutch burghers, but, whoever they were, by this act of symbolic obeisance, they appear to have been preparing for that eventual restoration and to have been reassuring themselves about its consequences. They put themselves into the space of history in order to keep history away.

In town halls of Leiden and Deventer or the justice chamber in The Hague, where versions of *The Continence of Scipio* could also be seen, its message was perhaps more general: less a reflection on Orangist rule as such than a model for the temperate exercise of power in whatever form. But even here a specific concern with the dangers militarism posed to a burgher republic seems evident. Scipio was, after all, not just any ruler but a conquering general. He governed by the force of arms, a fact that the many soldiers crowded around him in these paintings makes clear. And if militarism is the issue, that issue is represented in terms of sexual competition. Who is to possess this woman's body? Scipio or the fiancé? The stadholder or the regents of Holland? In early modern European culture—a culture that in many ways is still ours—that is how men talk, whether in pamphlets or paintings, about questions of power.

Exhibit B. The Rape of Machteld van Velsen. On January 3, 1638, Amsterdam inaugurated its magnificent new theater, the Schouwberg, with a play written especially for the occasion, Joost van den Vondel's *Gijsbrecht van Amstel*. Based loosely on chronicle accounts of events that followed the murder in 1296 of Count Floris V of Holland, Vondel's play is a sequel to Pieter Cornelisz Hooft's *Geeraerdt van Velsen* (1613), in which the murder itself takes place. Both plays are deeply engaged in the political conflicts of seventeenth-century Holland. Both concern tensions that oppose the party of the ruling count, a thirteenth-century protoabsolutist, to the aristocratic party, a medieval version of the burgher regents of Hooft's and Vondel's own time. And both trace the eruption of those tensions into murderous and destructive violence to an event of the sort we have come to expect: Count Floris's rape of Machteld van Velsen, the wife of Geeraerdt van Velsen and the cousin of Gijsbrecht van Amstel, both leading aristocrats.

Thinking of Holland's republican identity, one might imagine Machteld as a Dutch Lucretia and her rape as the event that brings the end of one-person rule. But neither poet develops the story that way. Hooft's Machteld does not commit suicide and does not approve the revenge her husband takes by murdering Count Floris. The son of a mayor of Amsterdam who wrote one of the earliest defenses of Holland's republican form of government, Hooft argues rather for a mixed constitution in which monarchic stadholder and aristocratic regents would together keep foreign princes and local rabble safely distant from power in Holland. Floris's rape of Machteld and Geeraerdt van Velsen's revenge both violate these principles and are thus both culpable, as Machteld herself is made to say. As for Vondel, his play ends not with the triumph of aristocratic/burgher rule but rather with its defeat: the return of Floris's troops and the burning of Amsterdam. Vondel's model is Troy, not Rome. From this perspective, Machteld, to whom the play only alludes, would be more another Helen (though a very unwilling Helen) than another Lucretia. And rather than prophetically anticipating William II's siege of Amsterdam or even remembering Prince Maurits's overthrow of Oldenbarnevelt (an event that nevertheless deeply affected Vondel and prompted an earlier play, his *Palamedes*), Vondel seems to be thinking back to the Spanish sack of Antwerp, his parents' home, and to be giving expression to his sense of the Dutch as a people of exile. But however the story gets told, whatever its particular ideological bearings, rape marks its originating moment for both Hooft and Vondel. And not just any rape, but a rape in which the relative positions of the rival men, rapist and husband, approximate those of stadholder and regent. This is the story that both poets present as the ground for national self-understanding.

Exhibit C. The Summoning of Bathsheba. Announcing the name of this exhibit spoils its effect, for at first glance the Jan Steen version I have chosen for display seems not to be a history painting at all (figure 16). Instead, we might easily suppose we are looking at another genre scene.

Figure 16   Jan Steen, *Bathsheba* (c. 1659). Oil on panel, 42 × 33 cm. Private Collection.

But that is just the point. What finally distinguishes a history painting from a genre painting is not so much the figures' heroic stance and gestures, their archaic costumes and setting, or the work's grandiose scale—though all these may come into play—as it is the fact that we can identify the painting with a text of the appropriate sort. *History* is defined by a certain relation between image and text; *genre*, by the apparent lack of such a relation. If Steen's painting must be pushed to the history side of the history/genre divide, it is only because of the barely visible words on the letter the central figure holds: "Alderschonte Barsabe—omdat" (Most beautiful Bathsheba—because). Those few words tell us not only who the woman is, but also who sent the letter and what is going to happen. They invite us to take this apparent genre scene as an illustration of 2 Samuel 11, where we find the biblical story of David and Bathsheba. They turn genre into history.

And what a history it is. "It happened," the Bible tells us, "late one afternoon, when David arose from his couch and was walking upon the roof of the king's house, that he saw from the roof a woman bathing; and the woman was very beautiful. And David sent and inquired about the woman. And one said, 'Is not this Bathsheba, the daughter of Eliam, the wife of Uriah the Hittite?' So David sent messengers, and took her; and she came to him, and he laid with her." From this not-so-delicate exercise of "erotic *force majeur*" flow many consequences: Bathsheba's pregnancy, David's murder of her husband, the marriage of David and Bathsheba, the birth and death of their child, the birth of a second child, the future King Solomon, and eventually, if one follows the genealogy of St. Matthew, the birth of the Messiah. Talk about a woman being made a vessel of destiny! But again the originating moment of this profoundly resonant historical sequence is marked by a royal intrusion into a private domestic interior and into the body of the woman identified with that interior. It is a scene, as Steen clearly recognizes, where history and genre meet.

But look back at Steen's painting. The details do not quite fit the biblical text. Not only are the costumes and setting surprisingly Dutch, but the messenger and letter also depart from the source. "David sent messengers, and took her," reads 2 Samuel 11.4. Steen shows just one messenger, an old woman hardly capable of "taking" anyone, and he adds a letter. Still more striking, his Bathsheba's manner suggests a far greater degree of agency than scripture allows. Why these changes?

Here, quite exceptionally, we have a contemporary explanation, a discussion not of Steen's painting itself—that would be too much to hope for—but of an earlier and obviously similar version (now lost) by Jan Lievens. In his *Praise of the Art of Painting* (1642), Philips Angel marvels at how a great painter like Lievens can read missing details into a text. His *Bathsheba* is a case in point. Faced with the brutal spareness of 2 Samuel 11.4, Lievens brilliantly intuited that the "messenger must have been an old woman experienced in the art of love, or a procuress, as one calls them," and that the message itself could not have been delivered only by word of mouth. A letter would have been needed "as proof of higher power" (tot bewijs van meerder macht). Nor could one suppose Bathsheba a wholly passive victim of David's will. "However powerful the monarch may be, no one has to be ready to serve in sin. . . . There must have been a hot fire of lust in Bathsheba when she was sought by the king."[38] Lievens thus showed her flushed with embarrassment and pleasure.

Cool triumph would more nearly describe the expression of Steen's Bathsheba, but otherwise he adopts just the understanding Angel attributes to Lievens. In doing so, he, like Lievens, pulls history firmly in the direction of genre. The old woman, the letter, and the willing wife all figure among the familiar narrative conventions of genre painting. But if history can so easily be read as genre, the reverse is no less true: genre can also be read as history. Indeed, that is precisely what Steen prompts us to do with those three crucial words: "Alderschonte Barsabe—omdat." Whether one thinks of Steen as turning history into genre or turning genre into history, the effect is the same. He connects the everyday world, the world of Maes's *Eavesdropper,* de Hooch's *Interior Scene,* and Vermeer's *Soldier and the Laughing Girl,* to the historical world of Scipio Africanus, Count Floris V, and Prince William II. But he could not have made that connection if the two worlds had not already been linked by a thick web of shared conventions and concerns. Which is not to say that the two were indistinguishable. On the contrary, it is only because they were distinguishable that their intersection could be so fraught with meaning—only for this that Scipio's restraint could be made the preeminent sign of virtuous rule, only for this that Count Floris's and King David's failure to exercise similar restraint could be made to resonate with such exemplary horror. And the point of intersection remains the same: the sexual encounter of a "genre" woman and a "history" man. It is in this encounter, at this point of intersection, that the most intense reflection on both worlds takes place.

Reading for the "True Freedom"

The triumphs of Jan Lievens's art, so wonderfully displayed in his *Bathsheba*, all flow, according to Philips Angel, "from the fountain of avid reading" (uit de fontein der lees-gierigheid).[39] To turn text into visual representation, the painter must be a passionately active reader. But what does active or avid reading mean? It means reading into. It means filling the empty spaces of unfinished narrative with plausibly explanatory detail. And when the source text contains unassimilable detail of its own—too many messengers, a too passive Bathsheba—it can even mean active misreading. Nor is the painter the only avid reader. While he makes pictures of texts by means of such reading, the viewer makes texts of pictures in much the same way. Seeing a young woman approached by an old woman in black, a viewer informed by the conventions of genre painting, comic drama, and historical narrative and concerned by political threats to republican freedom could easily read "procuress for lover, soldier, or king." And seeing another young woman reading a letter, the same viewer could as easily read "love letter" or even "Bathsheba." John Nash invites us to do just that when he presents all five of Vermeer's letter paintings, along with others by ter Borch and Metsu, in relation to the Bathsheba story.[40] And we could obviously extend the same invitation to viewers of a typical genre painting, like Quirijn van Brekelenkam's *Confidential Conversation* (figure 17), which lacks a letter but has an eager old woman in black.

Does this mean we should rename Brekelenkam's painting *Bathsheba?* Or that we should give that same name to all the dozens of paintings of young women reading letters, paintings like Vermeer's *Woman in Blue* (figure 18)? Obviously not—no more than we should go back to using the title long attached to Steen's *Bathsheba: The Love Letter*.[41] Steen's is a history painting; Brekelenkam's and Vermeer's are not. But it does mean that history lurks close to the edges of paintings like Brekelenkam's and Vermeer's just waiting to be read into them. We see a young woman listening intently to an older one or another young woman absorbed in her reading. What are we to understand? The older woman's talk, the writing the young woman reads, could be about almost anything. But powerful convention suggests love, perhaps illicit love. And who would the lover be? Hundreds of other paintings, including those we have already seen, supply an answer: a young man, a courtier, a soldier, a sword-bearing gallant— someone more readily associated with the court of a military ruler than with mercantile burghers. Perhaps the message comes from the ultimate figure of royal power. It could not be from King David. The prominent

Figure 17   Quirijn van Brekelenkam, *The Confidential Conversation* (1661). Oil on panel, 47 ×
36 cm. Rijksmuseum, Amsterdam.

maps of Holland in both Brekelenkam's painting and Vermeer's tell us
that this is not Jerusalem but rather Delft, Leiden, or Amsterdam. But
it could come from a Dutch David, from a future count of Holland or
king of the Netherlands, a ruler whose dynastic "house" will be born from

Figure 18   Johannes Vermeer, *Woman in Blue Reading a Letter* (1662–64). Oil on canvas, 46.5 × 39 cm. Rijksmuseum, Amsterdam.

the body of this young Dutch woman, as David's house was born from the body of Bathsheba.

Is this reading too active or avid? Does it cross too readily over into the territory of misreading? Perhaps so. But just as the interpretive conventions that make a map a sign of both patriotic pride and threatening worldliness can neither be turned off nor effectively controlled, so the conventions and concerns that prompt us—or that would have prompted a prosperous Dutch merchant and householder of the 1650s and 1660s—to read history into genre defy limits. Things do not, however, go all one way. There remains an equally powerful counterinclination: an inclination to refuse history all entry into genre, to condemn any reading of Dutch painting that goes beyond what we can actually see. We see three women talking or one woman reading. That is *all* there is. To attach a text to those scenes, however compelling the conventions and concerns that prompt it, is as violent and unjustified an intrusion as would be a message from King David—or from Stadholder William.

In *Reading "Rembrandt,"* Mieke Bal has distinguished between a way of looking at images based on the tenets of Western realism and what she calls "reading for the text."[42] More obviously than any artistic tradition that preceded it, Dutch painting of the seventeenth century—not only genre painting, but also landscape, townscape, still life, marine painting, and architectural painting—invites a realistic response. Such painting "describes," to adopt Svetlana Alpers's term, the world around us. Alpers's own book, *The Art of Describing,* defines the epistemological values that informed this painting, values that motivated Dutch painters to trust their eyes rather than their books; and a host of others, dating back at least to Hegel's lectures on aesthetics nearly two centuries ago, have joined in celebrating this Dutch birth of the real.[43] What we can now begin to understand is that realism not only differs from the text-based art of history painting but is also part of an ideologically motivated reaction against history, the history that kings and soldiers make. Dutch art participated in the Dutch Revolt, a revolt that reached its culmination in the Peace of Westphalia, the stadholderless 1650s and 1660s, and the paintings of ter Borch, Maes, Metsu, de Hooch, Brekelenkam, Vermeer, and the others.

But, for all these accomplishments, history did not go away, nor did reading for the text. Not only did the Dutch keep on producing works as deeply imbued with the style and values of international history painting as Gerbrandt van den Eeckhout's *Continence of Scipio.*[44] They also let history, dressed in the garb of the stadholder's mercenary soldiers, invade even those paintings apparently most immune to it. Against such invasion, champions of the real can, of course, continue to take a firm stand. "These women are not Bathsheba," the realists may rightly insist. "Their lovers are not King David. These are still genre paintings, unadulterated by the least intrusion of history." And so they are—as long as we can keep from reading for the text. Realism, both as a representational mode and as a mode of apprehension, is a mark of the "True Freedom," the political freedom from stadholder and king alike. But, as Pieter de la Court's *True Interest of Holland* makes clear, refusing to recognize the danger of a monarchic coup d'etat might be just the way to ensure its happening. From this point of view, realism is foolish complacency; reading for the text, a prudent precaution. So true freedom needs both: both the realism that excludes history and the reading for the text that sees the repressed staging its return.

With all this in mind, let's look at one final painting, Samuel van Hoogstraten's *Slippers* (figure 19). It may seem perverse to conclude a discussion of women and soldiers with a painting that shows neither, and still more perverse to read for the text where the art of realist illusion is so insistently and so convincingly displayed. To museum goers, Hoogstraten is best known as the maker of the marvelously intricate perspective box now at the National Gallery in London. And art historians cite him most often as the author of one of the very few early modern Dutch treatises on artistic technique, his *Introduction to the Advanced School of Painting* (1678). In neither role does he seem a likely candidate for a text-based historical reading. Nor does a first look at the painting itself encourage such a reading. What we see is a succession of three doorways leading to a brightly lit room. Along the way, we see a door handle and thumb latch, a broom and cloth, a pair of women's slippers on a woven mat, a set of keys hanging from the lock of the last door. In the room itself, we see a table with a heavy fringed tablecloth, a silver candlestick with an extinguished candle slightly askew, a book, a chair, a painting, and the frame of perhaps another painting or, more likely, a mirror—all rendered with such precision and care that we can easily find satisfaction in just looking.

But in this painting, as in any other, we are always looking at a representation of something. No painter, not even Hoogstraten, can give an illusion of light, space, and material surface without locating those qualities in or identifying them with a world we can imagine or know. And here that world is specifically domestic. When we look into—as opposed to read into—Hoogstraten's painting, we see the inside of a private dwelling, the inside of someone's home. And were we to look through the peephole of his London perspective box, that is again what we would see. Hoogstraten and the other Dutch painters of the 1650s and 1660s who were most interested in the precise rendering of interior light and space found the light and space that most appealed to them in private homes. Even Eman-

Figure 19 Samuel van Hoogstraten, *The Slippers* (late 1650s). Oil on canvas, 103 × 70 cm. Musée du Louvre, Paris. Photo: © RMN.

uel de Witte, who usually painted church interiors, made a house the focus of his most elaborate experiment in illusionistic perspective. Houses were by no means the only subject of Dutch realism, but they were a much favored subject. The real seems to have been more real at home.

By the very act of painting so many domestic interiors with such minute attention, Dutch genre painters made a powerful ideological statement. Whether ordered or disordered, whether the scene of behavior we ordinarily label virtuous or vicious, private homes demand attention. Their very representation puts them in competition with the grand scenes of history painting. Had it no other connection to history than this, Hoogstraten's painting would derive much of its cultural significance from such implicit competition. "Realism," "the art of describing," "the celebration of the everyday"—whatever term one chooses, Dutch art of Hoogstraten's sort owes its peculiar identity to its rivalry with another art shaped by quite other values. And because that other art was recognized as an art of power—religious and ecclesiastical power at first, but by the mid-seventeenth century still more the secular power of the monarchic state—its domestic rival appeared inevitably as the representational alternative to such power.

History of this sort, history as a rival art of painting, is, however, defined only by difference. What the maps and soldiers, the letters and messengers, the narrative and dramatic conventions do is to bring history into the genre painting itself, where we then "read" it. But what happens when there are no maps or soldiers, no letters or messengers? Interpretive convention seizes on whatever there is. Why have viewers called this painting *The Slippers?* And why do we nod with understanding when we first encounter the title? Because those slippers, more obviously than any other detail in the painting, suggest a story. The owner of the slippers has gone off with her lover. Equipped with Jacob Cats's *Zinne- en Minnebeelden* and a few other moral emblem books, any iconographer will tell us that the empty slippers, the open doors, the abandoned broom, the unlighted candle, the keys, the book, the mirror, and who knows what else all have amorous associations. But if we have seen many Dutch genre paintings, we hardly need this learned help. Love is their most persistent subject. And once we think of love, we may also begin to think of history.

As though to help us along in this direction, Hoogstraten has included an easily decipherable painting within his painting. Hanging at the back of the furthest room in *The Slippers* is a pastiche based on the painting we began with, ter Borch's *Paternal Admonition.*[45] The soldier/father and procuress/mother are both missing. But the mysteriously beautiful standing woman, the woman who so captured the imagination of Goethe and his characters, is still there, now accompanied by a young messenger who has brought the letter she appears to be reading. We do not have to think of Bathsheba or Machteld van Velsen to understand that, in the absence of the always absent male householder, history has once again found a way into the ill-protected fortress of burgher domesticity. The proof of higher power, as Philips Angel called the letter in Jan Lievens's *Bathsheba,* remains out of sight. We only imagine the letter, can only guess who may have written it, and have no way to be sure that the empty slippers are the sign of a story like the one represented in the painting-within-the-painting. Yet as soon as we invoke it, history is as actively and intrusively there as it would be if we saw a map of the Netherlands on the wall, a soldier offering money in the foreground, or a letter from King David in the hand of the now absent woman. If the Dutch "True Freedom" of the 1650s and 1660s had much to do with the genre paintings of those decades, with their intense focus on women and domestic interiors, the threats to that freedom—threats whose shared name is "history"—have just as much to do with the stories we still feel compelled to read into those paintings.

And what of Hoogstraten's empty room? Turned on it, such avid reading might easily find the desolation of the "True Freedom's" defeat. The tone is light, even comic. But, after eighty years of war and in the midst of intense civil strife, the implications were as serious as any a Dutch republican could have imagined.

Fables of Absolutism

Chapter Five

—⇥• ⇤—

The Liberty of Spanish Towns

SPANISH DIFFERENCE/SPANISH LIKENESS

Whether in England or the Netherlands, whether in drama or painting, whether in the 1590s or the middle decades of the 1600s, the bourgeois home and marriage were attracting unprecedented attention. For the first time, apart from annunciation scenes and saints' lives, these "everyday" homes and marriages were escaping the degrading confines of fabliau, farce, and comic novella, where cuckoldry was the endlessly repeated joke, to claim a seriousness of response that had long been reserved for the doings of gods, kings, saints, and nobles. They made this move not alone, but rather in close, if marginal, relation to those very figures of royal and aristocratic power whose exclusive right to the higher genres of history and tragedy was being forcefully reasserted at just this time. Expressly excluded from humanist history, from classical tragedy, and from history painting, the bourgeois home and marriage challenged exclusion with the story of its own disruption—whether actual or threatened—from above. In its barest outline, this story remained what it had always been: a story of sexual predation and adultery. But it was no longer funny—or, at least, not funny in quite the same way. As economic power, including the power vested in theater audiences and purchasers of paintings, shifted in the direction of merchants and tradesmen, so too did the inclination to regard the integrity of their homes and marriages with something like the concern commanded by the fate of the upper orders. Because those middling homes and marriages mattered more, so too did their violation.

But if class identity has its part in explaining why in the 1590s the murder of a provincial merchant, the sufferings of a city shopkeeper and his wife, or the triumphs of two virtuous small-town wives appealed to English theatergoers and why half a century later quietly troubled domestic scenes caught the attention of Dutch art buyers, what are we to make of the early seventeenth-century success in Spain of a strikingly similar artistic promotion of the nonaristocratic home and marriage? After all, the commonest of commonplaces about Spain's early modern social structure is that it lacked a large and productive urban middle class. A dominant antimercantile aristocratic ethos (underscored by caste-based tax exemption), the forced conversion and eventual expulsion of Jews and Moors (both identified with commercial activity), and an apparently unlimited supply of American gold and silver all discouraged the commercial and industrial development that would have given rise to such a class. And hardly less common is the understanding that Spanish theater in this period—the theater of Lope de Vega and Calderón de la Barca—consistently favored an ideology designed for the benefit of kings and nobles.[1] Yet not only did the Spanish theater produce a handful of plays that center on the sexual disruption of the nonaristocratic home by figures of aristocratic or royal power, but, unlike the English plays I have examined, these are widely acknowledged to be among the greatest theatrical works of their country's Golden Age: Lope's *Peribáñez y el comendador de Ocaña* (1610), *Fuenteovejuna* (1613), and *El mejor alcalde, el rey* (1621); and Calderón's *Alcalde de Zalamea* (1641).[2] Without some discussion of Dutch genre painting, any treatment of my topic would have been obviously incomplete. But it would be no less incomplete without these Spanish plays. They mark one of the indisputable high points in the early modern convergence of home, state, and history.

This is, however, a high point with a difference. The nonaristocratic home that intersected so memorably with the state and its history on the stages of Golden Age Spain was not bourgeois. It was, on the contrary, rural and agrarian—a peasant home rather than a burgher one. The protagonists of *Peribáñez*, *Fuenteovejuna*, and *El alcalde de Zalamea* are repeatedly and insistently identified—as they identify themselves—as *villanos* or *labradores*, terms that have no exact equivalent in English but mean something like "countryman," "peasant," "yeoman," or "farmer." And if the principal figures of *El mejor alcalde, el rey* pride themselves on being of *hidalgo* descent—that is, offspring of the nobility—they too labor as peasants and are generally accounted as such. Nor can we suppose, as we did for a play like Heywood's *Edward IV* or paintings like Vermeer's, that these plays were produced for people similar in social standing to those represented. However varied their audiences, the playhouses of Madrid and the other leading Spanish cities seem not to have been much frequented by peasants.

From these differences come still others, including a far sharper distinction between the sexually predatory soldier or lord and the just monarch than can be found in either England or the Netherlands and a far bolder response to such predation. Just imagine for a moment that the Falstaff of Shakespeare's *Merry Wives* is not merely a needy courtly interloper in Windsor but the resident lord of the town and its now peasant inhabitants. Then imagine that he not only pays court to Mistress Page and Mistress Ford but abducts and rapes both of them. Then imagine that instead of humiliating him with a buck basket, an old woman's hat and gown, and a comic shaming ritual, the wives and their husbands garrote him, stab him to death, or tear him limb from limb. And finally imagine that rather than remain an off-stage object of veneration, the monarch appears in the play's final scene to approve this bloody revenge. Imagine all this and you will have imagined the transformation of *The Merry Wives of Windsor* into a play Lope or Calderón might have written, the transformation of an English comedy into a Spanish *comedia*. Each element—the military or courtly intruder, the nonaristocratic home, the sexual abuse, the home's response, and the royal approbation—remains, but each is raised to a new level of violence and dramatic intensity.

The effect of such changes may be to suggest that we have entered a different world altogether, one so different that it can have no significant commonality with the English and Dutch worlds we have left behind. Mitchell Greenberg puts it succinctly in the opening sentence of a chapter on Lope's *Fuenteovejuna:* "Spain, as they say, is different."[3] Without disputing or ignoring such difference, I will be arguing that Spanish likeness is no less striking and no less helpful in understanding both the widespread early modern promotion of the nonaristocratic home and the ideological implications of that promotion. Spanish drama not only takes us where we have not been before. It also reveals with new clarity significant features of the territory we have already visited.

Consider, for example, the crucial issue of artistic genre. In both England and the Netherlands, significant departures from an emerging humanist, courtly, and neoclassical orthodoxy were undertaken with little acknowledgment and no sustained discussion. Terms like "domestic drama" or "genre painting" were applied decades or even centuries later to materials that had been produced in unspoken and perhaps unconscious defiance of hierarchical decorum. Spanish transgressions were no less significant, but they were acknowledged and discussed. The very title of Lope de Vega's *Arte nuevo de hacer comedias en este tiempo* (1609)—*The New Art of Making Plays in This Time*—insists on departure, on newness, and on the determining influence of present conditions. Addressing the Academy of Madrid, Lope clearly articulates orthodox expectation: comedy "treats low and plebeian actions, and tragedy royal and lofty ones"; "tragedy takes history for its subject matter, and comedy fiction"; "the doings of artisans" or "the love of a blacksmith's daughter" should never share the stage with a king; and so on.[4] But then, with rueful irony, Lope admits that of the 484 plays (no less!) he had by then written, only six obey such rules. The rest belong to the far more miscellaneous category of the Spanish *comedia nueva*, a form that freely mixes comedy and tragedy, history and fiction, high and low. Why this willfully "barbarous" infraction, as Lope himself calls it? Because Spanish audiences demand such rule breaking. These, Lope assures us, are the plays his audiences insist on seeing. Whatever the idealist claims of "art," plays are commodities and must be made to please the "vulgar" spectators who pay for them.[5] The influence of a newly invigorated market economy—an economy that had, we may suppose, as much effect on the form and content of English plays and Dutch paintings as it did on the Spanish *comedia*—is here acknowledged in a way that it rarely is in England or Holland. Spanish difference thus works to define a significant underlying likeness. Wherever it occurred, the representational rise of people of less than aristocratic status was a market-driven phenomena.

But from likeness we return to difference, to the peasant protagonists of Lope's and Calderón's plays and to the absence of peasants from the theater audience. How can Spanish peasants be thought comparable to English and Dutch burghers? How, in particular, can a socioeconomic group that was not strongly present in the artistic marketplace be thought to have exercised an influence comparable to groups that were? Yet here again difference helps reveal a broader and deeper likeness reaching across national borders. If people like the peasant protagonists of Lope and Calderón cannot be supposed to have had any large place in the theater audiences of seventeenth-century Spain, people who did attend plays—courtiers, government officials, landowning aristocrats and their retainers, the king himself—had a large stake in the prosperity and independence of Spanish peasants, especially the rich peasants favored by Lope and Calderón.

In the economic crisis of early seventeenth-century Spain, rich peasants were widely seen as the group on whose productive capacity the strength of the nation and its hopes for economic revival depended.[6] Like Thomas Mun, who in the mid-1620s argued for the essential role of merchants in securing "England's treasure," or Pieter de la Court, who in 1662 claimed that "the true interest of Holland" reposed on a mercantile base, Spanish economic thinkers were coming to the recognition that Spain's treasure, its true interest, derived from the contributions of rich peasants.[7] Rich peasants in Spain thus occupied something of the structural position held by such figures as Thomas Arden, Matthew Shore, Francis Ford, George Page, and their real-life counterparts in England or by the prosperous burghers in Holland whose homes resembled those represented in innumerable Dutch genre paintings. Indeed, the wealth of the peasants who command serious attention in the Spanish *comedia* makes more obvious the specificity of the comparable attention accorded burgher homes in England and the Netherlands. Not everyone qualified. The elevating intersections of home and state that push against the conventional limits of generic exclusion in all three countries are reserved for nonaristocrats of substantial income. Early modern plays and paintings may occasionally relax their status test, but only to replace it with a means test. With rare exceptions, the poor need not apply.

Still more revealing is the insistently municipal setting of the Spanish plays. Like English and Dutch burghers, Spanish peasants lived in towns. Their very name says so. As the root of *burgher* is *burgh,* so the root of *villano* is *villa*—"town" in both cases. Burghers and *villanos* are equally town dwellers. In England, the Netherlands, and Spain alike, the liberty of the nonaristocratic home depended on the liberty of the towns in which those homes were located. The Dutch, after all, rose up against their Habsburg overlord in the name of ancient municipal liberties, and the republic they founded was based on municipalities and their freedoms. No wonder then that townscapes joined genre paintings as one of the new forms popularized in seventeenth-century Holland. Home and town were the twin pillars on which Dutch republican identity was founded. Similarly in England, defending "the city's liberty," as well as maintaining the king's royalty and his own home's integrity, were, as we have already noticed, what motivated Matthew Shore to take arms against Falconbridge and his rebels. And the onstage representations of Faversham and Windsor resonate with a concern for municipal liberty that expressed itself still more directly in the new municipal charters that in this period both towns secured from the crown. But, with the single exception of Heywood's *Edward IV,* no English play or Dutch painting brings so fully to the surface the interdependence of domestic and municipal liberty as do the plays Lope and Calderón devoted to the affairs of Ocaña, Fuenteovejuna, and Zalamea, all of them Castilian towns threatened by a sexual marauder dressed in the aristocratic and military power of the state. Though the inhabitants of these Spanish towns are peasants, their preoccupation with municipal liberty and their sense that the safety of their homes and bodies depended on that liberty bring into sharp focus attitudes shared by the burgher inhabitants of Faversham, London, Windsor, Amsterdam, and Delft. "Bourgeois" or "domestic" drama and painting could, as we see more clearly with the help of these Spanish plays, be as accurately called "municipal." The interests and values these new genres represent belong as much to towns as they do to homes and their middle-class owners.

But this new label complicates our historical sense. "Bourgeois" and "domestic" seem inevitably to look forward. The rise of a prosperous middle class and the emergence of an autonomous domestic sphere associated with that class provide the chief elements of a story whose early chapters are, we may suppose, illustrated by domestic drama and genre painting. "Municipal," as in "municipal liberties," looks back. It recalls the patchwork polities of medieval Europe, the elaborate corporate and contractual structures that bound town dwellers to one another and defined their relation to their more-or-less sovereign lords. Where "bourgeois" and "domestic" imagine a world of capitalist growth and possessive individualism, "municipal" points rather to communal solidarity in the face of feudal imposition. What the Spanish drama reveals more clearly than either English drama or Dutch painting is that both were going on at once. The "bourgeois" and "domestic" future was being formed out of a tenaciously defended "municipal" past. As J. H. Elliott has remarked, "the defense of liberties could"—and in this instance did—"broaden into the defense of liberty."[8]

And, finally, the Spanish drama throws into high relief the monarchic absolutism that all over Europe served as a paradoxically enabling (even when antagonistic) support for the transition from municipal liberties to bourgeois domesticity and the individual liberty such domesticity supposes. The king appears in each of the peasant plays—as kings appear in a great many Spanish *comedias* of all sorts—to pronounce a final judgment, and in each the local and domestic action is played off against, and often intertwined with, a royal action of significance in the late medieval or early modern making of Spain. Enrique III in *Peribáñez* gathers troops for an assault on Moorish Granada; Ferdinand and Isabella in *Fuenteovejuna* fight to secure Isabella's Castilian inheritance; Philip II in *El alcalde de Zalamea* marches on Portugal to claim its crown; and in *El mejor alcalde, el rey*, Alfonso VII, by the very judgment he renders in the local and domestic case of abduction and rape that is the play's subject, proves his suzerainty over a rebellious lord of Galicia. The final words of *El mejor alcalde* announce that the story can be found in "the Chronicle of Spain"; "part four"—in case we want to check—"tells it."[9] But all four plays intersect with the royal history of Spain. As Lope and Calderón present them, these peasant dramas *are* history. The domestic and municipal liberty in whose interest they elicit our emotional engagement is at one with the consolidation of monarchic power.

Dutch liberty, including especially the liberty of Dutch towns, was won in battle against the Habsburg kings of Spain, who claimed the Netherlands as part of their royal domain. In marked contrast, the liberty of Spanish towns depended on the support of those very Habsburg kings. Yet underlying the difference, there is again a deep likeness. Royal authority and its real or attempted consolidation shaped both, as, in Tudor or Stuart guise, it shaped the similar claims of early modern English towns. In all three countries, royal charters—their maintenance or their abrogation—defined the bounds of municipal liberty. And in all three, royal absolutism supplied the frame for municipal self-assertion. But in Spain such absolutism played an unusually active role. Not only was the royal government of early seventeenth-century Spain becoming keenly aware of the economic importance of peasant agricultural production, but the crown also had long profited, as it continued to do through the seventeenth century, from the organization, multiplication, autonomous operation, and sale of Castilian towns.

Thinking of conditions elsewhere in Europe, one might imagine medieval and early modern towns as islands in a manorial sea. But in Spain towns were the sea. All of Castile was divided among cities and towns. Towns were the basic units of Castilian administration. Though a town might belong to the royal domain or the domain of a great lord or ecclesiastical body, each was a self-governing entity. Towns elected their own officials, including the *alcaldes* or "town judges" that figure so prominently in the peasant *comedias* of Lope and Calderón, and towns took full responsibility for the management of the lands under their jurisdiction. "These municipal governments, particularly in small towns and villages, remained," in the words of Helen Nader, the historian who has attended most closely to these matters, "the principal means through which Castilians exercised personal liberty in the sixteenth through the nineteenth centuries." Achieving autonomous township was thus the ambition of every Castilian hamlet or commune, an ambition Spanish kings were eager to reward. Armed with a novel theory of "absolute royal power," a theory shaped for the purpose from a fresh reading of Roman law, fifteenth- and sixteenth-century kings alienated rural communities and their surrounding farmlands from their ruling cities and towns to create new towns that could then form their own municipal governments, administer justice, collect and pay taxes, and regulate the local economy. Though existing towns understandably resented these high-handed heists, both the new townsmen and the king had reason to be pleased. The townsmen gained an increased measure of freedom, and the king collected a handsome fee. The result was an extraordinary proliferation of local self-government and a fundamental decentralization of authority, though always in relation to the crown and its absolute power. "Town liberty and royal absolute power were," as Nader has written, "necessary for each other."[10]

These interdependent forces—town liberty and royal absolute power—are what Lope and Calderón dramatize in their peasant *comedias*. As Marcelino Menéndez y Pelayo famously said of *Fuenteovejuna*, these plays are at once "profoundly democratic" and "profoundly monarchic."[11] But they are also profoundly domestic. They are as much concerned with homes as with towns and kingdoms. In dramatizing the interdependent dynamics of municipal liberty and monarchic absolutism, in bringing stories of peasant suffering and retribution to the stage, Lope and Calderón gave new dignity and new affective power to peasant homes, marriages, and families. The first of these accomplishments, the translation into theatrical terms of an emerging ideology of town and kingdom, made these plays the most eloquent and lasting expression of a particularly critical moment in Spain's social, political, and economic development. The second, the resulting dramatic emphasis on the peasant home, did still more. It joined English bourgeois drama and Dutch genre painting in opening a new field of artistic representation and cultural investment. But in attributing death-dealing agency to the nonaristocratic home and community, the Spanish plays outdid even their English and Dutch counterparts. Though this last accomplishment was variously contested on the seventeenth-century Spanish stage, it has survived to give these plays their uniquely powerful claim. They explode with a destructive energy that the governing classes of early modern Europe deeply feared and were usually successful in keeping far from sympathetic artistic expression. How and why that prohibition failed here is the concern of this chapter.

PEASANT TOWNS IN ACTION

Lope's *Fuenteovejuna* supplies what is no doubt the most extraordinary example of communal action in all early modern drama, of whatever country. Provoked by repeated acts of tyrannical abuse—abductions, rapes, and beatings, culminating in the arrest at his own wedding of the peasant Frondoso and the abduction of his bride, Laurencia—the townspeople of Fuenteovejuna rise up against their lord, Fernán Gómez de Guzmán, a commander of the knightly Order of Calatrava, break into his house, and murder him. When the king sends a judge to find out the ringleaders and punish them, all the judge can get the townspeople to say, despite his torture of women and men, of young and old, is "¡Fuenteovejuna lo hizo!"— "Fuenteovejuna did it!" With no choice but to execute everyone in the town or to pardon them all, King Ferdinand reluctantly chooses pardon.

Critics have hailed the "revolutionary" character of the play's action and identified its agent as a "collective hero," but they have less commonly remarked how both action and agent are defined by the familiar municipal order of a Castilian town.[12] The events that finally push the people of Fuenteovejuna to violence are the abduction of Laurencia, the daughter of their *alcalde,* and the disrespect shown the *alcalde* and his staff of office. The revolt itself is planned in a formal town meeting. And the resulting attack ends in the ritual replacement of the commander's arms on the town hall with those of Ferdinand and Isabella. But long before these culminating actions, the play had reminded its audience of how in happier times Spanish towns worked. At the opening of the second act, the *alcalde* and one of the councilmen come on stage talking of municipal business. Esteban, the *alcalde,* prudently suggests that, given the likely poor harvest, no more grain should be dispersed from the communal store. The councilman agrees that this is the way "to govern this republic in peace" (en gobernar en paz esta república).[13] Nearly two centuries later, León de Arroyal wrote, "We ought to consider Spain as a country composed of various confederated republics [*repúblicas*], under the government and protection of our kings. We should imagine each town as a small kingdom, and the whole kingdom as a large town."[14] Lope's councilman anticipates this view. Fuenteovejuna, like all other Spanish towns, is a republic, and men like the councilmen and the *alcalde,* peasants though they are, have a duty to govern it.[15]

The duty, mechanism, and pride of town government figures significantly in *Peribáñez* and *El alcalde de Zalamea* as well. *Peribáñez* includes no meeting of Ocaña's town council, but it does feature the closely comparable meeting of the brotherhood of the town's patron saint, San Roque. Here, once again, we see village democracy at work, with open and inclusive discussion, careful and pragmatic planning, and selection of a steward for the next year's fiesta—a job that goes by general acclaim to Peribáñez himself. This choice confirms what a follower of this play's predatory commander has already said. Peribáñez, according to this description, is

> a peasant of Ocaña, rich and of Old Christian descent, a man held in great esteem by his equals, and whose name, if there were ever an uprising in this town, would be followed by all those who go to the fields with their plows, because he is, though a peasant, highly honored.[16]

In this play, unlike *Fuenteovejuna,* there is, in fact, no such collective uprising. Peribáñez kills the commander, who is about to rape his wife, himself. But when, in the play's final scene, he justifies himself to the king, his local standing grounds his plea. "I was the best among my peers," he says. "Whatever they took up, they gave me the first vote. And for six years I held the [*alcalde's*] staff."[17]

Holding the municipal staff of office and exercising the judicial power associated with it are still more crucial to the action of *El alcalde de Zalamea.* Pedro Crespo, a proud and stubborn *villano* and the richest man in Zalamea, returns from the woods, where his daughter has been raped and abandoned by a captain in the king's army, to be congratulated on his election as the *alcalde* of Zalamea and to be given two bits of news requiring the attention of the new *alcalde:* first, that the king is coming to their town and, second, that soldiers have secretly brought the wounded captain—wounded, as Crespo knows, by Crespo's own son—to the town for treatment. Armed with the *alcalde's* staff, Crespo orders the captain's arrest and execution, actions which put him at odds with the equally proud and stubborn Don Lope de Figueroa, the famous commander of the king's Flanders regiment, to which the captain belonged. Their confrontation includes the following exchange between Crespo and Don Lope, who has so far heard only that some "petty *alcalde*" has arrested one of his officers and who insists that jurisdiction belongs to him alone.

CRESPO. You must not be aware, sir, what the status of a town judge is in a place like this.
DON LOPE. Can he be more than a loutish peasant?
CRESPO. A loutish peasant he may be, but if he stubbornly resolves that he must garrote [his prisoner], then, by God, he will do it.[18]

In his *Tesoro de la lengua castellana* (1611; *Treasury of the Castilian Language*), Sebastián de Covarrubias writes that the *vara*—the staff of office—at whatever step of the governmental hierarchy it may be held "represents royal authority and thus even the lowest of these ministers"—and by that he clearly means village *alcaldes*—"says on such occasions: 'Submit to the king.'"[19] That, in effect, is the answer Pedro Crespo gives when not only Don Lope but also the king himself questions his authority. "All your justice," says Crespo to the king, "is but one body, no more. If that body has many hands, then say, what does it matter if one of those hands puts to death a man another should have killed?"[20] Faced with the garroted body of the dead captain, the king can only agree. The king's justice may be one, but in *El alcalde de Zalamea*, as in *Fuenteovejuna* and *Peribáñez*, peasant authorities exercise that justice in ways the king finds shocking. Only with much reluctance does the king end by endorsing the actions a peasant magistrate takes on his own initiative.[21]

The one clear exception to this pattern announces retreat in its very title: *El mejor alcalde, el rey*—*The Best Judge, the King*. In all four plays, the king is, in some ultimate way, the sole font of justice. Here he is also its sole agent. Set in Galicia rather than Castile, *El mejor alcalde* tells once again the story of a beautiful peasant woman abducted on her wedding day by an obsessively infatuated lord. But in this new setting, the lord's tyrannical behavior results in no communal revolt, no village *alcalde*'s judgment, no violent act of vengeance or defense. The "place" (*lugar*) where the woman, her father, and her peasant groom live—ten households in a valley—hasn't even a name, much less the habits and institutions of self-government we have seen at work in Ocaña, Fuenteovejuna, and Zalamea. Instead of acting for themselves, these country folk take their sufferings to the king, who first sends a letter ordering the woman's release and, when the letter is scorned, comes in person to arrest and punish the offending lord. In terms of literary history, the king's specific remedy—

marrying the dishonored woman to her rapist and then executing him—
may have been borrowed from Pedro Crespo's action in an earlier, non-
Calderonian version of *El alcalde de Zalamea*.[22] But in *El mejor alcalde*,
Lope reclaims the judgment and the power for the king alone. If this king
owes his Solomonic cleverness to the theatrical example of a village *alcalde*,
the play keeps that debt a secret, expending all its energies in the celebration of an unshared royal justice.

Given that, chronologically, *El mejor alcalde* followed not only the original *El alcalde de Zalamea* but also *Peribáñez* and *Fuenteovejuna*, we may
feel that Lope is here drawing back from the bold attribution of agency
to the rural community that had marked those earlier plays and that was
to be so powerfully reaffirmed in Calderón's *Alcalde de Zalamea*. He draws
back, too, from the unequivocal identification of his rural protagonists as
peasants. As I have already mentioned, though the woman, her father,
and her lover are repeatedly referred to and often refer to themselves as
villanos or *labradores*, at a few crucial moments they claim *hidalgo* descent.[23] But if their status has risen, their wealth has declined. Sancho,
the wronged lover, is a mere herdsman for Don Tello, their tyrannical
lord. And Nuño, Sancho's prospective father-in-law, is too poor to give
his daughter, Elvira, a dowry. Only from the perspective of the comic
swineherd, Pelayo, does Elvira seem both "beautiful and rich."[24]

These differences between *El mejor alcalde* and plays it otherwise so
much resembles point to a significant cluster. In the theater of Lope and
Calderón, retributive and death-dealing agency, the kind of agency that
even a social inferior can wield at the expense of a criminally abusive superior, goes with being rich, peasant, and Castilian and with living in a town
capable of effective self-government. But the differences also point to the
remarkable audacity of those other plays. After all, the people of Fuenteovejuna consider sending to the king for help, but decide not to; with
the king in nearby Toledo, Peribáñez could also have sought royal intervention, but doesn't; and Pedro Crespo must actually rush the execution
of his prisoner to get it done before the king arrives. Not only do peasants
in *Peribáñez, Fuenteovejuna,* and *El alcalde de Zalamea* command our sympathy and respect—something that happens as well with the similarly
positioned figures in *El mejor alcalde*. In risky anticipation of the king,
they also take on themselves the job of enacting the king's justice. Written
and produced near the center of royal power in absolutist Spain, these
plays represent an edgily complementary countertradition of rural and municipal autonomy. In saying this, I go at least some way toward giving a

positive answer to questions Menéndez y Pelayo asked many years ago of Calderón's *Alcalde de Zalamea:* "Was *El alcalde de Zalamea* for its contemporaries, as it seems to be for ours, the incarnation of Castilian municipal liberty, battling with the established privileges of the nobility and the military? Can we give this domestic drama a truly political and even revolutionary scope?"[25] Though their revolutionary scope may be limited by ultimate adherence to royal power, *El alcalde de Zalamea, Fuenteovejuna,* and *Peribáñez* are clearly political, and their politics grants a surprising place to the peasant-governed "republics" that were Spanish towns.

Our surprise can only increase when we remember the virulent prejudice Spanish elite culture—the culture Lope and Calderón shared and to which their plays contributed—customarily directed toward peasants in general and small-town authorities in particular. Both prejudices are conveniently on view in Covarrubias's dictionary. Because *villanos* "have little contact with city dwellers," Covarrubias says, "they are . . . very rustic and troublesome. . . . From *villanos* we say *villanía* for a crude or discourteous act." As for village *alcaldes,* "because they are rustics, they often say stupid things in their pronouncements, from which we got the word *alcaldadas*"—that is, "alcaldisms" or "foolish sayings."[26] And what Spanish elite culture thought, the Spanish stage faithfully reproduced. As Noël Salomon shows in his massive and wonderfully informative study, peasants in the Spanish theater of the sixteenth and seventeenth centuries were most often portrayed as comic butts, as *villanos bobos*—"clowns" in the full early modern English sense, both countrymen and fools. Nor did village magistrates fare any better. Salomon lists some sixty plays and interludes, thirty of them by Lope, that feature a comic *alcalde.* "Nine times out of ten," Salomon remarks, "when an *alcalde* appears on stage, it is to get a laugh"—and given the evidence he so generously presents, the ratio may in fact have been more like nineteen out of twenty.[27] Peasant *alcaldes* were the Dogberrys of the Spanish stage, foolishly self-important municipal officials, whose pride was matched only by their ignorance and gullibility.

Lope and Calderón anticipate this prejudice, build it into their plays, derive dramatic energy from its spectacular overthrow. We have already heard Don Lope de Figueroa referring to the *alcalde* of Zalamea as an *alcaldillo,* a "petty town judge," who he supposes must be "a loutish peasant," a *villanote.* Before seeing her, the captain's idea of Crespo's daughter is no better: "Can she be more than a peasant girl with rough hands and feet?" Similarly, the commander in *Fuenteovejuna* expresses surprise that peasants care about their honor, calls Frondoso a "peasant dog," and

mocks the *alcalde*'s protests ("Oh, what an eloquent peasant!"), while the
king in *Peribáñez* is amazed that "such a humble peasant [as Peribáñez]
should so esteem his reputation."[28] Nor are these negative expectations
wholly misplaced. Pedro Crespo goes a long way toward living up to his
advance billing as "the vainest man in the world, one who is more pomp-
ous and presumptuous than a prince of Leon"; Peribáñez is made to lead
a "comically armed peasant troop"; and *Fuenteovejuna* and *El mejor alcalde,
el rey* each satisfies its audience by featuring a familiar peasant clown.[29]
Yet despite belittling expectations and sometimes real identification with
the comic stereotypes shared by early seventeenth-century Spanish elite
culture and the Spanish stage, Pedro Crespo, Peribáñez, Sancho and
Nuño, and the townspeople of Fuenteovejuna emerge to claim the serious
concern and even the admiration of their audiences.

What, we may ask, prompted that emergence? And how do Lope and
Calderón bring it off? A partial answer to the first question is already
before us. A sharpened sense of the economic value of peasant labor and
peasant self-government was pushing even elite attitudes in new directions. And there was also, especially in the wake of the 1609 expulsion
from Spain of thousands of converted Moors (the "Moriscos," as they were
called), a new urgency concerning *limpieza de sangre* (purity of blood), a
quality particularly identified with peasants and one that the peasant heroes of Lope's and Calderón's plays insistently claim.[30] But peasant labor,
peasant self-government, and even peasant purity of blood were mocked
far more often and with far greater conviction than they were praised. So
how in the face of such mockery do Lope and Calderón achieve their
striking reversals? Answering that question will be the work of the next
two sections. But let me anticipate the answer with two words that are
already familiar from our study of English drama and Dutch painting:
home and *history*. These plays, I will be arguing, engage our sympathy and
win our respect by making the peasant home a place of unquestionable
value and by aligning that value with the interests of the state, with pro-
cesses early modern Europe was learning to call "history."

ROYAL HISTORY AND MUNICIPAL LIBERTIES

Let's begin with history.

In a fine article on early modern Spanish historiography—an article
from which I have already borrowed León de Arroyal's remark on each
Spanish town being a "republic" or "small kingdom"—Richard Kagan sees

a split between two kinds of history: royal and municipal. Royal history, institutionalized in the office of *cronista del rey* (the king's chronicler), told, from a court perspective, the unitary and unifying story of the centuries-long reconquest of Spain, of the gradual assembly of the various Iberian kingdoms under a single monarch, and of the triumph of that monarch over various over-mighty subjects. Municipal history—or "chorography," as it was called—emphasized "local *fueros* [rights] together with the laws and institutions which accorded each city a separate and distinctive legal identity." Royal history aimed at winning a historiographic monopoly to match the royal monopoly on military and governmental power. From this vantage point, as Kagan says in summarizing the ideas of King Philip IV and his great minister the count-duke of Olivares, "all history should be royal history, a reflection of the monarchy's particular vision of past events." Municipal chorographers and their local patrons did not oppose royal power or even the royal account of the past. But they did claim "a historical 'space' denied them by historians employed by the crown. . . . [I]n order to defend and support municipal liberties, [they] underlined the importance of a mutually beneficial, reciprocal or contractual relationship between the monarchy and the municipalities."[31]

The peasant dramas of Lope and Calderón mark the theatrical intersection of these two historiographical modes. Chorography, with its emphasis on an ideally static local community, on unchanging municipal institutions and liberties, is in the foreground. Linear, goal-oriented royal history is in the background. But for there to be any drama at all, that background—or figures associated with it—must intrude on the foreground. Such intrusion and the consequences that follow from it justify the serious attention the chorographical object received on stages patronized by the crown and the court. Because the local peasant community was made the scene for actions related to one or another of the great themes of royal history, audiences who identified with that history could be brought, at least for the duration of a play, to set aside the comic disdain with which they usually responded to the theatrically imagined life of such people and such places. Even a village *alcalde* would seem less laughable if the municipal rights he embodied were somehow caught up in the ongoing march of royal history.

Lope and Calderón worked hard to make this connection. Stories like those they tell, stories of abusive power and sexual transgression, could just as easily have been told without it. But Lope and Calderón obviously wanted their "chorographic" attention to local peasant communities to be dignified and legitimized by a simultaneous attention to the monarchy and its imperial destiny. Take, for example, *Fuenteovejuna*. In the brief account he gives of the by-then proverbial phrase *Fuenteovejuna lo hizo*, the indispensable Covarrubias, writing a year or two before Lope, mentions the Castilian civil war raging in 1476, when Fernán Gómez de Guzmán was murdered, and suggests by implication that Fuenteovejuna's revolt was part of the general chaos, but he gives no direct role to the Catholic kings and leaves undefined any specific engagement either the commander or the people of Fuenteovejuna might have had in the dynastic conflict then dividing Castile. Nor does Lope's chief source, Francisco de Rades y Andrada's *Crónica de las tres ordenes de Santiago, Calatrava y Alcantara* (1572; *Chronicle of the Three Orders of Santiago, Calatrava, and Alcantara*), do more than set side by side, as largely unrelated events, Calatrava's armed support of the Portuguese pretender and the rebellion in Fuenteovejuna. Lope unites the two. By making the commander at once the oppressor of Fuenteovejuna and the chief instigator of his order's revolt against Ferdinand and Isabella, he gives further substance to the townspeople's cry of "Long live Ferdinand and Isabella! And death to traitors!" Their defense of their own rights becomes, at the same time, a defense of Isabella's right to the crown of Castile. And when we hear in the play's final scene that Ferdinand and Isabella will now be free to march on Granada, the ultimate triumph of the *Reconquista* adds its luster to the union of the crowns of Aragon and Castile and puts the people of Fuenteovejuna still more firmly on the "right" side of royal history.

The *Reconquista* figures once again in *Peribáñez*, where the marks of authorial intervention show up with even greater clarity. If the usual accounts of *Peribáñez*'s genesis are accurate, Lope began with neither municipal nor royal history but rather with no more than a single, four-line folk ballad stanza that he had quoted years earlier in his peasant saint's life, *San Isidro labrador de Madrid* (1598).

> Más quiero yo a Peribáñez
> con su capa la pardilla,
> que no a vos, Comendador,
> con la vuesa guarnecida.[32]
> (I love Peribáñez more with his little brown cloak than you, commander, with yours all adorned.)

From these few lines come the name and status of Peribáñez, the rivalry with a noble commander, and the woman's boldly expressed preference for her peasant lover. But it was Lope who put this love triangle in a particular and thickly described Castilian town, who drove the story on to its "tragicomic" ending, and who placed it against the background of King Enrique III's plans for an attack on Granada. So precise and so detailed are Lope's historical indications that he even assigns his seemingly timeless romantic intrigue a particular date, 1406, for it was then, shortly before his death, that Enrique, according to the chronicle account Lope versifies at the beginning of act 3, assembled bishops, lords, and knights in Toledo to prepare a major assault on the Moor. Listening to that account, Lope's commander of Ocaña is startled—as Lope himself may have been when he came on it in his source, the *Crónica de Don Juan II* (*Chronicle of King John II*)—to hear among the king's warriors the name "Periáñez." This verbal near echo of "Peribáñez" suggests a connection that Lope makes real when he has his commander respond to the king's call for troops by naming Peribáñez captain over one hundred peasant soldiers. The commander's purpose is simply to get Peribáñez out of the way, but the effect of his action is much like the effect Lope achieves by giving his story a historical resonance: it elevates Peribáñez's status and makes him a worthy opponent. And when, after the murder of the commander, the king confirms Peribáñez's commission, the one-time *alcalde* of Ocaña sets off for Granada as a full participant in the historic project of reconquest.

Behind both *Peribáñez* and *Fuenteovejuna* stands an issue that the shared crusade against the Moorish invader at least partially obscures: the crown's struggle to establish its authority over the feudal nobility, including commanders of the military orders of Santiago and Calatrava, who were the lords of Ocaña and Fuenteovejuna. This is the problem that comes most clearly to the fore in *El mejor alcalde, el rey*, the play Lope identified as having been based on "the Chronicle of Spain." Lope altered his chronicle source in many ways, but he fully retained and even sharpened its main point: the triumph of royal justice over the injustice of a rebelliously defiant lord. The king emerges here as "the image of God" in his realm, a position that in Galicia the abusive Don Tello would claim for himself. "Peasant," Don Tello says when Sancho brings a letter from the king ordering Elvira's release, "if I have taken that woman from you, I am who I am, and here I reign in all that I command as the king does in Castile."[33] "I am who I am"—"soy quien soy." This godlike assertion of absolute self-identity outdoes even the imperious "¿Mías no sois?" (Aren't you mine?) of Fernán Gómez de Guzmán in Fuenteovejuna or the commander of Ocaña's equally peremptory "Yo soy el comendador, / yo soy tu señor" (I am the commander, I am your lord) in *Peribáñez,* and it still hangs in the air an act later when the disguised and unarmed King Alfonso VII arrives at Don Tello's door and has himself announced simply as "Yo"—"I."[34] Who has the right to call himself *yo* in Galicia? Don Tello at first claims that he does. But confronted with the king, his pretension collapses. "My just death is at hand," he says. "I have offended God and the king."[35] In this glittering apotheosis of royal history, the municipal disappears, leaving the peasants who would have been its representatives with little to do but admire and be thankful.

Yet even here, though these Galician peasants, unlike their Castilian counterparts, have no way to enforce their rights other than appealing to the offending lord himself and then to the king, they do clearly have rights. In *El mejor alcalde,* as in *Peribáñez* and *Fuenteovejuna,* seignorial power has limits. Not even the greatest lord can justly lay claim to the wife of another man, however lowly that other man's status may be. The plays depend on their audiences sharing that sense of limits, and they cut strongly against the grain of social prejudice to make sure that it will be shared. What they do not do, however, is to wonder whether similar limits would also apply to the king. Instead Lope is careful in all three plays to keep his kings free of transgressive desire. Not that royal transgression was unimaginable. In a curious digression, *Peribáñez* alludes to the victim of just such a case: "La Cava," a legendary Spanish Lucretia, Bathsheba, or Machteld van Velsen, a woman whose rape by Don Rodrigo, the last Visigoth king of Spain, brought on the Moorish invasion and conquest.[36] According to this legend, Spain was lost by its ruler's sexual transgression. In Lope's peasant plays, Spain is won back—or put on the way to be won back—by rulers who are not only far from committing such an offense themselves but who punish or acquiesce in the punishment of those lords who do. By acting as the guarantor of individual and municipal rights, even the rights of peasants, royal history establishes its claim on a restorative imperial destiny, while errant lords play their assigned part as properly guilty scapegoats for monarchical and seignorial power in this ritual of national self-cleansing. Wanton abuse by some—the tyrannical lords—makes possible theatrical display of the rights and the righteousness of others—peasant subjects and their king.

Without wholly disrupting it, *El alcalde de Zalamea* complicates this pattern. This play's offending lord is no despotic territorial magnate in revolt against the crown and its authority but rather an officer in the king's own army, an officer billeted in Zalamea while on his way to Portugal as part of the force raised to secure the final parcel of King Philip II's pan-Iberian inheritance. Furthermore, the confrontation between Pedro Crespo and Don Lope de Figueroa over legal jurisdiction sets a town *alcalde* in opposition not to his feudal lord but rather to a military representative of the king. Royal power is thus directly implicated, as it never is in Lope's peasant dramas, in the disruption of municipal and domestic life. Perhaps that is why this seems an emotionally more complex play than the others. Calderón's captain may be a less socially and dramatically significant figure than any of Lope's three despotic lords, but the antagonist's space is more than filled by Don Lope de Figueroa, the legendary hero of Spain's sixteenth-century wars in the Mediterranean, the Atlantic, and the Netherlands, a man who shows up in at least four other plays of the period and who would have been known to every member of Calderón's audience. That Pedro Crespo turns out to be a civilian mirror image of Don Lope, the great general's equal in pride and stubbornness and his match with words and sword, not only makes the two surprising friends but also contributes enormously to Crespo's dramatic elevation. This peasant *alcalde*, whose very name would have had comic echoes on the Spanish stage, belongs in the most heroic company imaginable.[37] Indeed, he outdoes that company. In the play's final scene, as Don Lope threatens to destroy Zalamea rather than allow a mere *alcaldillo*, whatever his own friendship and esteem for that *alcaldillo*, to hold and punish one of his men, Crespo calmly proceeds with the captain's execution and then, with considerable effrontery, defends his action before the king himself. On both Don Lope's and Pedro Crespo's side their difference is so much a matter of principle that audiences may well have felt themselves invited to translate the play's conclusion into abstract terms: municipal liberty trumps military privilege.

Two centuries later and an ocean away, the congress and states of the newly independent American republic included as the third article in their Bill of Rights the following: "No soldier shall, in time of peace, be quartered in any house without the consent of the owner, nor in time of war, but in a manner prescribed by law." The Bill of Rights is about the limitation of governmental power. *El alcalde de Zalamea* does not suggest limiting the Spanish government's power to quarter troops in peasant households, but it does expose the danger of such power, and it remarkably celebrates a peasant *alcalde*'s initiative in punishing a soldier who abuses it. Certainly the question of military mistreatment of the civilian population was current both at the historical moment represented by Calderón's play and at the time when the play was written. In a decree issued in 1580 in conjunction with the march on Portugal, Philip II ordered that "no soldier or other person of whatever rank or station dare or be so bold as to commit any violence toward women of whatever status," while the records of the late 1630s and early 1640s present numerous complaints of military abuse, such as this "Notice" (*Aviso*) of May 1639: "Not a day arrives without revealing casualties or deaths due to thieves or soldiers, houses broken into and virgins and widows bemoaning rapes and thefts. Such is the confidence soldiers have in [the leniency of] the military tribunal [*el consejo de guerra*]."[38] Calderón's captain puts his trust in precisely that leniency, but he finds that peasant justice, justice King Philip is brought to accept as his own, is less pliable. Whatever may have happened to his real-life counterparts in early modern Spain, this captain dies for his crime, a fate he shares with the oppressive lords of *Peribáñez*, *Fuenteovejuna*, and *El mejor alcalde, el rey*.

As represented in the peasant dramas of Lope and Calderón, contact with royal history at once disrupts and elevates Spain's rural communities. But it also redefines royal history itself. No longer can that history be seen only as the progressive expansion and consolidation of monarchic power. It now has a countertheme more nearly associated with chorographic municipal history. Against royal power must now be set municipal liberties and subjects' rights. More than any other lord, the king is entitled to say, "I am who I am," "You are mine," "I am your lord." But not even the king can use those imperious claims to justify as gross an infringement on subjects' rights as those dramatized in these plays. Not that any of the kings featured by Lope and Calderón has any such intention. They don't. But once we are taught that peasants are not merely objects of fun, that their sufferings are as worthy of our concern as those of their betters, that they too are capable of self-government, the way has been opened to something like a bill of rights that would limit a monarchic government just as the American Bill of Rights limits a republican one. In the terms I quoted earlier from J. H. Elliott, plays like these put us on the road from "liberties" to "liberty." This may not be what we expect from absolutist Spain in the age of the Inquisition and what Protestant Europe erected into the Black Legend of Spanish tyranny. It may not even be what either Lope or Calderón intended. But the affective dynamics of these plays, the way they shape our emotions and values, make such an opening inevitable.[39]

PEASANT HOMES

Underlying the affective dynamics of Lope's and Calderón's peasant dramas is a powerfully engaging representation of the peasant marriage and home, a representation that has moved critics to identify many scenes in these plays as "genre paintings."[40] Village festivities, like the weddings featured in *Peribáñez*, *Fuenteovejuna*, and *El mejor alcalde, el rey*, particularly attract that label. But it could be applied just as well to the frequent images of everyday peasant life: Peribáñez and Casilda sharing their garlic and onion soup, Elvira washing linen in a stream, Isabel joining her father and his guest at dinner, Laurencia reciting the homely pleasures of an ordinary day. Yet attractive as they are, such images never stand alone. They are always caught in a dialectical relation to that which they are not, to the aristocratic, courtly, and military world that surrounds and threatens them. Sometimes the relation turns violent. Fernán Gómez first attacks Laurencia as she rests from her washing; Isabel is abducted from her father's house where she and he and her cousin sit by the street door enjoying the evening cool; and each of the three weddings is disrupted by the arrival of the predatory lord. Here and elsewhere, desecration of an idealized, yet paradoxically realistic, "genre" scene doubles the transgressive effect of violent sexual oppression. But even when there is no actual intrusion, genrelike scenes of everyday peasant life are always defined by difference. Their meaning and value are made known to the nonpeasant audiences of Lope's and Calderón's plays through constant contrast with a world more like the one those audiences inhabited.

On at least one occasion Lope builds the audience into his play. In *Peribáñez*, one of the commander's servants, who has infiltrated Peribáñez's house as a pretended harvest laborer, describes to his master a scene remarkably like an actual genre painting we have already considered, Nicolaes Maes's *Young Girl Sewing* (figure 13). In her bedchamber, Casilda sits alone at her needlework. In pursuit of Casilda, the commander will later break into this room, and he will die here at the hand of Peribáñez. But already he penetrates its intimacy not only through the voyeuristic report of his spy but also through the presence on the room's back wall, in the place of Maes's map of Holland, of tapestries decorated with his own arms. Looking at Dutch genre paintings, we speculated about the relation of the maps to the foreground scene. Here the commander and his servant engage in a similar exercise in iconographic interpretation. These hangings, says the servant, are signs of Love's victory over the commander.

No, says, his master, they stand rather for my own coming triumph over Casilda. And because this is a play rather than a painting, elements of the scene figure in the ongoing action. Indeed, the very idea of a painting serving as a surrogate object of desire is enacted when the commander orders a surreptitious portrait of Casilda. Alerted to the commander's love by his accidental discovery of this portrait in the artist's studio, Peribáñez returns home to order the removal from his chamber wall of the commander's arms. "A crest and plumes go badly," he says, "between a plow and spade, a winnowing rake, a thresher, and a hoe. On our white walls should hang no crosses of silk"—like those that stood for the commander's military order—"but rather of wheat and straw with poppies, camomile, and broom."[41] But maintaining this separation proves impossible. Though by the end of the play the commander is dead and his arms cast down, Peribáñez himself has been made a captain in the king's army, and Casilda is about to be recostumed in dresses from the queen's wardrobe. No longer would either qualify for the kind of genre painting of ordinary peasant life they had once fit so well. Through no ambition of their own, they have exchanged peasant straw for aristocratic silk.

Early in the play, before the commander has made his first appearance, the newly wed Peribáñez says that "a peasant who has peace in his soul is a king."[42] This proverbial-sounding phrase has reminded one recent editor of another Spanish proverb, one from which Lope took the idea for a whole play: "He is a king who never sees the king."[43] In that other play, El villano en su rincón (1611; The Peasant in his Corner), the allegorically named Juan Labrador founds his identity on this happy autonomy, going so far as to have his tombstone carved in advance with an epitaph that begins, "Here lies Juan Labrador, who never served an [earthly] lord, nor saw the court or king."[44] But neither the king nor Juan Labrador's own socially ambitious children will let this rich and self-satisfied peasant remain independent of the court and its interests. To be "a king in one's own small corner," as Juan Labrador aspires to be, is to excite the envy and desire of the court and its followers, among whom are Lope and his audience. Like the commander of Ocaña, enthralled with the self-absorbed image of Casilda at her needlework, they want to get into the picture, to post their own arms as a sign of possession. But, in a sense, those arms are already there in the very terms the rich peasant uses to declare his independence. To be a king, even if only in a small corner, is to accept a conceptual dependence on the monarchic order that one is pretending to ignore. Freedom is what the king has. All other freedom, including freedom from the king, is understood as an imitation of his.

In ways like these, the dominant discourse reveals and extends its dominance. Just try reversing the operative terms: "A king who has peace in his soul is a peasant" or "He is a peasant who never sees a peasant." Grammatically the sentences still work, but they have become culturally incomprehensible. Kings, not peasants, supply the standard of happiness and autonomy. Yet, without reaching all the way to the king, these plays do undermine and even overturn that standard, as when Juan Labrador calls his lazy workers "courtiers" or when Pedro Crespo's son reminds the captain that without peasants there would be no captains.[45] Though even the proudest of Lope's and Calderón's peasants have internalized something of a monarchical-seignorial ideology, they do not wholly forget the material base in agricultural labor and production on which kings and lords depend. If the usual historical understanding of the emergence of these peasant dramas is right, Lope, Calderón, and their audiences had not forgotten it either. An economic crisis that menaced them all insisted that rich peasants be taken seriously, that they be accorded a value that inevitably put them in competition with the otherwise uncontested value invested in the rule of kings and nobles.

Nowhere is that competition weighed more heavily in the peasant's favor than in the depiction of his marriage and home. What we glimpse here, most clearly in *Peribáñez* but to a significant degree in all these plays, is a vision of unalienated wholeness that contrasts strikingly with both the destructive self-division of the predatory lords and the hieratic emptiness of the justice-dealing kings. In part this has to do with *limpieza de sangre*. Only peasants are true "Old Christians," "never stained," as Peribáñez says of his own lineage and Casilda's, "with [trace of] Jew or Moor."[46] But it also has to do with the reciprocal love of husband and wife, with the integration of home and community, with economic self-sufficiency and the proud acceptance of one's station in life. However miserable and harsh the existence of actual Spanish peasants in the sixteenth and seventeenth centuries—and there is much evidence that it was often very harsh—these stage peasants represent an ideal of abundance and contentment.

They are, however, never allowed to stay "in their own corner." Juan Labrador's children are ennobled and he is made royal steward; Peribáñez becomes, as we have seen, a captain in the king's army; Pedro Crespo's son Juan enters the service of Don Lope de Figueroa as a soldier; and Elvira inherits half the vast estate of her noble tormentor, Don Tello. Only the peasants of Fuenteovejuna remain peasants, and even they end their play at court. The theatrical "genre painting" of the peasant household is staged only to be disrupted and consumed. Though the very appeal of these rich peasants derives from their self-sufficient wholeness, their harmonious relation to one another and to the land they farm, that appeal is tinged with the threat that a truly autonomous peasantry would rise up against their parasitic lords. So to contain and avert that threat these stage peasants are made to pay the symbolic equivalent of a feudal due. They are made to acknowledge, by their own participation in it, their subservience to a monarchical-seignorial organization of power. In this, the plays do something not altogether unlike what the marauding lords do. They look on the peasant home and community with a desire that ends in appropriation. Now, there are of course bad lords and good ones, and Lope and Calderón carefully range themselves, their plays, and their audiences on the side of the good. But in their ultimate aims, the good and bad may differ less than we are led to suppose.

The mark of badness is sexual oppression. The mark of goodness, the upholding of peasant honor. But the very focus on sexual oppression and honor may represent an avoidance of more general issues of dominance and subordination. As Walter Cohen has written, "the transfer of social and economic struggles to the arena of sexual relations . . . helps avoid the full tragic implications of irreconcilable [class] antagonism."[47] Such transfer is an incontestable fact about the genesis of these plays. "Carrying off by force daughters and wives" is only one item in a long list of offenses committed by Fernán Gómez de Guzmán in Lope's chronicle source for *Fuenteovejuna,* while the source of *El mejor alcalde, el rey* does not so much as mention sexual oppression. The Galician peasant in the *Cronica general*—Lope's "Chronicle of Spain"—complains that his lord has taken not his wife but his estate.[48] But in Lope, as in Calderón, attention is focused exclusively on sexual abuse. Why the change? As Lope explains in his *Arte nueva,* it makes for good theater. "Questions of honor are the best subjects because they strongly move everyone."[49] But where everyone is moved, no one is implicated. The oppressor is an aberration, a monster whose destruction, even if it must come at the hands of his peasant victims, frees the courtly and seignorial spectators from guilt. Nor, in such a case, is peasant action as threatening as it would otherwise be. Theirs is not, after all, a political uprising but rather a more "private" expression of offended honor. As the king's acquiescence and the peasant's incorporation into the aristocratic body proves, this is no revolution.

Emphasis on the peasant home and marriage thus enables sympathy but limits change, particularly the kind of fundamental change that would upset the familiar hierarchical relations on which Spanish society was based. In words George Mariscal has used to characterize Golden Age *comedia* in general, "social power is allowed to pass through marginal and subordinate figures . . . so that once on the other side aristocratic power is reasserted in a newly configured and revitalized form."[50] For all the remarkable and historically significant concessions they make to peasant honor, dignity, and even agency, these plays are not really of, by, or for the peasantry, not even the rich, burgherlike peasants whose homes they feature and whose values they celebrate. Rather they arise from the needs and serve the interests of the politically and culturally dominant court and aristocracy.

CONTRADICTION

The last few pages would seem to have led me into self-contradiction. After some very whiggish talk of peasant rights and municipal self-government, I have been brought to acknowledge that even idealizing, genrelike representations of the peasant home and marriage, the very sites where the discourse of rights and self-government should be most firmly grounded, are hedged about with the desires and interests of kings and lords. Such contradiction is endemic to the territory these plays occupy. As royal history must, in the process of legitimating itself, limit its own power to make a place for subjects' rights, so drama must yield to the sovereign claims of the governing hierarchy. Indeed, in this Spanish setting, domestic drama may owe its very existence to those sovereign claims.

But if these plays pull in two directions at once, their opposed inclinations have been unevenly assessed at different times. In our own century, *Fuenteovejuna* in particular has been prized over all other Spanish Golden Age *comedias* for its extraordinary collective and revolutionary energy. And at an earlier moment, as we will see in the next chapter, *El alcalde de Zalamea* was called on to play a similarly transformative role. But in seventeenth-century Spain, reception seems to have run the other way. Not only do these plays represent a tiny fraction of the total output of early modern Spanish drama—something that is true as well in their respective fields of English domestic drama and Dutch genre painting—

but their most audacious departure, their attribution of reformative agency to the peasant community itself, was vigorously redirected and contained.

We have already noticed the retreat represented by Lope's *Mejor alcalde, el rey* and the denial of peasant autonomy more comically achieved in his *Villano en su rincón*. But we might also remember the rewriting of *Peribáñez* as *La mujer de Peribáñez* (1667; *The Wife of Peribáñez*) by three anonymous "wits" and of *Fuenteovejuna* by Cristóbal de Monroy (1629). *La mujer de Peribáñez* still has Peribáñez kill the commander of Ocaña but introduces both a comic subplot of *villanos bobos* and a worthy lord, Don Sancho, to balance the erring commander and give feudal patriarchalism an authoritative voice, while the new *Fuenteovejuna* reduces the peasant townspeople to a secondary role and makes aristocrats the chief victims of the tyrannical commander and the chief avengers. Nor are these the only plays to dilute or deny the part of peasant agency in the correction of lordly sexual oppression. In *La Santa Juana II* (1613; *2 Saint Juana*), *La dama del Olivar* (1614; *The Lady of the Olive Grove*), and *El burlador de Sevilla* (1622; *The Trickster of Seville*), Tirso de Molina replays the story of peasant wrongs but attributes their righting to divine intervention: to a miraculous conversion of the oppressive lord by Sor Juana de la Cruz in *La Santa Juana II;* to another conversion, this one helped along by an apparition of the Virgin, in *La dama del Olivar;* and to punishment at the hands of an animated statue in *El burlador de Sevilla.* That two of these plays, *La Santa Juana II* and *La dama del Olivar,* draw heavily on *Fuenteovejuna* and the third introduces a scene reminiscent of the disrupted peasant weddings in *Fuenteovejuna, Peribáñez,* and *El mejor alcalde, el rey* testifies to the remarkable appeal of Lope's peasant dramas, but that all three shy away from the licensing of peasant retribution shows how transgressive such agency was felt to be. Better to leave justice to the king, as Lope does in *El mejor alcalde, el rey,* or to the nobility, as Cristóbal de Monroy does in his *Fuenteovejuna,* or to God, as Tirso de Molina does in all three of his oppressed-peasant plays.

And yet, despite this deep and enduring resistance, *Peribáñez, Fuenteovejuna,* and *El alcalde de Zalamea* do nevertheless take the radically different turn that continues to attract our attention.[51] In the face of Spanish Habsburg absolutism—perhaps even prompted by Habsburg dependence on the self-governing agricultural towns of Castile—these plays locate peasant honor and the homes whose integrity honor is meant to represent on a trajectory that leads, with whatever hesitations and indirections, from ancient municipal liberties to modern bourgeois liberty. Not only do they value the peasant home and community in a way that undoes the comic stereotypes common in this aristocratic culture. They also grant peasants the power to resist seignorial tyranny, a power that may notionally depend on the king's justice but that is exercised independently by such figures as Peribáñez, Pedro Crespo, and the people of Fuenteovejuna. And, what is more, to justify these actions they supply words that can still ring with defiant conviction. Peribáñez:

> I am a vassal. He is my lord. I live under his protection and defense. But if he intends to take my honor, I will take his life.

Pedro Crespo:

> To the king, one owes one's estate and one's life. But honor is the patrimony of the soul, and the soul belongs only to God.

And the people of Fuenteovejuna:

> *¡Fuenteovejuna lo hizo!*[52]

Are the stories mere vehicles for such ringing statements, the last of which had currency even before Lope wrote? Or do the statements arise almost by necessity from the stories and their dramatization? No doubt a bit of both. But here, it seems to me, the story is, if not pushing out words the culture would otherwise not have spoken, at least putting them in the mouths of people who would not otherwise have been taken seriously speaking them. And that in itself is an accomplishment of real consequence.

Chapter Six

—◦— ● —◦—

From *Tartuffe* to the French Revolution

In 1788, Hans Konrad Escher von der Linth, an ardent Swiss patriot just back from a trip to Rome, wrote in his diary: "We must not let ourselves be put to sleep by the love of art. Among us a friend of mankind can still look freely and with satisfaction at the man and the citizen in real life, and a responsible judge is worth more to society than a Raphael. But there, where only oppression, misery, and vice exist, it is a relief to distract oneself with beautiful paintings."[1] Escher might have been surprised to learn that the very figure he took such satisfaction in admiring, "the man and the citizen," the "responsible judge" working for the benefit of society, had a century and a half earlier been put on stage with a striking semblance of "real life" in one of those southern and Catholic lands of "oppression, misery, and vice." Calderón's Pedro Crespo is just such a figure. No wonder then that others who shared Escher's civic values were giving *El alcalde de Zalamea* new and vigorous currency. Just a year after Escher wrote, a fateful year in French history, the Théâtre de la Nation in Paris put on an adaptation by Jean Marie Collot d'Herbois under the suggestive title *Il y a bonne justice ou le paysan magistrat* (*There is Good Justice or the Peasant Magistrate*), and many others found the play equally appealing. From 1768, when the *Mercure de France* published a lengthy summary—a summary that was read with "extraordinary pleasure" by Gotthold Ephraim

Lessing, who enthusiastically recommended the play be adapted for the German stage—to the 1790s, when Pedro Crespo dropped his monarchic allegiance and began talking like the citizen of a revolutionary republic, no less than fifteen separate versions of Calderón's peasant drama appeared in France, Holland, Sweden, Denmark, Poland, Austria, Italy, and, as Lessing wished, Germany.[2]

In late eighteenth-century Europe, *El alcalde de Zalamea* found a remarkably receptive audience. The image of a peasant magistrate and father defending his and his family's honor against lordly oppression and military force spoke powerfully to both sides of views like Escher's: to both the positive regard for virtue as expressed in the common stations of society and the negative association of oppression, misery, and vice with the hierarchical order of an old regime that lived on in many parts of Europe other than Rome. But *El alcalde de Zalamea* not only represented the two sides. It also staged a conflict between them, a conflict that resulted in the gratifying victory of plebeian civic and domestic virtue over aristocratic prerogative and vice. And were this obvious ideological appeal not enough to explain its remarkable popularity, Calderón's play had the additional advantage of readily adapting itself to a dramatic mode that, despite significant opposition, had been steadily gaining favor and clarity of purpose since the early part of the century.

Pushed to its logical extreme, the opposition Escher posits between looking at real life and looking at art might have resulted in a devaluation of drama to match his devaluation of painting. That, in fact, is what happened in the work of a far more celebrated Swiss patriot. Responding to Jean Le Rond d'Alembert's complaint that Geneva had no theater, Jean-Jacques Rousseau argued that it should have none. A free people living in a society of equals does better to regard one another—just the idea Escher would echo thirty years later—than to gaze on deceptive theatrical shows. "Let the spectators become an entertainment to themselves; make them actors themselves; do it so that each sees and loves himself in the others so that all will be better united."[3] But, as even Rousseau acknowledged, in less happy societies a properly reformed theater might have uses more valuable than the relief and distraction beautiful paintings afforded Escher in Rome. Achieving such reform, in painting as well as drama, was the self-consciously assumed task of Rousseau's fellow *philosophe*, Denis Diderot, the coeditor with d'Alembert of the *Encyclopédie* where d'Alembert's article on Geneva appeared—a task taken up by a host of Diderot's followers, including Collot d'Herbois, Lessing, and the many others who adapted *El alcalde de Zalamea* for their various national theaters. These men created a new form of drama—a "bourgeois" drama, as they often called it—and celebrated a new mode of painting that together gave audiences all over Europe the opportunity to see and love themselves in much the way Rousseau imagined the citizens of Geneva doing in the streets and squares of their virtuous republic. Deprived of a real Geneva, they made art serve as a virtual Geneva in the midst of what they saw as a corrupt and declining old regime.

This chapter concerns the drama and painting written and promoted by Diderot and his followers. Even in a book that has already done much jumping from place to place and from time to time, this may seem an objectionably large leap. But it only follows the material itself. In late eighteenth-century France, English domestic drama, Dutch genre painting, and Spanish peasant drama finally come together. This is not to say that English, Dutch, and Spanish work exercised an irreplaceable influence on the French drama and painting we will be examining, though it certainly did have some influence. Social, political, economic, and artistic forces like those that prompted Thomas Heywood, Gerard ter Borch, and Lope de Vega more than a century earlier were acting as well on Diderot and his contemporaries and might have had much the same effect had the English, Dutch, and Spanish never written or painted. But the French did know the earlier work, whether directly or indirectly, and they recognized in it a welcome precedent for what they were trying to accomplish.

Such recognition would be reason enough to study them together. But there is a still better reason. The eighteenth-century French gave a central and polemically active role to representational departures that in sixteenth- and seventeenth-century England, Holland, and Spain had been marginal and unassertive. Though Heywood defended actors, he never defined or defended the domestic drama he pioneered; the Dutch were equally silent about the genre painting they boldly developed; and even Lope's discussion of his "new art of making plays in this time" is more rueful than combative, and it has, in any case, no more application to his few peasant dramas than to the hundreds of other *comedias* he wrote. In marked contrast to this reticence, Diderot and his followers issued manifestos as readily as they wrote plays, and in their manifestos they discover how the virtual Geneva of domestic and bourgeois painting and drama might transform the old regime after its own image. Flatly denying the preeminent claims of the state and its history, they put the bourgeois—or "bourgeoisified"—home in their place. They thus revealed in domestic drama and painting a radical potency their English, Dutch, and Spanish predecessors could scarcely have imagined.

But in adopting this stance and producing the works that would justify it, the French had to confront a theatrical history in their own language that loomed much larger than any native accomplishment the English, Dutch, or Spanish had been obliged to acknowledge—a theatrical history that had strong associations with the monarchic state and the hierarchy that maintained it. Where the Elizabethans, Lope de Vega, and the seventeenth-century Dutch themselves created the works that were to dominate the dramatic and artistic canons of their respective countries, that job had been done for France long before Diderot and his contemporaries arrived on the scene. Theirs was not the Golden Age of French drama. That distinction belonged rather to what Voltaire called "le siècle de Louis XIV"—which, as it happened, was also the *siècle* of Corneille, Racine, and especially Molière. I say "especially Molière" because, unlike the classical and heroic tragedies of Corneille and Racine, Molière's comedies defined for French drama the territory of ordinary life. Were Diderot and the others to succeed in making a place for their bourgeois drama, they had necessarily to contend with the enormous precedence of Molière. Indeed, the very theater where they hoped to see their work played, the Comédie Française—which, by the end of the eighteenth century, had become the Théâtre de la Nation—was Molière's. He and his company founded it, and his plays continued, as they do even today, to dominate its repertory. Nor was playing at the Maison de Molière, as the Comédie Française was familiarly known, merely a matter of prestige. Thanks to a royal decree of 1680, a decree that remained in force until the Revolution, the Comédie Française enjoyed a monopoly on both the classical French repertory and new plays in the "great genres" of comedy and tragedy. The old regime, at whose heart Diderot and his followers hoped to locate their virtual Geneva, was, theatrically at least, the regime of Molière.

How then in that old regime was the nonaristocratic home represented? What place, if any, did Molière allow aspirations like those the English, Dutch, and Spanish found a way to reward?

BEING BOURGEOIS IN THE HOUSE OF MOLIÈRE

No one who knows plays like *George Dandin* (1668) or *Le bourgeois gentilhomme* (1670; *The Bourgeois Gentleman*) will long hesitate in answering.

Molière gave those aspirations an extraordinarily large and a still more extraordinarily uncomfortable place in his work. George Dandin occupies precisely the same social status as Pedro Crespo, Peribáñez, and the leading figures of Fuenteovejuna. He is a rich peasant. But he has made a mistake those Castilian peasants never make. He has married above his station, and for that he is made to suffer. A young nobleman, the lord of the surrounding country, courts Dandin's highborn wife, and she, much to her husband's dismay, welcomes his advances. Monsieur Jourdain, the bourgeois gentleman, suffers less, but only because he is still more of a fool. His courtly pretensions make him an easy mark for a titled schemer and the unconscious butt of every joke. And if cuckoldry is never a threat, Monsieur Jourdain is tricked out of his daughter by a bourgeois suitor disguised as the son of the Grand Turk, who satisfies Monsieur Jourdain's longing for social promotion by elevating him to the lofty but wholly imaginary rank of *mamamouchi*.

Fabliau, farce, and the comic novella shadow English domestic drama, Dutch genre painting, and Spanish peasant drama. The newer forms necessarily remember and variously reform their predecessors. They thus play against expectation. Not so Molière. Rather than depart from the familiar expectation that the private world of the nonaristocratic home will be a scene of extravagant and degrading mirth, he grandly fulfills it. Where even Shakespeare's farcical *Merry Wives* evokes fabliau cuckoldry only to deny it, *George Dandin* amplifies the humiliation. And, as for Molière's bourgeois gentleman, he joins the *précieuses ridicules*, the jealous guardian, the provincial lawyer, the hypochondriac, the learned ladies, and many ignorant and pretentious doctors in a lengthy parade of everyday folly. The parade does of course include its share of silly aristocrats—Molière's *petits marquis* are justifiably famous—but it also celebrates the hierarchical order of society and ridicules any attempt to violate that order. Indeed, in the figure of the misanthrope, Molière even makes fun of outspoken rectitude, the uncompromising sincerity that would unmask the polite world's fundamental mendacity.

This last entry in Molière's parade of fools particularly upset Rousseau, who may have seen something of himself in the misanthrope and who certainly saw his own values in the misanthrope's attack on worldly accommodation and insincerity. But even without the prompting of self-identification, Rousseau found *George Dandin* and *Le bourgeois gentilhomme* similarly offensive. "Who," he asks, "is more criminal, a peasant so mad as to marry a lady, or a wife who seeks to dishonor her husband?"

And "who is more blameworthy, the unintelligent man of the middle class who foolishly plays the gentleman, or the rascally gentleman who dupes him?"[4] In both instances, Rousseau would have us answer "the latter." But in both, Molière's target is the former, with the result that, from Rousseau's Genevan perspective, Molière offered a theater more to be avoided than embraced. Nor was Rousseau alone in this view. Louis Sébastien Mercier, one of Diderot's most ardent disciples in the project of creating a bourgeois drama, argued strongly that Molière could not furnish their model. In support of that argument, Mercier again turns to *George Dandin* and *Le bourgeois gentilhomme*. In *George Dandin,* as Mercier describes it, "an honest man, pained by the dishonor of his house, becomes the object of public laughter, because, being very rich, he married a gentlewoman who had nothing, an event one sees every day and that serves, politically, to undo the horrible inequality of fortunes." And in *Le bourgeois gentilhomme,* Molière "wanted to humiliate the bourgeoisie, the most respectable order in the state, or, to put it better, the order that makes the state."[5] Clearly, Molière's comedy, where, with the audience's laughing complicity, aristocratic vice regularly triumphs over what is unfairly made to appear bourgeois folly, is the very antithesis of the morally, socially, and politically useful drama Rousseau thought impossible and Mercier, following Diderot, hoped to produce.

Or so it would appear from these sharply critical remarks. But Enlightenment writers also saw another Molière, one who was more their progenitor than their antithesis. Voltaire, who wrote a life of Molière, hailed the seventeenth-century playwright as a fellow *philosophe.* Rousseau admitted that he never willingly missed a performance of any of Molière's plays. Diderot despaired of being able to write at all when he read Molière and drew heavily on *Tartuffe* in his own showpiece for the new drama, *Le père de famille* (1758; *The Father of the Family*).[6] Mercier made a performance of *Tartuffe* the subject of a bourgeois drama he called *La maison de Molière* (1776; *The House of Molière*). And Pierre Augustin Caron de Beaumarchais, easily the most successful of Diderot's many followers, found a theatrical space midway between Diderot's bourgeois drama and Molière's laughing comedy for his three Figaro plays, the last of which he named *L'autre Tartuffe* (1792; *The Other Tartuffe*).[7]

The prominence of *Tartuffe* in these more positive responses, particularly in the three that come from leading proponents and practitioners of the new bourgeois drama, is striking. Of all the plays from the seventeenth-century Golden Age of French theater, *Tartuffe* most clearly anticipates the Enlightenment and its bourgeois drama. But *Tartuffe* is also and no less clearly the seventeenth-century French play that shares most with the English and Spanish drama we have been studying, the one in which the intersection of the state and its history with the private, nonaristocratic home is most marked, the one in which the audience's sympathy is most firmly engaged on the side of that home rather than on the side of the predator who menaces it. In this, *Tartuffe* reverses the pattern of *George Dandin* and *Le bourgeois gentilhomme*, just as a few remarkable English and Spanish plays reversed the familiar comic pattern of fabliau and farce. Audiences do, of course, still laugh at Orgon, the rich bourgeois who foolishly welcomes Tartuffe into his house, but the laughter quiets when Tartuffe claims the house as his own, turns Orgon and his family out at the door, and accuses Orgon before the king of a capital offense. Nor does Molière's bourgeois drama, if we may call it that, neglect the sexual predation that had been the usual way of dramatizing conflict. But Tartuffe's would-be seduction of Orgon's wife is only a step—though, given the violence of Tartuffe's passion, a grotesquely chilling step—on the way to Orgon's total dispossession.

It may not be what comes first to mind when we think of Tartuffe, but he, like so many of the libertine adventurers of early modern comedy, is not only a penniless con artist, but also an aristocrat—or, at least, that is what Orgon, with no contradiction from the play's other characters, insists: "You can tell by his appearance that he is truly a *gentilhomme*."[8] I have left Orgon's *gentilhomme* in French because the French word, as it was used in the seventeenth century, had a much more exclusive meaning than the English *gentleman*. According to Furetière's dictionary, a *gentilhomme* is "a nobleman by descent, who does not owe his nobility either to the office he holds or to letters from the prince."[9] One might, that is, bear a title of nobility—be, for example, a *marquis* or a *comte*—without being a *gentilhomme*. Thus in *Le bourgeois gentilhomme*, Cléonte must admit that, though his parents occupied honorable offices, though he himself held a military position of honor, and though he has sufficient wealth to maintain a respectable station in the world, he is not a *gentilhomme*—and for that, Monsieur Jourdain foolishly refuses him the hand of his daughter: "I want a *gentilhomme* as my son-in-law."[10] Orgon also wants a *gentilhomme* as his son-in-law.[11] But Orgon goes still further than Monsieur Jourdain. Not only does he offer his daughter to Tartuffe. He also disinherits his son and even dispossesses himself in Tartuffe's favor. Yet were we to ask a version of Rousseau's question of *Tartuffe*—"Who is more blameworthy, the unperceptive man of the middle class who lets a gentleman scamp take over his house, or the rascally gentleman who dupes him?"—the answer this time would clearly be the one Rousseau would prefer.[12] The rascally gentleman is more blameworthy than the middle-class fool. Though Molière once again makes fun, as Mercier charged him with doing, of the bourgeoisie, he reserves his most biting satire for a noble imposter preying on bourgeois folly, wealth, and (Tartuffe hopes) women. In the end, the bourgeois family, including the foolish father, is more an object of concern, and perhaps even sympathetic identification, than of ridicule or scorn.

But my account has so far ignored what is most obvious about Tartuffe, the specific nature of his scam, his mask of severe piety. From its first performance in 1664, a performance before the king of just three acts of the still unfinished script, *Tartuffe* achieved renown as the play "Molière had written against hypocrites."[13] But hypocrisy proved a dangerous subject. That same first performance resulted in an immediate royal prohibition that was only definitively lifted five years later in 1669. In the meantime, the play was the target of repeated attacks, including a 1667 order from the archbishop of Paris proclaiming the excommunication of anyone in his diocese who "put it on, read it, or heard it recited, whether in public or in private." And Molière himself was denounced by still another clergyman as "a demon dressed in flesh . . . the most signal atheist and libertine of all time."[14] Besides making *Tartuffe* unavailable in the public theater, the most obvious effect of these prohibitions and attacks was to excite such interest in the play that, when its public performance was finally permitted, it became the greatest draw of Molière's long and spectacularly successful career. But a no less significant, if more subtle, effect was to transform the play into an allegory of its own troubled history. As Tartuffe, through the hypocritical assumption of a show of piety, gains temporary control of Orgon's house and fortune, so the ecclesiastical hypocrites who demanded the prohibition of Molière's play gained at least temporary control of the king and the church. In the first of his three appeals to the king, Molière makes this connection himself: "The tartuffes"—a name Molière invented for his hypocrite and that became with his help an instant common noun—"underhandedly managed to win grace with your majesty, and in the end the originals got the copy suppressed."[15]

Tartuffe began, according to Molière, as just another of his comic attacks on "the vices of [his] age." "Correct[ing] men while entertaining them" is, as he points out, no more than "the duty of comedy."[16] But none of his other targets struck back, or at least not with the same effect. No cabal of *précieuses*, misers, libertines, doctors, learned ladies, or even social-climbing peasants or burghers ever got one of his plays forbidden. The hypocrites' success, where all others despaired of even trying, provided an irrefutable demonstration of their extraordinary power. That success made *Tartuffe* forever after a work of history, one that told of a danger lurking at the very apex of royal government. But, of course, *Tartuffe* was already, from its very inception, a work of history in the sense that, more directly than any other of Molière's plays, it addressed an issue of great political moment. Though Molière may have thought that in attacking an ostentatious excess of devotion he was doing the work of the libertine court at odds with the *parti dévot* and may thus have been genuinely surprised by the king's quick prohibition of his play, he had to know that every act of supposed piety he attributed to Tartuffe—indeed, Tartuffe's very presence in a private home as a director of conscience—was a topic of intense controversy.[17] Were the Jansenists Molière's prime target? Or the Jesuits? Or some more particular figure or figures? Centuries of scholarship have provided no simple answer to such questions.[18] But it is clear now, as it has been from *Tartuffe*'s first performance, that in staging a religiously grounded usurpation of "tyrannical power" within the confines of a bourgeois home, Molière was enlarging the reach of comedy to embrace matters of state.[19]

Nor is *Tartuffe*'s engagement with history only allegorical. In a scene that recalls the closing moments of each of the four Spanish peasant dramas but that has no counterpart in Molière's other comedies, the king intervenes to rescue Orgon and his family from Tartuffe's machinations. Unlike the Spanish kings, he does not appear in person. Where they were figures from the past, this king is Louis XIV himself. He is thus represented by an officer of the royal guard. But his intervention is no less direct and no less decisive for that. Indeed, in only *El mejor alcalde, el rey*, does the achievement of what the audience is prepared to accept as a just outcome depend so completely on the king. And not even Lope's Alfonso VII performs an act of such blatantly absolute authority as Molière's Louis XIV. After all, the Galician nobleman Alfonso executes is unquestionably guilty of capital crimes. As he admits himself, he deserves to die. Tartuffe is guilty of no crime, unless pretending to be pious is a crime, while Orgon has in fact committed the treasonous act of which he stands accused. He has knowingly hidden the property of a state criminal in flight from justice.

In ordering the arrest of Tartuffe, in pardoning Orgon, and in annulling the donation by which Orgon had conveyed all his worldly goods to Tartuffe, the king rises above the law to attain a summit of equity answerable only to his own conscience and the audience's applause. But by these acts, he not only reverses the play's outcome. He also repositions himself with regard to its chief antagonists. Before being arrested as the king's enemy, Tartuffe had appeared as an instrument of the king's justice. The royal officer arrives at Orgon's house at Tartuffe's instigation and in Tartuffe's company, and Tartuffe defends his disloyalty toward Orgon in the name of duty to the king. Royal power thus seems firmly aligned with Tartuffe, and, were we not able to count on Molière to give us a happy ending, the very different way power does finally align itself would appear the less probable alternative. In the real world, kings do not normally pardon criminal offenders and arrest their accusers, however unpleasant those accusers may be.

But that very violation of real-world expectation intensifies the drama of *Tartuffe*, heightens the *éclat* of its abrupt shift in direction. In the *Lettre sur la comédie de l'Imposteur* (1667; *Letter on the Comedy of the Imposter*), a detailed discussion that came out after the single public performance that the play enjoyed before 1669, the anonymous author makes much of this sudden reversal. "The spirit," he writes, "of the whole [fifth] act and its only effect and aim [up until the king's intervention] has only been to represent the affairs of this poor family in the most extreme desolation." Molière's solution, his introduction of the king as the savior from this extreme desolation, deserves, this commentator insists, the most extravagant praise.

> It seems to me that if, in all the rest of the play, the author has equaled all the ancients and surpassed all the moderns, one can say that in this denouement he has surpassed himself, there being nothing greater, more magnificent, and more wonderful, and yet nothing more natural, more felicitous, and more just, since one can say that were it permissible to dare to draw the character of the soul of our great monarch, it would undoubtedly be in that plenitude of light, that prodigious penetration of mind, and that marvelous discernment of all things that it would consist.[20]

But others were not so sure. Nicolas Boileau, who had defended *Tartuffe* from those who would censor it, nevertheless thought the whole fifth act needed rewriting. Instead of introducing "the authority of the king," Molière could have left Tartuffe's punishment up to Orgon and his family, ending perhaps in a good solid beating. That, says Boileau, would have been much funnier. As is, the play "leaves the spectator in tragedy"— "dans le tragique."[21]

What the anonymous letter writer celebrates and Boileau deplores is the generic transformation of comedy into tragedy and royal panegyric. But this transformation is precisely what saves the bourgeois home from ridicule. Foolish as he has been, Orgon comes to stand for the state— and perhaps for society at large—menaced by the threat of hypocrisy. As I have already remarked, Orgon's story becomes history, and Orgon himself quite unexpectedly attains a pathos and grandeur that separates him from the likes of George Dandin or Monsieur Jourdain. That Molière, stung by earlier attacks on the supposed licentiousness of *L'école des femmes* (1662; *The School for Wives*) and in solidarity with a court that had suffered its own antilibertine reproach, chose to strike back at what appeared to him religious hypocrisy is remarkable enough. But that he made a bourgeois family both the victim of the hypocrisy and the beneficiary of an extraordinary royal intervention is more remarkable still. Instead of ridiculing the bourgeoisie, as Rousseau and Mercier rightly charged him with doing in his other plays, he identifies with it and invites his audience to do the same.

A century later this identification was made the basis for Mercier's own bourgeois drama *La maison de Molière*, a play that reverses Mercier's evaluation of Molière just as Molière reversed his depiction of the bourgeois family.[22] Not only does Mercier make a performance of *Tartuffe* his subject. He also retells a version of the *Tartuffe* story with Molière and his house at its center in the place of Orgon and his. In Mercier's play, Molière is menaced by his own tartuffe, a religious hypocrite who has flattered and bribed his way into Molière's house in the hopes of causing sufficient disruption to prevent the performance of *Tartuffe*. But moved by the spectacle of Molière's virtuous behavior in the most hidden recesses of his private life, even the hypocrite must finally testify on Molière's behalf. Though the frivolous marquis and count whom Mercier introduces as courtly foils may object that Molière lives "bourgeoisement," that his plays are marred by the excessive attention they give the middle class, and that, as a result, they will survive only among "the thick-headed bourgeoisie" (l'épaisse bourgeoisie) Mercier makes it clear that Molière's middle-class identity underlies the exemplary force of both his life and his art.[23] The

Molière of *Tartuffe*, the man who courageously sets the naive and honest simplicity of bourgeois virtue against religious hypocrisy and courtly pretension alike, emerges as the very model of the progressive, reforming dramatist Mercier hoped to become, a man more of the new order Mercier imagined than of the old. "Our theater," wrote Mercier in the preface to his *Molière*, "is moving toward a necessary and inevitable revolution," and in the play itself Molière is made prophetically to object that "my name itself will be used to stop the progress of art and to block those who will come after me."[24] If *Tartuffe* provided the opportunity to transform the reactionary Molière into a guide toward the impending revolution, it was precisely because in this play, as in no other, conventional farce is made to border on something approaching bourgeois tragedy. The tragedy is of course averted, but only by an intervention that deploys the absolute power of the state to satisfy the sympathies of the play's ideal audience, an audience that identifies with the belatedly enlightened Orgon and cares little for the treasonous behavior that has made Orgon vulnerable to Tartuffe's denunciation. In *Tartuffe* the state has in effect been made to abandon its own interests and embrace those of the bourgeois family.

Seventeenth- and eighteenth-century French dwellings took, in the words of the *Encyclopédie*, "different names according to the different estates of those occupying them. We speak of *la maison* of a bourgeois, *l'hôtel* of a noble, *le palais* of a prince or a king."[25] Most of Molière's plays were produced, as *Tartuffe* was, in the Palais Bourbon, and they accordingly adopt a *palais* or *hôtel* perspective on the *maisons* they portray. *Tartuffe*, where so much of the plot turns on the occupancy and ownership of Orgon's *maison*, largely maintains that aristocratic perspective through the first four acts. But, as Boileau complained, the fifth act alters it radically. That alteration prepared the way for the ideologically self-conscious construction a century later of a new "theater of the nation," a refashioned *maison de Molière*, which would house in place of the hierarchical "estates" comedy of the old regime—the comedy to which the actual Molière had devoted most of his career—a universalizing bourgeois drama. As Robert Darnton has provocatively suggested, "One of the most important tasks of the French Revolution was to rewrite Molière."[26] With *Tartuffe*, Molière could be seen as having begun that task himself.

TEARS, TRUTH, AND PICTURES OF VIRTUE

In Calderón's *Alcalde de Zalamea*, followers of Diderot recognized and welcomed a play that fit or could easily be made to fit the emerging taste of their moment. As antagonist and as model, Molière helped shape that moment. But so too, in a more purely positive way, did rule-breaking precedents from England and the Netherlands. From England came the heady mix of bourgeois tragedy, sentimental comedy, and Richardsonian fiction, all of which reach back, whether directly or indirectly, to the domestic drama of the 1590s. And from the Netherlands came what the eighteenth-century French were the first to call "genre" painting, the painting of everyday domestic life. Even before Diderot began his campaign for theatrical reform in the 1750s, both found French imitators. Pierre-Claude La Chaussée and Françoise de Graffigny brought English-style weeping comedy to the French stage in the 1730s and 1740s, and in the same decades Jean-Baptiste Siméon Chardin gave the French their own Dutch-style genre painting. In formulating his program for a new theater, Diderot drew on both.

At once the most obvious and the least expected element in this multinational set of influences is genre painting. What, after all, have drama and painting to do with one another? Not so much as is commonly thought, Lessing was soon to argue in his *Laokoon* (1766). But the practice of Dutch painters and the theoretical declarations of French dramatists suggested otherwise. In borrowing figures, poses, and situations from comic drama and in creating images that invite a narrative interpretation, Dutch genre painters established the connection in one direction. Diderot, with much greater fanfare, renewed it in the other. Among the central undertakings of his reforming program was the replacement of the *coup de théâtre*, which in his view had characterized the court-oriented drama of the preceding century, with the *tableau*. As Diderot defines the two terms in his *Entretiens sur "Le fils naturel"* (1757; *Conversations on "The Illegitimate Son"*), "an unexpected incident, which happens as part of the action and suddenly alters the standing of the characters, is a *coup de théâtre*. An arrangement of those characters on the stage, so natural and so true that, faithfully rendered by a painter, it would please me on a canvas, is a *tableau*."[27] But for Diderot not any *tableau* would do. What he clearly favored in his own plays and what his followers were most eager to imitate were touching scenes of ordinary family life. That is where "nature" and "truth," the qualities that he and they sought as the most effective antidote to the artificiality, hypocrisy, and oppression of the old regime, were most likely to be found.

We have already encountered in an earlier chapter a distant product of Diderot's new aesthetic in the *tableau vivant* described in Goethe's *Elective Affinities*, for, as we can see now, Diderot and his circle were the essential relay station on the circuit that linked Gerard ter Borch's genre painting to Goethe's novel. Not only was Goethe's sensibility shaped by Diderot's theories and the plays that emerged from those theories; Goethe also learned to know ter Borch's painting and to think of it as *The Paternal Admonition* (rather than as the brothel scene its first Dutch viewers might have seen) from an engraving by Diderot's longtime friend and collaborator Johann Georg Wille.[28] But we need go no further than the example Diderot himself supplies in the *Entretiens* to see what he meant by a *tableau*. He points to the second act of *Le fils naturel*, where Rosalie calls her maid, Justine. A stage direction follows: "Justine approaches a tapestry loom. Rosalie leans unhappily on the loom. Justine sits on the other side. They work. Rosalie interrupts her work only to wipe the tears that fall from her eyes. She then goes back to work. The silence lasts for a moment, while Justine leaves off her work to look at her mistress."[29] Take away the bit of movement—there is not much—and this could easily pass for the description of a genre painting. Scenes of women engaged in ordinary household labor were a favorite of both the Dutch and Chardin. Chardin's *Diligent Mother* (figure 20) tells a different story than Diderot's stage direction, the story of a mother and daughter rather than of a young woman and her maid. But the painting and the play share the same precisely realized domestic setting, the same quiet intensity and absorption, the same striving after the natural and the true—all qualities that both share as well with Goethe's *tableau vivant*, with ter Borch's *Paternal Admonition*, and with hundreds of other Dutch genre paintings of the seventeenth century.[30]

Diderot worked hard to make these painterly qualities a feature of drama. As a measure of his success, consider the opening stage direction of Collot d'Herbois's adaptation of *El alcalde de Zalamea*. Crespo's daughter Isabelle and her cousin Inés "are busy with embroidery or lacework; they look at one another several times as though they wanted to speak, but don't; finally . . ." Inés breaks the silence, just as Justine did in *Le fils naturel*.[31] Clearly, Collot is here drawing far more heavily on Diderot than on Calderón, whose play had begun with soldiers marching toward Zalamea. Though they have since become commonplace, detailed stage directions of the sort that fill Diderot's two bourgeois dramas and that became a mark of followers like Collot had little precedent in the plays of earlier writers. Equally novel and equally popular with his followers were the extended silences Diderot wrote into those stage directions and the elaborate pantomime that often took the place of speech. By these means, Di-

Figure 20 Jean-Baptiste-Siméon Chardin, *The Diligent Mother* (1740). Oil on canvas, 49 × 39 cm. Musée du Louvre, Paris. Photo: © RMN.

derot hoped to achieve a more powerfully natural communication than the formal declamation of classical French theater could manage, a greater and more immediate involvement of the spectator in the action—the kind of response Diderot himself had to the paintings he most admired. Chardin's certainly fell into that category. For Diderot, Chardin was the "great magician," the master of nature and truth.[32] But by the time Diderot began his *Salons*, the reviews he wrote from 1759 to 1781 on the biennial shows of the Royal Academy of Painting and Sculpture, Chardin was no longer producing new genre paintings. In the *Salons*, Jean-Baptiste Greuze is the painter—"my painter," as Diderot calls him—whose work elicited the responses that tell most of what Diderot sought to accomplish in his own plays.

Take, for example, Diderot's comments on the most ambitious of the paintings Greuze presented at the Salon of 1763, his *Filial Piety* (figure 21).

> Greuze is really a man after my own heart. Leaving aside for a moment his smaller works, which will give me plenty of pleasant things to say to him, I come directly to his picture of *Filial Piety*, which would be better called *Payment for the Gift of a Good Upbringing*. First, I like the genre. This is a moral painting. And why not? Hasn't painting been devoted to debauchery and vice long enough? Shouldn't we be pleased to see it finally competing with dramatic poetry to move us, instruct us, correct us, and lead us to virtue? Keep at it, my friend Greuze! Go on teaching morals in painting, and always do it as you do here! When you reach the end of your life, there will be none of your works that you won't be able to recall with pleasure. How I wish you had seen the girl who, looking at the head of your paralytic, cried with a charming vivacity: "Oh, my God, how it moves me! If I look any longer, I'm sure I'll start crying." And how I wish that girl had been mine! I'd have known her just from that response. When I saw that eloquent and pitiful old man, I felt, as she did, that it touched my soul and that tears were about to fall from my eyes.[33]

From here, Diderot goes on to comment on the painting in lengthy and enthusiastic detail, but this should be enough to give us a sense of what he valued. Most obvious is an intense emotional response to the image of virtue. Virtue not vice is now to be the subject of painting and drama. And that image of virtue—suffering virtue is what Diderot likes best— is charged with a pathos that draws us to itself as it draws our tears, a pathos that makes of its audience a community of fellow weepers.

From the reform of art, its redirection toward everyday, domestic, and suffering virtue, is to come a reform of society. But in this reform the

Figure 21   Jean-Baptiste Greuze, *Filial Piety* (1763). Oil on canvas. The State Hermitage Museum, St. Petersburg.

reformers themselves are granted a remarkably prominent role. As Diderot presents it, what he and Greuze seek to accomplish through their paintings and plays is precisely what the "good upbringing" provided by the "eloquent and pitiful old man" has accomplished in his family. They seek not only to bring into being a new world of goodness; they also expect that new world to turn its gaze on them. What else can Diderot's surprising image of Greuze near his death, like the old man near his, mean? Or the introduction of the charmingly sensitive girl? Or the sudden claim Diderot himself lays on the girl and her emotions? With an audacious lack of reserve, first Greuze, then Diderot is slipped into the place of the dying old man as "the principal figure, the one who occupies the center of the scene and who fixes our attention."[34] Our tears of admiration, sympathy, and gratitude are now shed as much for them as for him. Nor is this an isolated incident, an odd and insignificant turn of phrase. The self-promoted cult of Rousseau is only the century's most obvious example of this sentimental exaltation of the artist.[35] Mercier's substitution of Molière for Orgon in his retelling of *Tartuffe* as *La maison de Molière* has a similar effect on a smaller scale. And that effect recurs with still more passionate conviction in Diderot's amazingly fulsome *Éloge de Richardson* (1762; *Praise of Richardson*), where the English novelist is hailed as the God-like author of a new gospel, a man whose claim on our interest and attachment is even more compelling than that of his heroically virtuous characters. "Who has read the works of Richardson," asks Diderot, "without wanting to know this man, to have him for a brother or friend? Who has not wished him every blessing?"[36] Like Greuze's old man, Richardson collects a rich payment for the gift of a good upbringing, the upbringing he has given his many readers. But again, as he did with Greuze, Diderot cannot resist imagining himself in Richardson's place. His praise is qualified only by a jealous fear that while he is enthralled by Richardson "the years of work and the harvest of laurels are passing, and I approach my last hour without attempting anything that can similarly establish my claim on future ages."[37]

This emergence of the artist—whether painter, novelist, playwright, or even critic and philosopher—as the hero of a new culture of bourgeois virtue sets Diderot and his contemporaries off from the English and Spanish dramatists and the Dutch painters of the sixteenth and seventeenth centuries. And so too does the artist's reforming mission. English bourgeois drama, Dutch genre painting, and Spanish peasant drama may in fact have expressed and perhaps even enabled significant social change. But there is little evidence that they were meant to do more than satisfy the demands of some particular audience. In defending *Tartuffe*, Molière could claim a bit more, but not even he envisioned the kind of fundamental reordering of art and society that is central to Mercier's work as a dramatist and that is clearly anticipated by Diderot in the *Encyclopédie*, the *Salons*, the *Éloge de Richardson*, and the two bourgeois dramas and their accompanying manifestos. Heywood, Vermeer, Lope, and Molière are at most accidental and reluctant reformers. Diderot and Mercier could hardly be more deliberate. As Mercier never tired of repeating, the writer—and particularly the writer of bourgeois drama—was to be the "legislator" of a world remade both morally and politically. To his irresistible lawgiving will, kings and governments would necessarily bend.[38]

But if Enlightenment writers' artistic, social, and even political aims and their sense of their own role distinguish them sharply from their predecessors, the means to those ends derive from representational forms that had been forged in various parts of Europe over the preceding two centuries: domestic drama, genre painting, and a more recent fictional mode that had obvious affinities with both. Whether he is talking about Greuze's paintings, Richardson's novels, or his own plays, Diderot singles out precisely those qualities we have seen characterizing the drama and painting of the sixteenth and seventeenth centuries, the combination of realism and pathos in a domestic and bourgeois setting. And no less familiar from what we have examined before is the sense of generic transgression. The scramble to find names for the new dramatic forms—"weeping comedy," "mixed genre," "bourgeois tragedy," "serious genre," "*drame,*" "domestic tragedy," "intermediate genre"—suggests the unsettling breakdown of the old bipolar system, a breakdown heralded by Heywood's Jane Shore, Lope's and Calderón's tragic peasants, the fifth-act pathos of Molière's *Tartuffe,* and the unexpected solemnity of genre scenes by Vermeer, ter Borch, and de Hooch, a breakdown Diderot's followers turned into a *cri de guerre:* "Down, down, you walls between the genres!"[39]

But many resisted this act of aesthetic demolition: "Good taste has long accepted and shown that between tragedy and comedy there exists *nec ultra, nec infra.*" Enter that void, couple "the only two genres that can actually exist," and "you become monstrous."[40] Nor was the resistance any less fierce in the realm of painting. At the shows of the Royal Academy, paintings were hung according to kind: history on top, genre and still life on the bottom. And painters themselves were ranked according to the kind in which they worked, again with history painters on top and genre and still life painters on the bottom. When Greuze had the pretension to choose a subject from ancient history as his formal reception piece, he was firmly put back in his place—admitted to the Academy but only as a genre painter, a humiliation that marked him for the rest of his life. On the appearance eight years later of his two most self-consciously heroic genre paintings, *The Father's Curse* and *The Punished Son,* one critic remarked in a cruel echo of the Academy's decision, "Greuze is the Molière of painting, but he is neither the Corneille nor the Racine."[41] But for Diderot, Greuze had always been a history painter, as much a Corneille or Racine as a Molière. Citing several works similar to *Filial Piety,* Diderot writes that "for me these are as much history paintings as *The Seven Sacraments* of Poussin, *The Family of Darius* of Lebrun, or the *Susanna* of Van Loo."[42] And he thought a similar claim should be made for Richardson: "The novel, as you have written it, is a good history."[43]

Tragedy and comedy, history painting and genre painting, history and the novel—none of these hierarchical pairs survives Diderot's scrutiny. Differences fade. Values shift. New kinds emerge.[44] Nor is this only a matter of aesthetics, a mere question of genre theory. Diderot's deep, if not always consistent, blending of artistic forms accompanies and supports an equally radical mixing of social orders. Sophocles's Philoctetes, Racine's Clytemnestra, Lillo's George Barnwell, and a peasant woman whose story is told by Diderot's fictional interlocutor in the *Entretiens* are—or so Diderot claims—united by their common humanity in suffering. Each is as able as any of the others to furnish the model for one of Diderot's *tableaux*. Considerations of rank would only be a distraction. "If for a moment the mother of Iphigenia"—Clytemnestra—"showed herself to be the queen of Argos and the Greek general's wife, she would appear to me only as the lowest of creatures. Real dignity, that which strikes me, which knocks me over, belongs to the picture of maternal love in all its truth." And at the other end of the social scale: "Do you think a woman of another rank would have been more pitiable [than this peasant]? No. The same situation would have inspired in her the same words."[45] In the genre theory against which Diderot was reacting, tragedy was distinguished from comedy, history painting from genre painting, history from the novel by the rank of those each represented, by their differing attention to public or private life, and by their dissimilar truth claims. Diderot upsets all such distinctions. Rank does not matter. The public is shoved to the side, allowed only as a cause for private grief. And truth belongs not to the state and its history but rather to universal suffering humanity.

"Is it possible," asks Diderot's spokesman in the *Entretiens*, "not to feel that the effect of suffering is to bring people together?"[46] Bringing people together is Diderot's goal. The leveling of conditions and genres in drama, painting, and fiction is meant to accomplish a similar leveling of society. As the still more political Mercier put it, "whatever mixes the different levels of society and works to break down the excessive inequality of conditions, the source of all our misery, is good, politically speaking. Whatever brings citizens closer together is the sacred cement that unites the many families of a vast state, which must look on them all with an equal eye."[47] In their pictures of suffering and virtue, bourgeois drama, genre painting, and Richardsonian fiction were, in effect, anticipating by several decades the revolutionary transformation of the Estates General—the divided polity of clergy, aristocracy, and commons, each separately summoned by the king—into a single National Assembly, the representative of a nation of free, equal, and fraternally united citizens. Literature and painting thus imagined what revolutionary politics would soon enact. "The Revolution," in the words with which Scott Bryson closes his valuable study of bourgeois drama, "did not just *suddenly* happen: it was rehearsed for many years on the stage, on canvas, in those scenes which we can see in Diderot's theater or Greuze's paintings of the family united around the aged or dying father. Their loss is ours, their tears provoke ours and imperceptibly, yet indubitably, we find that we are now one with them, joined by our shared emotion, beyond the proscenium, beyond the frame: a new family regenerated by the imaginary."[48] In that moment—the moment of cultural and political regeneration—the virtual Geneva of bourgeois painting and drama became the real France.

But, as that revolutionary culmination unhappily suggests, the sentimental union prompted by drama and painting could easily lead to new division. Huge crowds drawn from all ranks of society may have pushed into the Louvre's Salon Carré to weep over Greuze's *Filial Piety*. But what of those who remained unmoved? What of those who mocked instead of crying? Diderot raises just this issue in the *Éloge de Richardson*.

> Should I say it? . . . From differences of judgment [over Richardson's characters], I have seen secret enmity born, hidden disdain, in a word, the same divisions among people otherwise united as if it had been a matter of the greatest seriousness. Then I recognized the likeness between Richardson's work and a still more sacred book, a gospel brought on earth to separate husband from wife, father from son, daughter from mother, brother from sister; and his work was thus at one with the most perfect creations of nature.[49]

Like a new gospel, the new forms of drama, painting, and fiction unite us across old barriers and divide us according to new ones. Whatever your rank in the old regime, weep with Rosalie as she leans unhappily on her tapestry loom, prefer the fate of Clarissa to that of her triumphant tormentors, feel the pathos of Greuze's paralytic old man, and you are a citizen of the new nation of egalitarian sentiment, a nation led by its poets, painters, and philosophers. Resist those tears, that identification, that pathos, insist on the old hierarchical divisions of people and of artistic kinds, and you sacrifice that universal citizenship, reveal yourself as a traitor to the new regime. Mercier makes the point as clearly as anyone: "You can judge the soul of each man by the degree of emotion that he shows in the theater: if his face remains impassive, if his eye is not moist . . . he is certainly a bad person." In response to judgments like these—mere matters of taste, one might suppose—the bloody "civil storm" Mercier was already prepared to welcome would soon rage.[50]

BEING BOURGEOIS IN THE HOUSE OF DIDEROT

The names most often given the plays, paintings, and fictions around which the new regime of sentiment was gathering and affirming itself were *domestic* and *bourgeois*. But what exactly do these terms mean? *Domestic* is easy enough, though its resonance is surprisingly broad. It refers to the home and the family, to private as opposed to public life, and to the virtues and travails characteristic of that intimate sphere. *Bourgeois* is more difficult. While the literary and artistic works that get labeled *domestic* and *bourgeois* do normally confine their attention to actions that take place within the home and the family, they are less consistent with regard to rank. In only a few plays—Michel Sedaine's *Philosophe sans le savoir* (1765; *The Philosopher without Knowing It*), Beaumarchais's *Deux amis* (1770; *The Two Friends*), and Mercier's *Brouette du vinaigrier* (1775; *The Vinegar Merchant's Wheelbarrow*) are obvious examples—do the commercial activities characteristic of the bourgeoisie figure significantly, while in others, including Diderot's *Père de famille* and Beaumarchais's *Eugénie* (1767), the central characters are not only not engaged in commerce, they are not even bourgeois. They are, on the contrary, titled aristocrats. Peter Szondi, who makes much of this anomaly, argues that these plays nevertheless deserve to be called "bourgeois" because their characters live, in the term Mercier applied to Molière, *bourgeoisement*. They have adopted bourgeois values, including most obviously the primacy they grant domesticity.[51] Indirect, but nevertheless telling, support for this expansive view of what counts as bourgeois comes from Robert Mauzi's massive study of the eighteenth-century idea of happiness, the utopian happiness that by contrast gave value to bourgeois suffering. "If," writes Mauzi, "one wishes to define the most commonly accepted notion of a happy life according to the eighteenth century, the idea of *bourgeois happiness* clearly imposes itself." But he then goes on to make an important qualification: "It would be imprudent to define too sharply or to give too much weight to the social content of this notion, since bourgeois happiness flows beyond the limits of the bourgeoisie."[52] To be happy in the eighteenth-century way was to live like a bourgeois, whatever one's actual status. And, once again, the overflowing social demographics of bourgeois value found revolutionary political expression before the century was over. In 1789, sympathetic clergymen and aristocrats joined representatives of the Third Estate in proclaiming that they were, in effect, *all* of the Third Estate. Henceforth, the Third Estate was to be recognized as the nation itself.[53]

Bourgeois drama, like bourgeois painting and bourgeois fiction, thus had a hegemonic ambition. Its values were no longer to be the values of one social order or even of one of the three estates. They were to be the values of everyone. Seen this way, the very erasure of generic distinctions so central to the aesthetic program of Diderot and his followers can be seen as bourgeois. Raymond Williams makes much this point in *Marxism and Literature.* The formally rigid, sharply distinguished, and hierarchically arranged genres, based (or so it was supposed) on unimpeachable classical precedent, "belonged," Williams suggests, "to feudalism and post-feudalism in decline." "Bourgeois society" undermined such prescriptive genre theory, as it undermined its social equivalent, the theory of "estates," replacing both with notions of individual accomplishment and mobility.[54] Yet, paradoxically, this new emphasis on individual freedom and creativity, an emphasis we have seen expressed both in Diderot's praise of Richardson and Greuze and in his own yearning for fame, was accompanied in the plays themselves by a dispersal of individual particularity into social relations, the replacement, as Diderot urged, of "characters" by "conditions," of a miser or misanthrope by, to mention only Diderot's own favorite example, a father of a family. This shift, an important part of the new drama's rewriting of Molière, was, as Julie Candler Hayes has remarked, also part of that new drama's bourgeois identity. Instead of the theatrical "despotism" exercised by the characters whose oddities Molière put on display, the theater was now to show a flexible system of conditions "structured by exchange and interdependency"—structured, that is, in a way that recalls the bourgeois marketplace.[55]

Diderot's own justification for favoring conditions over characters points to still another facet of what he and his contemporaries meant by *bourgeois.* From characters of the extravagant sort Molière specialized in presenting, we can, Diderot argued, easily detach ourselves, as we can detach ourselves from the kings and queens of classical and neoclassical tragedy. "That's not me," we say. In seeing a theatrical representation of the ordinary conditions of life, such detachment becomes impossible. We necessarily see ourselves. Beaumarchais makes much the same argument in his *Essai sur le genre dramatique sérieux* (1767; *Essay on the Serious Dramatic Genre*). The prosaic realism of the "serious genre," including the literal adoption of prose rather than verse, is meant to heighten identification and thus to touch the audience more directly. To be bourgeois and domestic is, both Diderot and Beaumarchais assume, to be like me, whoever *I* may be.[56] Bourgeois and domestic reality is everyone's reality—or if it isn't, it should be. Universality, whether actual or imposed, is also what they meant by the bourgeois.[57]

And linked to the identification of spectator with spectacle in what made bourgeois drama bourgeois was a new antitheatrical theatricalism, the replacement of histrionic extravagance with everyday truth. Elaborate stage properties contribute to this effect. Not only Rosalie's tapestry loom but also a harpsichord, some chairs, card tables, a game of trictrac, and a sofa—objects that might have been taken from the prop room of Vermeer or Chardin or, for that matter, from any bourgeois salon—appear on stage at the opening of *Le fils naturel.* To us these props may seem unsurprising and unobjectionable, but contemporary theatergoers could mock them with something like the virulence Charles Gildon directed at the tragic pretensions of Rowe's Jane Shore. One critic claimed to be "wholly disgusted" by "the doors, tables, windows, trictracs, harpsichords, cupboards, [and] chests of drawers" that littered Diderot's stage, while another sarcastically charged that "Clairville's salon" was in fact the main character of *Le fils naturel.* But, as a defender pointed out, these are precisely the elements that render the scene "truer and more natural."[58] Nor was that appearance of truth produced only by objects. There was also to be a new style of naturalistic acting that ignored the audience and gave the impression of total absorption in the ongoing action, the style of acting Diderot calls for in his description of Rosalie and Justine at their loom, a style of acting that has a deep affinity with the genre painting of Chardin, Greuze, and their Dutch predecessors.[59] On this antitheatrical theatricalism, on these everyday props and this naturalistic acting, was to be based the "domestic and real spectacle," the bourgeois spectacle, that Diderot and his followers sought to put in the place of the artificial and aristocratic theater of the old regime.[60]

But none of this, important as it is, can quite explain the overwhelming emotional effect the new drama was meant to incite, the effect its authors experienced in reading Richardson's novels or seeing Greuze's paintings. After all, bourgeois happiness and virtue, however presented, could seem anything but appealing, even to those most committed to their representation. Here, for example, is Diderot in a passage from his *Salon* of 1767:

> Happy, a hundred times happy, . . . Monsieur Baliveau, the magistrate of Toulouse! It's Monsieur Baliveau who drinks well, eats well, digests well,

sleeps well. It's he who takes his morning coffee, who keeps the market in order, who perorates to his little family, who rounds out his fortune, who preaches the virtue of money to his children, who sells his oats and his wheat on time, who keeps his wine in his cellar until a frost in the vineyards boosts the price, who knows just where to place his investments, who is proud never to have been caught in any bankruptcy, who lives unknown and for whom the happiness uselessly envied by Horace, the happiness of dying unknown, was invented.[61]

Why do the virtues of private, bourgeois life seem suddenly so flat and so unappealing? Why has celebration turned to mockery? Because the terms of difference have changed. Here Diderot sets the contented burgher not against some lordly oppressor but rather against the man of genius, against poets, painters, and philosophers, "rare and divine fools who make poetry out of life, and suffer in the process." What would lift a Monsieur Baliveau out of his repellantly fortunate mediocrity and make him deserve serious artistic attention? A touch of suffering. Only when she has "lost her honor," writes Diderot, does Richardson's Clarissa attain sublimity.[62] Like Clarissa, like Jane and Matthew Shore, like Pedro Crespo, like Orgon, like the domestic figures in ter Borch, de Hooch, or Vermeer, Monsieur Baliveau needs a Lovelace, an Edward IV, a libertine captain, a Tartuffe, a prince of Orange to give his bourgeois virtue dramatic and cultural value.

What does *bourgeois* mean in bourgeois drama? It means domestic sentiment and virtue. It means a leveling of social distinction and the substitution of conditions for characters. It means audience identification and affection. It means a claim to universality. And it means antitheatrical realism and truth. But for these meanings to have their effect—an effect that is as much political as artistic—*bourgeois* must also mean oppression and suffering. "The poet," writes Mercier with an eye particularly on the writer of bourgeois drama, "is the interpreter for the unfortunate, the public orator of the oppressed."[63] Without oppression he has no purpose, and his plays have no effect.

Where then in the bourgeois drama of the French eighteenth century is the required oppression and suffering to be found? It is a question that is surprisingly hard to answer. Though Diderot, Mercier, and Beaumarchais all professed great admiration for English domestic tragedy and talked as though they were writing plays of that sort themselves, none of their bourgeois dramas, with the single exception of Mercier's *Deserteur* (1770; *The Deserter*), ends unhappily—and even *Le deserteur* was rewritten, reportedly at the request of Queen Marie-Antoinette, to get rid of its final unpleasantness. Just as hard to find are the adultery, abduction, and rape that marked English and Spanish plays. Closest is probably the false marriage in Beaumarchais's *Eugénie,* but that marriage is made good by the end of the play, leaving us with something closer to the complacent satisfaction of *Pamela* than the tragedy of *Clarissa.* And even when the French take over an English or Spanish play directly, they soften its sharper edges. Mercier makes the most extraordinary claims for his re-casting of George Lillo's *London Merchant* as *Jenneval ou le Barnevelt français* (1769; *Jenneval or the French Barnwell*). He calls it "a *tableau* offered to the nation" and expects that it will "enlighten" the nation "by the force of sentiment" and "give it healthier ideas in politics and legisla-tion." He even alludes to Greek tragedy and its success in nourishing "the republican genius and making monarchy odious."[64] But from the play itself both the murder and the execution that had given *The London Merchant* its tragic force are removed. In the end, this "French Barnwell," unlike his English model, is left happily free, after a brief flirtation with a worldly seductress, to marry his master's virtuous daughter. And Collot d'Herbois does much the same to *El alcalde de Zalamea.* Calderón's speeches of defi-ant peasant self-assertion are still there, but the rape and the execution that motivated them aren't. This time, instead of dying at Crespo's hands, the erring captain marries Crespo's daughter, who had fallen in love with him even before the opening embroidery scene.

An odd mix of boldly rebellious programmatic declarations and timid theatrical realization characterizes this drama. The sway of convention—what Mercier calls "French delicacy"—was too strong to be thrown over by theory and foreign example.[65] Just look at the names these writers give their characters. Can Jenneval, Durimel, Dorval, and Lysimond really make any greater claim to bourgeois realism than Molière's Orgon, Har-pagon, Philinte, or Alceste? And if the stage furniture of Diderot's plays and their mixing of genres rubbed against accepted standards of theatrical *bienséance,* their strict adherence to the unities of neoclassical drama—the unities of time, place, and action—didn't.[66] Nor do these plays follow through on their loudly announced project of abandoning *coups de théâtre* in favor of *tableaux.* Though they do unquestionably provide plenty of heartrending and heartwarming *tableaux,* they are no less filled with *coups de théâtre.* Indeed, hardly a play ends without the revelation of unsuspected relationships. Dorval in Diderot's *Fils naturel* turns out to be the half-brother of the weeping Rosalie, with whom he had been in love; Sophie in *Le père de famille* is discovered to be the niece of the commander who had been bent on her destruction; Mercier's deserter is the long-lost son of the officer who must execute him; his indigent maiden in *L'indigent* (1772; *The Indigent*) is really the sister of her aristocratic would-be seducer; and his middle-class judge in *Le juge* (1774; *The Judge*) is, for no good dramatic reason, revealed to be the son of the lord whose despotic property claims he had courageously dismissed. On the day of his marriage, even Beaumarchais's Figaro finds a hitherto unknown mother and father. So, again: where in this mass of romantic discoveries and contrived happy endings is the sense of oppression and suffering to be found?

We might look first in a seemingly unlikely place, at the genre paintings Diderot so much admired. What keeps them from being so many pictures of Monsieur Baliveau and his family? Not much, one might suppose— except perhaps the fact that in Chardin's genre paintings *Monsieur* Baliveau is never seen. So far are Chardin's domestic images of women and children from admitting anything even remotely like oppression and suffering that they shut down even those few suspect openings to the outside world that mark the Dutch genre scenes they otherwise nearly resemble. No amorous soldiers here, no ambiguous maps, few wall hangings of any sort, no windows, rarely even an accessible door. Yet that very exclusion speaks forcefully of that which is excluded, particularly when we imagine these untroubled little scenes surmounted, as they would have been in the biennial Salons, by oversized history paintings depicting a world of violence and intrigue. What Chardin shows is not merely the home, but rather the home actively fending off the world. Look back at the painting we have already evoked, his *Diligent Mother* (figure 20). The needlework the diligent mother teaches her daughter is as much a barrier against that world and its temptations as are the screens that block off the door. The form such temptation might eventually take, once this little girl has grown up a bit, is suggested by the sewing scenes in *Le fils naturel* and the French *Alcalde de Zalamea*: Rosalie weeps over a guilty attraction to her fiancé's closest friend, while Isabelle is distracted by thoughts of the officer she met on a visit with her father to the royal court.[67] No wonder then that Chardin makes a child's exercise in embroidery appear such a solemn affair. If his simple domestic scene moves, in the words of the *Mercure de France*, the viewer to "feel far more that he can express," it is in part at least because that viewer knows the world the painting so scrupulously excludes.[68]

The pathos in Greuze, though far more evident, is similarly motivated. Only once—in *The Father's Curse*, where the eldest son is drawn from his

Figure 22   Jean-Baptiste Greuze, *A Father Reading the Bible to His Family* (1755). Oil on canvas. Hottinguer Collection, Paris. Photo: Courtesy of Edgar Munhall.

duty to the family by the lure of a military recruiting officer—does an outsider disrupt the domestic space. Otherwise these scenes, though usually centered on a father rather than a mother, a governess, or a child, are no more open to the world than Chardin's. But they, too, take their force from exclusion, from a sense of difference between the virtuous home and the licentious and despotic world that surrounds it, a sense that is heightened in paintings like *A Father Reading the Bible to His Family* or *The Betrothal* (figures 22 and 23) by the suspicion that these figures are Protestants.[69] From an Enlightenment perspective, the Protestant polities that surrounded France—Switzerland, Holland, and England—offered the model of the political and civil liberties for which the *philosophes* yearned, while Protestants in France were the most conspicuous victims of the ignorant and arbitrary old regime they hoped to transform. Here, for exam-

Figure 23 Jean-Baptiste Greuze, *The Betrothal* (1761). Oil on canvas, 92 × 117. Musée du Louvre, Paris. Photo: © RMN.

ple, is the marquis de Lafayette writing to his friend George Washington in 1785: "Protestants in France live under an intolerable despotism. Though there is at present no open persecution, they are subject to the whim of the king, of the queen, of the courts, or of a minister. Their marriages are not legal; their wills have no standing before the law; their children are considered bastards; their persons, good for hanging."[70] Forbidden to assemble, Protestants replaced public worship with the private Bible-reading Greuze portrays; forbidden to marry, they made do with a vow pronounced at home before a notary. Thus oppression, without ever entering the domestic scene, hovers over it.

Even more unequivocally than Greuze's heroically moral genre paintings, the bourgeois drama of the French eighteenth-century was enrolled in the cause of Enlightenment, including the defense of Protestant liberty. Recall what Bartholo includes in his anti-Enlightenment list of the "follies" of the age in Beaumarchais's *Barbier de Seville:* "Freedom of thought, gravity, electricity, toleration, inoculation, quinine, the *Encyclopédie*, and *les drames.*"[71] "Toleration" points right to the persecution of Protestants, and so too does "freedom of thought." Voltaire wrote articles on both for Diderot's *Encyclopédie*. Even "gravity" and "electricity" would have reminded eighteenth-century audiences of accomplishments associated with Protestant freedom, with the English Isaac Newton and the American Benjamin Franklin. If bourgeois drama—the *drame*, as Bartholo calls it— belongs on this list, it is because it too sought the goals of liberty, progress, and enlightenment. However improbably, *Le barbier de Seville* itself claims a place in that great cause. Though a laughing comedy rather than a bourgeois drama, it makes its strike for freedom by liberating its heroine, Rosine, from the tyrannical sway of the aggressively unenlightened Bartholo. In that regard, *Le barbier de Seville* inscribes itself, or so Beaumarchais would have us think, in the line of its two predecessors in his playwriting career, *Eugénie* and *Les deux amis*, both of them bourgeois dramas. The first exposed, as he says, the vices of a libertine lord; the second revealed the virtues of two provincial merchants. "Whether he moralizes while laughing," as in *Le barbier de Seville*, "or weeps while moralizing," as in the two bourgeois dramas, the dramatist's duty remains the same: to unmask the vices and abuses of his age and to display their opposing virtues. And in late eighteenth-century France, that was an Enlightenment undertaking, one that shared political objectives with the defense of Protestants and of other victims of arbitrary power and privilege generally. For Beaumarchais, it is thus a mark of his success that he can announce that *Le barbier de Seville* was accused of having "shaken the state."[72]

The charges against Beaumarchais's next play, *Le mariage de Figaro* (1781; *The Marriage of Figaro*), were still sharper and came from a more exalted source. At an early reading of the play, Louis XVI is said to have risen to his feet and exclaimed, "This is detestable. It will never be played. The Bastille would have to be destroyed for the performance of this play not to be a dangerous contradiction."[73] This report may well have benefited from hindsight; the allusion to the Bastille is a little too pat to be believed. But what is sure is that the king did prohibit the play's production, a prohibition that was not lifted until three years later, after an assiduous campaign on Beaumarchais's part. In this, *Le mariage de Figaro* nearly resembles *Tartuffe*. And, like *Tartuffe*, it has the distinction of being the single most successful play of its century. In his preface, Beaumarchais asks, "What mathematician can calculate the force and length of the lever it would take, in our days, to hoist onto the stage the sublime work *Tar-*

tuffe?"[74] That same massive force was, he implies, needed to get *Le mariage de Figaro* staged, with the result that it too became an allegory of its own impeded production history. In the words of Elizabeth MacArthur, "both as a text and as an event, the *Mariage de Figaro* is about the relationships between the individual, the State, and a new kind of public that is invoked to challenge the authority of the State."[75] As for the event, contemporary accounts certainly confirm that sense. The king's last-minute interdiction of a private performance scheduled for the Salle des Menus Plaisirs in June 1783 "seemed," according to one witness, "an attack on public liberty. All the disappointed hopes provoked such discontent that the words *oppression* and *tyranny* were never spoken, in the days preceding the fall of the throne, with more passion and vehemence."[76] Nor did the text fail to do its part. Once made available, it provided an ideal vehicle for just such feelings of outrage.

"One achieves," wrote Beaumarchais in the preface to *Le mariage de Figaro*, "neither great pathos, nor profound morality, nor good and true comedy in the theater without intense situations, which always arise from a social conflict."[77] The social conflict in *Le mariage de Figaro* might be taken as the historical epitome of the bourgeois and peasant drama and painting that had been produced in various parts of Europe over the preceding three centuries. The count of Almaviva, the king's chief deputy, governor, and judge in Andalusia, the man Figaro had helped get a wife in *Le barbier de Seville*, wants to revive his ancient seignorial right and sleep with Figaro's bride on her wedding night. If one believes—and I see no reason not to—Alain Bourreau's recent study, no such right ever existed, certainly not in France, and probably not elsewhere.[78] It was the invention of the Enlightenment and its campaign against aristocratic privilege of all sorts, an invention that was given its single most memorable expression (where else?) in *Le mariage de Figaro* itself—and, of course, in the opera Mozart based on Beaumarchais's play. But if the notorious *droit de cuissage*, the *jus primae noctis*, never in fact existed, something like the idea of such a "right" had haunted the European imagination for centuries, just waiting to be reduced to pseudo-legal form. Lope's three peasant *comedias*, each with an interrupted wedding and a seignorial attempt to appropriate the bride, verge so nearly on the familiar pattern that their closest student, Noël Salomon, in his great book on the peasant in Golden Age Spanish drama was moved to argue that a long tradition of popular resistance to the supposed *droit du seigneur* must lie behind them.[79]

Doubtful as that argument may now seem, it points to the way oppression and conflict of all sorts got expressed in stories of sexual abuse, not only in Spanish drama but also in Heywood, Shakespeare, Molière, and Dutch genre painting. By now, the point should be obvious. But it remains important to insist that a similar pattern, however varied or attenuated it may be in specific instances, also underlies eighteenth-century French bourgeois drama.[80] Here, as elsewhere, oppression occurs at home and is most often represented by the violation of sexual property. In his *Essai sur le genre dramatique sérieux*, Beaumarchais insists repeatedly that a *drame* should present "a domestic misfortune," an image of "suffering humanity," "the unhappiness of an honest man," "an unfortunate event that has happened among us." And when he imagines who might be the protagonist of such a play, it is "he whose wife, daughter, honor, or goods have been stolen away."[81] *Eugénie*, the play to which this essay is attached as preface, tells a story of just this sort, and so, were it not for Figaro's cleverness and the support of all the other members of Almaviva's household, would *Le mariage de Figaro*. More *Merry Wives of Windsor* than *Peribáñez* or *Fuenteovejuna*, *Le mariage de Figaro* nevertheless makes its accusation with sufficient force to have provoked the king's prohibition and to be credited after the fact with being "yet another of the causes of the Revolution."[82] If *Le barbier de Seville* "shook the state," this new play, as Beaumarchais remarks in joking imitation of his critics, "turned it upside down from top to bottom."[83] Maybe those critics were not so far wrong. Clearly, stories like the one Beaumarchais tells in *Le mariage de Figaro* have had—and continue to have—a powerful effect.

Once acclimated to the political atmosphere of Enlightenment and pre-Revolutionary France, we can begin to sense how even the apparently timid bourgeois dramas of Diderot, Mercier, and Beaumarchais participated, along with a more conventional laughing comedy of romantic intrigue like *Le mariage de Figaro*, in building antipathy to the old regime. As Robert Darnton's recent study, *The Forbidden Best-Sellers of Pre-Revolutionary France*, vividly demonstrates, virtually any exposure of arbitrary power or libertine behavior could be read as an attack on the ecclesiastical and political structures of the French state. At the very top of Darnton's list of forbidden best-sellers is a book by the most prolific of our bourgeois dramatists, Sébastien Mercier's *L'an 2440* (1771; *The Year 2440*). In that futurist utopia, Mercier's dream traveler visits a theater in the new Paris, where he sees, in Darnton's words, "a tragedy about the Calas Affair (the judicial murder of a Protestant that horrified Voltaire) and a comedy glorifying Henri IV (after defeating the Catholic League, the populist king enjoys a feast and clears the table himself)."[84] Mercier would later write a play on Henri IV's victory over the Catholic League, *La destruction de la Ligue* (1782; *The Destruction of the League*), and another, *Jean Hennuyer* (1772), on the St. Bartholomew's Day Massacre of 1572. But already, in his *Deserteur* the bourgeois victims of a libertine aristocrat and of the libertine's still more brutally oppressive father are Protestants. The libertine and the tyrant on one side, the bourgeois and the Protestant on the other—this is the highly politicized opposition that underlies this whole dramatic field.[85] Even a play like Diderot's *Fils naturel*, where the sexual menace is expressed through the otherwise virtuous central character, evokes, if only to deny as a present reality, the criminal barbarity of the old regime, the "monster," as the play calls it, whose "fury and illusions," armed with law and religion, "bathed this land in blood."[86]

So what does *bourgeois* mean in the bourgeois drama of the French eighteenth-century? It means appearing as the victim and defining opposite of that barbaric monster, a monster who embodies the ignorance, superstition, privilege, licence, and arbitrary power of the old regime. In this sense, *bourgeois* is less the name of a particular social class, just as *Protestant* is less the name of a particular religious community and *domestic* less the name of a specific physical space, than all three are names for a shared position of difference and deprivation. Diderot's Monsieur Baliveau, bourgeois though he is, does not occupy that position; but Diderot's *père de famille* does, and so too do Greuze's Protestant families, Collot's Pedro Crespo, Sedaine's philosopher without knowing it, Mercier's deserter, indigent, and judge, and Beaumarchais's Figaro and Eugénie. It was from this bourgeois and domestic position, this position of suffering and virtue, that the Enlightenment mounted its artistic and theatrical assault on the old regime. Rather than a particular legal and material status, though it could mean that as well, *bourgeois* names an oppositional state of mind, citizenship in the virtual Geneva the new drama and the new painting were working so hard to construct, citizenship that might be claimed by the sympathetically inclined whatever their rank or status in the old regime.

But if something of this sort is what *bourgeois* meant in pre-Revolutionary French drama, what it most decidedly did *not* mean was identification with a specific urban place and its traditional rights, privileges, and municipal government. I mentioned in an earlier chapter that *Arden of Faversham* was perhaps the first English play whose action could be easily followed on a map. Heywood's London and Shakespeare's Windsor are also mappable places, as are Lope's Ocaña and Fuenteovejuna and Calderón's Zalamea. And Dutch genre paintings are themselves full of maps, including many maps of the province where the domestic scene is presumably located. French bourgeois drama has none of that geographical specificity. Nor does it ever evoke, as the English and Spanish plays commonly do, the governing structure of the town where the action takes place. As a bit of local color and with perhaps a gesture toward Calderón, Beaumarchais brings in an *alcalde* at the end of *Le barbier de Seville*, but that municipal officer has no significant part in the action. And no other play by any of these French dramatists goes so far. The one apparent exception, Mercier's *Juge*, features a judge who is the judge of no place in particular. In part this difference can be attributed to an abstracting quality in early modern French drama generally, a quality obvious already in Molière. The French everyday, whether in seventeenth-century comedy or in eighteenth-century bourgeois drama or, for that matter, in eighteen-century genre painting, is never as geographically particular as the everyday in English and Spanish drama or in Dutch painting.

But there is more at work here than the tyranny of French *bienséance*, the feeling that naming specific places in works of art is bad form. The English, Dutch, and Spanish emphasized municipal particularity because what mattered to them was municipal liberty, threatened by the encroachment of an invigorated monarchic state bent on extending its power. Even when, as in *Fuenteovejuna*, the town's oppressor is also an enemy of the crown, municipal liberty, including the town's freedom to rise in its own defense, has in the end to be seized from the king as much as from the seignorial oppressor. But in France—or, at least, in French bourgeois drama—municipal liberty never matters. Instead, "the defense of liberties" has, in words I borrowed in an earlier chapter from J. H. Elliott, broadened "into the defense of liberty."[87] The French are interested not in the particular rights of Parisians or Lyonnais or Marseillais but rather in the rights of man.[88] Persecution of Protestants, Almaviva's pretended *droit du seigneur*, ecclesiastical obscurantism, aristocratic libertine abuse, antibourgeois prejudice, arbitrary royal power (including the infamous *lettres de cachet* brandished in both *Tartuffe* and *Le père de famille*)—all these stand for that denial of the rights of man that made the old regime odious to writers like Diderot, Mercier, and Beaumarchais. Together these writers were engaged in what Simon Schama has called "the cultural construction of a citizen," an enterprise that involved the dismantling not only of seignorial and ecclesiastical privileges but also of municipal privileges, the very privileges that had defined citizenship under the old regime.[89]

Where the bourgeois and peasant drama and painting of the sixteenth and seventeenth centuries had given new artistic attention to the rights and values of particular social groups in particular places, its eighteenth-century French descendants aspire to represent all mankind, or at least that part of universal mankind—call it *bourgeois*—that felt itself deprived under the old regime and ready to join the new. It is a group whose voice can be heard with particular clarity in a statement Beaumarchais made in the course of a trial in 1774: "I am a citizen, which is to say that I am neither a courtier, nor a clergyman, nor a *gentilhomme,* nor a tax collector, nor a favorite, nor anything that one calls a man of power today. I am a citizen, which is to say something altogether new, something unknown, unheard of in France. I am a citizen, which is to say what you should have been for the last two hundred years, what in twenty years you will perhaps be!"[90] This is a statement none of Beaumarchais's sixteenth- and seventeenth-century English, Dutch, or Spanish predecessors could have made. But its representational equivalent in plays and paintings does nevertheless draw on the domestic realism and pathos those predecessors developed. The new universal citizenship of Beaumarchais and the French Revolution took inspiration from plays and paintings about the old municipal citizenship so fiercely defended by the inhabitants of places like Faversham, London, Windsor, Amsterdam, Delft, Ocaña, Zalamea, and Fuenteovejuna.

Moving into History

And what of history? Hanging above Chardin's and Greuze's genre scenes on the walls of the Salon Carré, history was a kind of painting. Serving as the privileged source for neoclassical tragedy, history was a mark of generic superiority. But with the exception of Mercier's two "national plays" on the French persecution of Protestants, history did not intersect with the *drame bourgeois* in quite the way it had with the English and Spanish plays we have studied, or even with Molière's *Tartuffe.* No actual French king or his representative ever enters one of these plays, nor are their plots taken from the chronicles of France. *Le fils naturel* contains an offstage echo of the war then in progress with England; *Le deserteur* takes up an issue current in the military life of the old regime; and *L'autre Tar-*

tuffe refers, appropriately enough for a play produced in 1792, to revolutionary debates, to the new divorce law, and to a bust of the idolized George Washington. But the characters in these plays are all fictional, and the domestic scenes those characters inhabit stand at a far greater remove from the monarchic center of power than did the homes of Heywood's Jane and Matthew Shore, Calderón's Pedro Crespo, or Molière's Orgon. With the ever-present threat of a renewed and strengthened stadholdership, even the Dutch interiors of the republican 1650s and 1660s seem engaged with a historically more precise menace. In the bourgeois drama of the French eighteenth century, the particularity of historical events and persons has, like the particularity of places and institutions, been replaced by a universality of condition and situation, a universality now represented by the middle-class home. The oppression these plays denounce is less the work of specific historical malefactors than of a whole system of power. And the bourgeois virtues they proclaim no longer need a king's endorsement to establish their dignity and worth.

But as the plays moved further from the specificity of history, their authors became more fully and directly engaged in a historical process that was not predominantly literary. Where Shakespeare, Heywood, Lope de Vega, Calderón, and Molière lived—and live on—almost exclusively as men of the theater, the eighteenth-century bourgeois dramatists played much broader cultural and even political roles. With Voltaire and Rousseau, Diderot was one of the three most prominent and influential Enlightenment *philosophes*. And the others were, if anything, even more variously engaged in nontheatrical activities. Watchmaker, inventor, musician, speculator, secret agent, merchant, diplomat, and magistrate, Beaumarchais supplied arms to the American Revolution, edited the complete works of Voltaire, joined Rousseau's campaign to get mothers nursing their own children, and claimed membership as a "citizen soldier" in the revolutionary "bourgeois guard of Paris."[91] Known as "the Rousseau of the gutter" (le Rousseau du ruisseau), Mercier, who wrote two of Robert Darnton's forbidden best-sellers of pre-Revolutionary France, *L'an 2440* (number one on Darnton's list) and the twelve-volume *Tableau de Paris* (number four), was elected to the National Convention in 1792 and served a few years later on the Council of Five Hundred.[92] And Collot d'Herbois, the adapter of *El alcalde de Zalamea*, moved the abolition of the monarchy in 1792, was elected president of the National Convention, led the savage repression of the antirevolutionary revolt in Lyon, and served with Robespierre on the notorious Committee of Public Safety. Furthermore, Diderot, Beaumarchais, and Mercier were each either imprisoned under the old regime or driven into exile as a result of their writings. Their personal encounters with history were thus painfully direct. And a charge like the one the king's council lodged against Diderot's *Encyclopédie*—that it was a work "tending to destroy royal authority, to establish a spirit of independence and revolt, and . . . to raise the foundations of error, corruption of morals, irreligion, and disbelief"—was at one time or another aimed at the writings, including the dramatic writings, of each of them.[93] In this sense, both their lives and their works were engaged with history, whether or not they based their plays on historical sources or filled them with figures from history. In them, bourgeois drama self-consciously assumed the role—a role it shared with their other writings and actions—of a historical agent in its own right.

Which is not to say that these men were all committed, much less effective, revolutionaries. They weren't. Indeed, of the four only Collot d'Herbois, the least significant as a dramatist, comes close to fitting that description. Diderot died five years before the fall of the Bastille, and his *Salons* were written for manuscript distribution to an extraordinarily small and select group of subscribers, including the Russian empress, the kings of Sweden and Poland, and the rulers of several German states—hardly a revolutionary assembly. Deeply mistrusted by the actual French revolutionaries, Beaumarchais was involved in the 1780s in a scandalous affair that put him publicly on the wrong side of a real-life story of adultery and the bourgeois home. Despite his membership in the National Convention and the Council of Five Hundred, Mercier never exercised much influence in revolutionary deliberations, and he ended his life as an opponent of one of the central tenets of the Enlightenment, the progress of scientific thought. (He thought the earth was flat!) And were we to add the names of other significant contributors to French bourgeois drama—Simon-Nicolas-Henri Linguet, who first translated Calderón; Nicolas Restif de la Bretonne, who campaigned for the moral reform of the theater; and the marquis de Sade, who, odd as it may seem, wrote a number of plays in Diderot's new vein—the inconsistencies would be still more obvious.[94] Sade, in particular, might well figure as the nightmare embodiment of the monstrous aristocratic and libertine oppressor that had so long haunted bourgeois drama, Figaro's Almaviva gone mad with unlimited sexual power.

Yet for all these inconsistencies—and more could easily be adduced from both the plays and the lives of their creators—French bourgeois drama and the theoretical writings that supported it do mark a decisive turn from the theatrical and artistic evocation of history to an active and deliberate intervention in it. Instead of contenting themselves with a marginal enclave in a system of power and representation otherwise bent on their exclusion or oppression, they aimed at taking over the system altogether, leaving whatever remained of the old political and artistic regime as little more than an empty and powerless figurehead. Not even the Dutch Revolt and its accompanying representational forms had gone so far, while the English, Spanish, and seventeenth-century French never came close. Deliberate historical agency may, of course, not translate into aesthetic durability. We have learned to resist the sentiment and even the realism that are meant to engage us in French eighteenth-century drama and painting. But knowing that such ambitions were once attached to such works retrospectively redefines the broad, various, and historically discontinuous field from which they arose. Thanks to Diderot and his contemporaries, the local, particular, and even nostalgic citizenship of earlier drama and painting has taken on the trappings of progress, enlightenment, and universality. With the further vantage of another two centuries, even these qualities have lost much of their appeal. To many, universal bourgeois value now seems as oppressive as the old regime ever did to those once bent on its displacement. But if our own far less distinct virtual Geneva (if we even have one) is no longer theirs, stories like the ones they told, stories of the home and its disruptive encounters with history, remain a powerful site for the expression of fears and longings that continue to trouble and inspire us.

"From the beginning," writes Nancy Armstrong in the opening words of *Desire and Domestic Fiction*, "domestic fiction actively sought to disentangle the language of sexual relations from the language of politics and, in so doing, to introduce a new form of political power."[1] With a beginning that precedes Armstrong's by about a century and a half, my argument would seem to have been just the opposite. From this earlier beginning, domestic drama and painting actively sought not to disentangle the language of sexual relations from the language of politics but rather to entangle them in every way possible. Despite strenuous resistance from humanist historiographers and neoclassical genre theorists, the nonaristocratic home attained dignity and force precisely as a result of its often unwilling, adulterous alliance with the state. But even here we may find common ground. Entanglement of the sort I describe depends for its effect on the supposition of a prior disentanglement. The sense that a particular sexual violation has more than local significance derives from the home's difference and distance from the state. The sexual predation of a soldier, a courtier, an aristocrat, or the king takes on broad cultural and political meaning because the object of that predation belongs to a different and more vulnerable social order, whether bourgeois or peasant. The purpose of such stories may be, as Sébastien Mercier said of ancient Greek tragedy, to make monarchy odious.[2] Or it may be, as in *El mejor alcalde, el rey* or *Tartuffe*, to glorify monarchy as the protector of the commoner home.

But, whatever the intent, the ultimate effect is to give value to domesticity itself—domesticity apart from the state—and thus "to introduce," as Armstrong puts it, "a new form of political power."

"Bourgeois," "domestic," and (prior to the eighteenth century) "municipal" are the names I have been giving this new form of political power. To these, Armstrong would add a term that has been at least implicit in much of what I have been saying: "female." "This power emerged," she writes, "with the rise of the domestic woman and established its hold over British culture"—which we might, with whatever local qualifications, better call European culture—"through her dominance over all those objects and practices we associate with private life. To her went authority over the household, leisure time, courtship procedures, and kinship relations, and under her jurisdiction the most basic qualities of human identity were supposed to develop."[3] Armstrong credits the novel with a large role in this change. But contemporaries noticed something similar happening in the theater. As early as 1758, Rousseau reported that "a natural effect" of the new love-centered domestic drama "is to extend the empire of the fair sex, to make women and girls the preceptors of the public, and to give them the same power over the audience that they have over their lovers." But to Rousseau this effect was anything but welcome: "Look through most contemporary plays; it is always a woman who knows everything, who teaches everything to men. . . . A child would not be able to eat his bread if it were not cut by his governess. This is the image of what goes on in our new plays. The governess is on the stage and the children in the audience."[4] Being treated as one of those children was not at all what Rousseau wanted—or at least not what he claimed to want. (Readers of his *Confessions* may doubt that claim.) Though Rousseau agreed that instructive value, the kind of value on which a reformed polity must be based, should take a sentimental, bourgeois, and domestic turn, he had no wish to hand the determination and propagation of that value over to women.

Among the plays Rousseau blames for exciting unreasonable expectations regarding the wisdom of women is Diderot's first bourgeois drama, *Le fils naturel*, whose turning point comes in Constance's spirited attack on the old regime and celebration of the Enlightenment. But, in general, eighteenth-century French bourgeois dramatists were scarcely less resistant to the rule of women than Rousseau himself. Dorval and his father, the long-absent Lysimond, are the dominant figures in *Le fils naturel*, and Diderot's next bourgeois drama, *Le père de famille*, centers, as its title suggests, on another enlightened father. Similarly, Beaumarchais made Figaro's the controlling intelligence of the three plays in which he appears (though, in fact, only the women's plots succeed in *Le mariage de Figaro*), while Mercier not only preferred fathers and other men as protagonists but also spoke out, with no less virulence than Rousseau, against the feminization of drama.[5] And where Chardin and the Dutch had put women in very much the role Armstrong and Rousseau both describe as the teachers of civility, Greuze shifted the focus to fathers. Nor was the Revolution to which eighteenth-century domestic drama and painting contributed any more sympathetic to women. "The Declaration of the Rights of Man and the Citizen," enacted by the National Assembly in August 1789, was notably silent concerning the rights of women. And when Olympe de Gouges, herself the author of several *drames,* attempted to rectify this omission with a "Declaration of the Rights of Woman and the Citizeness," she was rewarded with a fatal trip to the guillotine as a counterrevolutionary and "unnatural" woman.

Does this mean that no new form of political power was in fact invested in women? Not necessarily. It does, however, suggest that, in France at least, the emergence of a political power that could fairly be called female was resisted even by those who were most interested in promoting the domestic and the bourgeois as a counter to the hierarchical order of the old regime. Indeed, it was precisely when domestic drama, painting, and fiction became conscious of themselves as the platform for a reforming and eventually even for a revolutionary political force that they shied away from their identification with women. In this sense, the French eighteenth century at once made manifest the political power of the domestic as the subject of serious artistic and literary attention and worked to suppress what had been most characteristic of earlier domestic drama and painting: the predominant role of women—a trait that continued to characterize the Richardsonian novels that give Armstrong her starting place and that so affected Diderot and his followers.

From the beginning—that is, from the point at which this book begins in the sixteenth century—the underlying social, economic, and political issues that were expressed through domestic drama and painting concerned relations between men: relations between burghers (or rich peasants) and aristocrats, between townsmen and soldiers, between men of the new regime of sentiment and fraternity and men of the old regime of hierarchy and oppression, between male subjects and their king. But the effect of representing those issues and those relations in stories about

rivalry over the sexual possession of women inevitably resulted in the promotion of women to positions of great consequence. Alice Arden, Jane
Shore, and Mistresses Page and Ford, like the women of ter Borch, Vermeer, de Hooch, and Chardin, are easily the most powerful and the most
affecting figures in the works in which they appear. And if the women
in the peasant dramas of Lope and Calderón and in Molière's *Tartuffe*
cannot make quite the same claim, they too attain a position and exercise
an influence that clearly anticipates what Armstrong would discover in
eighteenth- and nineteenth-century domestic fiction and Rousseau would
deplore in the bourgeois drama of his own time. Preceded by early modern
domestic drama and painting, paralleled by the novels of Richardson, and
followed by the great flow of nineteenth-century domestic fiction, the
Enlightenment deflection of representational authority to fathers and
brothers thus appears to be a short-lived aberration rather than a fundamental and lasting transformation, an aberration belied not only by Rousseau's *Confessions* but also by his own Richardsonian novel, *La nouvelle
Héloïse,* in both of which women exercise much the role he would have
denied them in the theater.

  The artistic power and cultural significance of this promotion of bourgeois and domestic women is undeniable. What is less clear is whether
it should count as a promotion of women in any broader sense. There is,
after all, something deeply paradoxical in Armstrong's claim that by being
wholly removed from politics, domestic women were made the basis for
a new form of political power. More familiar is the attitude expressed by
Jane Tompkins: "The public-private dichotomy, which is to say, the public-private *hierarchy,* is the founding condition of female oppression. I say
to hell with it."[6] And can even works like those I discuss, where entanglement rather than disentanglement underlies the promotion of the domestic household and domestic woman, be thought any more liberating?
What, after all, are the terms of entanglement but the identification of
male honor and the sanctity of male-owned property with female chastity?
Such terms may grant women representational significance. But do they
contribute to women's liberation? As we have seen, the adulterous alliances of early modern drama and painting are all about liberation, about
the exposure of oppression and its undoing, whether by ruse, rebellion,
or affective bonding. But does the liberation of burghers and rich peasants
mean the liberation of burgher and rich peasant women? Or does it mean
their still straighter confinement in the seemingly ahistorical and apolitical
realms of domesticity and sexuality?

Answering such questions in any adequate way would carry us far beyond the evidence presented in this book. But the very necessity of asking
them suggests the instability of this representational field, an instability
that stands out in sharp relief if we set Armstrong's *Desire and Domestic
Fiction* next to an earlier book that examines much the same generic and
historical territory from a very different perspective, Tony Tanner's *Adultery in the Novel.*[7] Where Armstrong writes of how desire makes the bourgeois home, Tanner explores desire's part in the home's unmaking. Men,
in Armstrong's account, are drawn to the desirable figure of the domestic
woman. Women, in the works Tanner examines, themselves desire a freedom, including a sexual freedom, that radically disrupts the domesticity
they represent. Both impulses are anticipated in early modern drama and
painting. If we think of Pamela, Elizabeth Bennet, and Jane Eyre as standing in the line of Jane Shore, Shakespeare's merry wives, de Hooch's
mothers and homemakers, Lope's Casilda, and Molière's Elmire, then we
must also recognize the links joining Emma Bovary, Anna Karenina, and
(glancing back to drama) Hedda Gabler to such women as Alice Arden,
Jan Steen's Bathsheba, and (depending on our understanding of her) Vermeer's laughing girl. Though it was the favored site for a theatrical and
artistic discourse of liberty and human rights, the bourgeois home could
also be experienced as a prison—not the place where desire is satisfied
but rather where it is frustrated and quelled.[8] Such self-division belongs
inescapably to a politics which at once bases itself on the private, nonaristocratic home and undermines both home and marriage by extending notions of liberty and contract (a key term in Tanner's book) to the individual.[9] Clearly, the male householder of middling status is to be freed from
the oppression of king and lord. In that understanding, all these works
agree. But what of his wife? Is her freedom to be no more than an extension of his? Or is she rather to enjoy a freedom like his, the freedom, for
example, to escape the confines of the home and to engage as fully as he
not only in the sphere of sexual pursuit but also in that of politics and
history?

Issues like these, which surfaced massively in nineteenth-century fiction
and drama and have surfaced still more massively in twentieth-century
public life, are no more than shadowed in the early modern plays and
paintings examined in this book. But a tradition—if we may call it that—
that has Alice Arden and her defiant cry that "marriage is but words" at
its head cannot avoid them altogether.[10] Stories of the home's disruption
by a sexual marauder dressed in the garb of oppressive political power can

still be told with great effect. In the introduction, I alluded to Mel Gibson's *Braveheart*, which, news reports suggest, may even have had a small part in the recent vote to restore Scotland's parliament.[11] Shortly before *Braveheart*, a film version of *Rob Roy* used a dramatic account of sexual predation to excite similarly nationalistic feelings. Nor are such stories set only in the unenlightened past, as though the sins of the old regime must remain forever their unique target. A low-budget independent film that came out the year after *Braveheart* recycled the familiar motif to direct anger not at some abusive king or lord but rather at the CIA's role in Central America.[12] The possibilities are as endless as oppression itself. But whatever sympathy the home is made to attract, it may also figure as the source, as well as the scene, of oppressive subjection. In this regard, Diderot's Monsieur Baliveau furnishes a hint that many subsequent works have amplified, a hint of bourgeois domesticity's complacent and stifling mediocrity. As we celebrate the early modern emergence of the nonaristocratic home as the basis for a new and revolutionary political power, we should also remember the home's own oppressiveness. Pathos and reality belong finally to both.

Scattered through the notes to this book can be found thanks for many specific favors. Here I have the pleasure of thanking those whose generous assistance cannot be properly acknowledged within the limits of a single endnote. David Bevington, Heather Dubrow, Patricia Fumerton, Elizabeth MacArthur, Mark Rose, and William Warner read and commented helpfully on the whole book. Ann Bermingham, Julie Carlson, Barbara Fuchs, Alan Liu, Michael O'Connell, David Harris Sacks, and Gary Schwartz did the same for individual chapters. Anneke Bart, Paula Skoe, and Véronique Otto helped make up for the inadequacies of my German and Dutch. Barbara Fuchs and Harvey Sharrer saved my Spanish translations from some embarrassing slips. Ann Jensen Adams, Harry Berger, Jr., Stephen Greenblatt, Wayne Franits, Lena Cowen Orlin, Ricardo Padrón, and Georgianna Ziegler provided valuable support of other sorts. And Alan Thomas and the editorial staff at the University of Chicago Press have done much to smooth the book's production. The book has also benefited greatly from the encouragement and advice of the thirty or so audiences who have heard bits of it given as talks—including especially the first audience for all of those talks, the person whose yawns, blank looks, and howls of protest have saved other listeners and readers from many stretches of unnecessary tedium, my wife, Marie-Christine Helgerson.

This book was begun on a fellowship, sponsored by the National Endowment for the Humanities, at the Folger Shakespeare Library in Washington, D.C. It was completed with the help of an NEH Research Fellowship, a University of California President's Fellowship in the Humanities, and a grant from the College of Letters and Science at the University of California, Santa Barbara. Without the time made available by those fellowships, I would have had far greater difficulty following leads into areas I had never before explored. Several parts of the book have been previously printed. A longer and quite differently focused version of chapter 1 appeared as "Murder in Faversham: Holinshed's Impertinent History," in *The Historical Imagination in Early Modern Britain,* edited by Donald R. Kelley and David Harris Sacks and published by the Woodrow Wilson Center Press and the Cambridge University Press in 1997; chapter 2 came out under its present title in the *South Atlantic Quarterly* 98 (1999); a shorter version of chapter 3 appeared as "The Buck Basket, the Witch, and the Queen of Fairies: The Women's World of Shakespeare's Windsor," in *Renaissance Culture and the Everyday,* edited by Patricia Fumerton and Simon Hunt (© University of Pennsylvania Press, 1999); and a version of chapter 4 was published under the title "Soldiers and Enigmatic Girls: The Politics of Dutch Domestic Realism, 1650–1672," in *Representations* 58 (1997). Thanks are due to their original publishers for permitting their reappearance here.

Throughout the text of this book, spelling and punctuation have been modernized in all quotations and titles. In the notes, titles are presented as they appear on the particular edition being cited, with the result that a title may be spelled differently in the text than in the notes. Unless otherwise indicated, all translations are the responsibility of the author.

INTRODUCTION

1. "La liberté de penser, l'attraction, l'électricité, le tolérantisme, l'inoculation, le quinquina, l'Encyclopédie et les drames." Pierre Augustin Caron de Beaumarchais, *Théâtre complet*, ed. Maurice Allem and Paul Courant (Paris: Éditions Gallimard, 1957), p. 176.

2. Lena Cowen Orlin, *Private Matters and Public Culture in Post-Reformation England* (Ithaca: Cornell University Press, 1994), pp. 15–84.

3. John Payne Collier, *The History of English Dramatic Poetry to the Time of Shakespeare*, 3 vols. (London: John Murray, 1851), 3.49–60; Arthur Eustace Morgan, *English Domestic Drama* (Folcroft, PA: Folcroft Press, 1912); Henry H. Adams, *English Domestic or Homiletic Tragedy, 1575–1642* (New York: Columbia University Press, 1943); Andrew Clark, *Domestic Drama: A Survey of the Origins, Antecedents, and Nature of the Domestic Play in England, 1500–1640*, 2 vols. (Salzburg: Universität Salzburg, 1975); Frances E. Dolan, *Dangerous Familiars: Representations of Domestic Crime in England, 1550–1700* (Ithaca: Cornell University Press, 1994); Viviana Comensoli, *"Household Business": Domestic Plays of Early Modern England* (Toronto: University of Toronto Press, 1996); and Frank Whigham, *Seizures of the Will in Early Modern English Drama* (Cambridge: Cambridge University Press, 1996). Though not primarily concerned with domestic drama as such, Heather Dubrow, who has the further distinction of having once lived in Arden's house, has addressed many closely related issues in two recent books: *A Happier Eden: The Politics of Marriage in the Stuart Epithalamium* (Ithaca: Cornell University Press, 1990); and, especially, *Shakespeare and Domestic Loss: Forms of Deprivation, Mourning, and Recuperation* (Cambridge: Cambridge University Press, 1999).

4. *Paradise Lost*, 4.750–2. Quoted from John Milton, *Complete Poems and Major Prose*, ed. Merritt Y. Hughes (New York: Macmillan Publishing Company, 1957), p. 296. In the next several

lines, Milton goes on to say, "By thee"—that is, by wedded love—"adulterous lust was driv'n from men / Among the bestial herds to range." He thus not only makes marriage and particularly the husband's possession of his wife's body the originating type of all private property but also immediately suggests, by its very denial, the adulterous threat to that property. After all, were there no wedded love there could be no adultery, adultery itself being defined as the violation of wedlock. Humans are the only "bestial herd" capable of adultery.

5. Edward W. Said, *Culture and Imperialism* (New York: Vintage Books, 1994), p. 45. For examples of the incarnation story treated as a domestic drama, a drama that includes Joseph's fears of cuckoldry, see "The Shearmen and Tailors' Pageant" in the true Coventry Cycle, "Joseph's Trouble about Mary" in the York Cycle, the Wakefield "Annunciation," the Chester "Nativity," and the N-Town "Joseph's Doubt" and "The Trial of Joseph and Mary." Thanks to Michael O'Connell for directing my attention to these plays.

6. A sociological explanation of this sort has long been central to discussions of the rise of the novel, a form that shares so much with domestic drama and painting that it might be considered a successor genre. For a good recent examination of these issues, see William B. Warner, *Licensing Entertainment: The Elevation of Novel Reading in Britain, 1684–1750* (Berkeley: University of California Press, 1998), pp. 1–44.

CHAPTER ONE

1. For a map that shows Paul's Walk, the location of White's shop, and Cheapside, see Peter W. M. Blayney, *The Bookshops in Paul's Cross Churchyard* (London: Bibliographical Society), figure 1 (facing p. 3).

2. Raphael Holinshed, *The Third Volume of Chronicles* (London: J. Harison et al., 1587), sig. Kkkkki^v. Holinshed's 1577 account of Arden's murder differs mainly in lacking the extensive marginal glosses that distinguish the 1587 edition.

3. Many of these subsequent appropriations of the Arden story are described in the introduction to M. L. Wine's edition of *The Tragedy of Master Arden of Faversham* (London: Methuen, 1973), pp. xlv–lvii, where the reference to *Arden* as Faversham's "own passion play" occurs (p. xlvii). For the Arden story's relation to subsequent crime literature, see Victor E. Neuberg, *Popular Literature: A History and Guide from the Beginning of Print to the Year 1897* (Harmondsworth: Peguin Books, 1977), p. 87. For examples of its inclusion in local history, see Thomas Southouse, *Monasticon Favershamiense in Agro Cantiano* (London: T. Passenger, 1671); Edward Jacob, *The History of the Town and Port of Faversham in the County of Kent* (London: J. Marsh, 1774); C. E. Donne, *An Essay on the Tragedy of "Arden of Feversham": Being the Substance of a Paper Read at a Meeting of the Kent Archaeological Society Held at Faversham in July, 1872* (London: Russell Smith, 1873); Lionel Cust, "Arden of Feversham," *Archaeologia Cantiana* 34 (1920): 101–38; and Arthur Percival, "Arden of Faversham: The Man and the Play," *Bygone Kent* 13 (1992): 187–92 and 278–82. The opera is Alexander Goehr's *Arden Muss Sterben* (New York: Associated Music Publishers, 1967); the novel, Diane Davidson's *Faversham* (New York: Crown Publishers, 1969). I owe the jingle to the present owner of Arden's House, Roy Pleasance.

4. I survey the innovative critical and historical uses to which *Arden of Faversham* and the Arden story have been recently put in "Murder in Faversham: Holinshed's Impertinent History," in *The Historical Imagination in Early Modern Britain: History, Rhetoric, and Fiction, 1500–1800,* ed. Donald R. Kelley and David Harris Sacks (Cambridge: Cambridge University Press, 1997), pp. 133–58, a differently focused and considerably expanded version of the present chapter. Among the books and articles I cite there are: Catherine Belsey, *The Subject of Tragedy: Identity and Difference in Renaissance Drama* (London: Methuen, 1985); Betty S. Travitsky, "Husband-Murder and Petty Treason in English Renaissance Tragedy," *Renaissance Drama* n.s. 21 (1990): 171–98; David Attwell, "Property, Status, and the Subject in a Middle-class Tragedy: *Arden of Faversham,*" *English Literary Renaissance* 21 (1991): 328–48; James R. Keller, "Arden's Land Acquisitions and the Dissolution of the Monasteries," *English Language Notes* 30 (1993): 20–24;

Frances E. Dolan, *Dangerous Familiars: Representations of Domestic Crime in England, 1550–1700* (Ithaca: Cornell University Press, 1994); Peter Holbrook, *Literature and Degree in Renaissance England: Nashe, Bourgeois Tragedy, Shakespeare* (Newark: University of Delaware Press, 1994); Lena Cowen Orlin, *Private Matters and Public Culture in Post-Reformation England* (Ithaca: Cornell University Press, 1994); Garrett A. Sullivan, Jr., "'Arden lay murdered in that plot of ground': Surveying, Land, and Arden of Faversham," *ELH* 61 (1994): 231–52; Julie R. Schutzman, "Alice Arden's Freedom and the Suspended Moment of *Arden of Faversham*," *Studies in English Literature* 36 (1996): 298–314; and Frank Whigham, *Seizures of the Will in Early Modern English Drama* (Cambridge: Cambridge University Press, 1996).

5. On English humanist historiography, see F. Smith Fussner, *The Historical Revolution: English Historical Writing and Thought, 1580–1640* (London: Routledge, 1962); F. J. Levy, *Tudor Historical Thought* (San Marino, CA: Huntington Library, 1967); Arthur B. Ferguson, *Clio Unbound: Perception of the Social and Cultural Past in Renaissance England* (Durham, NC: Duke University Press, 1979); Antonia Gransden, *Historical Writing in England*, vol. 2, *c. 1307 to the Early Sixteenth Century* (Ithaca: Cornell University Press, 1982); Joseph M. Levine, *Humanism and History: Origins of Modern English Historiography* (Ithaca: Cornell University Press, 1987); and D. R. Woolf, *The Idea of History in Early Stuart England: Erudition, Ideology, and "The Light of Truth" from the Accession of James I to the Civil War* (Toronto: University of Toronto Press, 1990).

6. These phrases come from Peter Heylyn, *Microcosmus, or A Little Description of the Great World* (Oxford: John Lichfield and James Short, 1621), sig. C1; John Donne, *The Satires, Epigrams, and Verse Letters*, ed. W. Milgate (Oxford: Clarendon Press, 1967), p. 17; and Edmund Bolton, *Hypercritica, or a Rule of Judgment for Writing and Reading our History's*, in *Critical Essays of the Seventeenth Century*, ed. J. E. Spingarn, 3 vols. (Oxford: Clarendon Press, 1908), 1.97–98. I have borrowed them from the epigraph to Annabel Patterson's "Rethinking Tudor Historiography," *South Atlantic Quarterly* 92 (1993): 185.

7. Bolton, *Hypercritica*, 1.83. A year or two later, in his commendatory letter prefaced to Augustine Vincent's *Discoverie of Errours* (London: W. Jaggard, 1622), John Selden remarked that, with the exception of Camden's *Annals* and Bacon's *Henry VII*, "we have not so much as a public piece of the *History of England*" (sig. ai^v).

8. Thomas Blundeville, *The True Order and Methode of Wryting and Reading Hystories* (London: W. Seres, 1574), sig. Aiv^v.

9. F. J. Levy, "Hayward, Daniel, and the Beginnings of Politic History in England," *Huntington Library Quarterly* 50 (1987): 1–34.

10. Sir John Hayward, *The First Part of the Life and Raigne of King Henrie the IIII* (London: J. Wolfe, 1599), sig. A3.

11. Francis Bacon, *De Augmentis Scientiarum*, bk. 2, chap. 9, in *The Works of Francis Bacon*, ed. James Spedding, 14 vols. (London: Longmans, 1857–74), 4.310; William Camden, *Annales, or the History of the Most Renowned and Victorious Princesse Elizabeth, Late Queen of England*, trans. R. N. (London: B. Fisher, 1635), sig. c3^v; Sir George Buck, *The History of the King Richard the Third (1619)*, ed. Arthur Noel Kincaid (Gloucester: Alan Sutton, 1979), pp. 7–8; and Bolton, *Hypercritica*, 1.96.

12. Edward, Lord Herbert of Cherbury, *The Life and Raigne of King Henry the Eighth* (London: T. Whitaker, 1649), sig. A3.

13. Bacon, *Works*, 10.250 and 4.300–312.

14. Sir John Hayward, *The Lives of the III Normans* (London: R. B., 1613), sig. A4.

15. Camden, *Annales*, sig. c3^v.

16. John Trussell, *A Continuation of the Collection of the History of England* (London: E. Dawson, 1636), sig. A4. Compare Bacon's *Advancement of Learning*: "It doth not a little embase the authority of a history to intermingle matters of triumph or matters of ceremony or matters of novelty with matters of state" (3.339).

17. T. I., *A World of Wonders* (London: W. Barley, 1595), sig. A2.

18. Samuel Daniel, *The First Part of the Historie of England* (London: N. Okes, 1612), sig. A2ᵛ.

19. Trussell, *Continuation,* sig. A4.

20. Richard Baker, *Chronicle of the Kings of England from the Time of the Romans Government unto the Raigne of our Soveraigne Lord King Charles* (London: Daniel Frere, 1643), sigs. Lll3–3ᵛ and A2 (my emphasis).

21. The precise extent of Arden's landholding in and around Faversham has been carefully studied by Patricia Hyde, who questions whether he owned quite as large a share of the former abbey property as has usually been claimed. See Hyde's *Thomas Arden in Faversham: The Man behind the Myth* (Faversham: Faversham Society, 1996). Hyde usefully reprints many of the surviving documents relating to Arden.

22. Orlin, *Private Matters,* p. 31.

23. *Acts of the Privy Council, 1550–52* (London: HM Stationery Office, 1891), p. 230.

24. Peter Clark, *English Provincial Society from the Reformation to the Revolution: Religion, Politics, and Society in Kent, 1500–1640* (Hassocks, Sussex: Harvester Press, 1977), pp. 83–84. In *Private Matters,* Lena Orlin adds still another distinguished name to the list of possible suspects, Arden's own patron Sir Thomas Cheney (pp. 53–62).

25. Belsey, *Subject of Tragedy,* pp. 137–44.

26. Holinshed, *Third Volume of Chronicles,* sig. Kkkkkiᵛ.

27. Ibid.; and British Library, Harleian MS 542, fol. 34 (reprinted in Hyde, *Thomas Arden,* p. 117).

28. *Arden of Faversham,* ed. Wine, pp. 4–5.

29. Holinshed, *The First Volume of the Chronicles of England, Scotland, and Ireland* (London: John Hume, 1577), sig. iiii.

30. George Puttenham, *The Arte of English Poesie* (1589), in *Elizabethan Critical Essays,* ed. G. Gregory Smith, 2 vols. (London: Oxford University Press, 1904), 2.27.

31. Holinshed, *Third Volume of Chronicles,* sig. Kkkkkiii.

32. For a discussion of the monopolists and the parliamentary attack on them, see David Harris Sacks, "Private Profit and Public Good: The Problem of the State in Elizabethan Theory and Practice," in *Law, Literature, and the Settlement of Regimes,* ed. Gordon J. Schochet (Washington, DC: Folger Institute, 1990), pp. 121–42. Holinshed's language in the passages where he talks of Arden's economic oppression of his neighbors strikingly echoes the attacks on monopolists reported by Sacks (Holinshed, *Third Volume of Chronicles,* sig. Kkkkkiii–Kkkkkiiiᵛ).

33. Quoted by Orlin, *Private Matters,* p. 41.

34. Holinshed, *Third Volume of Chronicles,* sig. Kkkkkiii and Kkkkkiiiᵛ.

35. British Library, Harleian MS 542, fol. 36 (reprinted in Hyde, *Thomas Arden,* p. 120).

36. *Arden of Faversham,* ed. Wine, pp. 5–6.

37. On the likeness between Arden and Mosby, see Whigham, *Seizures of the Will,* pp. 65–74.

38. Arden makes the comparison himself in an exchange with Mosby, who has asked him about the title to the abbey lands in Faversham: "As for the lands, Mosby, they are mine / By letters patents from his majesty. / But I must have a mandate for my wife; / They say you seek to rob me of her love" (*Arden of Faversham,* ed. Wine, p. 22).

39. In speaking of "the early modern invention of private life," I do not mean to suggest that, whether as category or as lived experience, private life had never existed before the sixteenth century. That clearly is not the case, as any reader of the five-volume *History of Private Life,* ed. Philippe Ariès and Georges Duby, trans. Arthur Goldhammer (Cambridge: Harvard University Press, 1987–91), will know. But I would suggest that the particular forms of private life and, especially, of its representation do change, and that the European sixteenth and seventeenth centuries witnessed a particularly striking instance of such change, one

significant enough to be called an "invention." In early modern European drama and paint-ing, the private life of commoners came to mean something quite different than it had meant before.

40. Richard Brathwait, *The Schollers Medley, or, An Intermixt Discourse upon Historicall and Poeticall Relations* (London: G. Norton, 1614), sigs. B1, B2ᵛ, and O4–4ᵛ.

41. *The Riverside Shakespeare*, ed. G. Blakemore Evans, 2nd ed. (Boston: Houghton Mifflin, 1997), p. 1816.

42. On the relation of the Lucretia story to the development of early Italian civic humanism, see Stephanie H. Jed, *Chaste Thinking: The Rape of Lucretia and the Birth of Humanism* (Blooming-ton: Indiana University Press, 1989).

Chapter Two

1. James Boaden, *Memoirs of Mrs. Siddons* (London: Gibbings and Co., 1893), p. 195.

2. For a comprehensive listing of the many works, including ballads, complaints, elegies, plays, chapbooks, novels, an opera, a puppet show, and even several films, based on the Jane Shore story, see James L. Harner, "Jane Shore in Literature: A Checklist," *Notes and Queries* n.s. 28 (1981): 496–507. Harner discusses the early treatments of Shore's wife in "Jane Shore: A Biog-raphy of a Theme in Renaissance Literature" (Ph.D. diss., University of Illinois at Urbana-Champaign, 1972). This material is also described at length by Esther Yael Beith-Halahmi, *Angell Fayre or Strumpet Lewd: Jane Shore as an Example of Erring Beauty in Sixteenth-Century Literature*, 2 vols. (Salzburg: Institute für Englische Sprache und Literatur, 1974); and, more briefly, by Samuel M. Pratt, "Jane Shore and the Elizabethans: Some Facts and Speculations," *Texas Studies in Language and Literature* 11 (1970): 1293–1306.

3. Thomas More, *The History of King Richard III*, ed. Richard S. Sylvester as volume 2 of *The Complete Works of St. Thomas More* (New Haven: Yale University Press, 1963), p. 56.

4. More, *History*, pp. 56–57.

5. As quoted by James Harner, who surveys these views in "Jane Shore: A Biography of a Theme in Renaissance Literature," p. 25.

6. Tucker Brooke in *A Literary History of England*, ed. Albert C. Baugh (New York: Appleton-Century-Crofts, 1948), p. 398.

7. *The Mirror for Magistrates*, ed. Lily B. Campbell (1938; reprinted New York: Barnes and Noble, 1960), p. 387; and Thomas Nashe, *Strange Newes* (1592), in *The Works of Thomas Nashe*, ed. Ronald B. McKerrow and F. P. Wilson, 5 vols. (Oxford: Blackwell, 1958), 1.309. Such praise continued to be heard for at least another decade. In 1601, Ingenioso, a character in the Cambridge University play *The Return from Parnassus*, says of Churchyard, "Hath not Shore's wife, although a light skirts she, / Given him a chaste long-lasting memory?" *The Three Parnassus Plays (1598–1601)*, ed. J. B. Leishman (London: Ivor Nicholson, 1949), p. 245.

8. The larger traditions to which these poems may be thought to belong have been expertly surveyed by Lawrence Lipking, *Abandoned Women and Poetic Tradition* (Chicago: University of Chicago Press, 1988); and John Kerrigan, *Motives of Woe: Shakespeare and "Female Complaint"* (Oxford: Clarendon Press, 1991).

9. Samuel Daniel, *Poems and A Defence of Ryme*, ed. Arthur Colby Sprague (1930; reprinted Chicago: University of Chicago Press, 1965), p. 39; *The Works of Michael Drayton*, ed. J. William Hebel, 5 vols. (Oxford: Shakespeare Head Press, 1931–41), 1.215; and *Willobie His Avisa*, ed. G. B. Harrison (1922; reprinted New York: Barnes and Noble, 1966), p. 34.

10. *The English Works of Giles Fletcher, the Elder*, ed. Lloyd E. Berry (Madison: University of Wisconsin Press, 1964), p. 124.

11. Thomas Churchyard, *Churchyards Challenge* (London: John Wolfe, 1593), p. 126.

12. Cecilia Ann Infante discusses male competition in relation to several of the Shore's wife poems in "Sappho and Jane Shore as Male Models of Female Speech and Subjectivity, England 1513–1624" (Ph.D. diss., University of Michigan, 1994), pp. 64–101.

13. Daniel, *Poems*, p. 40. Compare the link introducing *Shore's Wife* in the 1587 edition of the *Mirror for Magistrates*, where Shore's wife thinks first of Baldwin as a possible teller of her tale, then rejects him because, as "a minister and a preacher," his "function and calling disdains to look so low," before turning to Churchyard, a "martial man, who hath more experience both in defending women's honor and knows somewhat more of their conditions and qualities" (p. 372).

14. *Mirror for Magistrates*, p. 386.

15. *The Works of Thomas Deloney*, ed. Francis Oscar Mann (Oxford: Clarendon Press, 1912), p. 304.

16. As further evidence of the deliberateness of Shakespeare's exclusion of Shore's wife, it is worth noting that the two earlier Elizabethan plays on Richard's reign, Thomas Legge's *Richardus Tertius* (1580) and the anonymous *True Tragedy of Richard the Third* (1594), both included her.

17. For a list of these plays, see Richard Helgerson, *Forms of Nationhood: The Elizabethan Writing of England* (Chicago: University of Chicago Press, 1992), p. 234. Daryl W. Palmer raises similar issues with regard to Shakespeare's *Richard III* and Heywood's *Edward IV* in "Edward IV's Secret Familiarities and the Politics of Proximity in Elizabethan History Plays," *ELH* 61 (1994): 279–315.

18. More, *History*, p. 55; and Chute, *Beawtie Dishonoured Written under the Title of Shores Wife* (London: John Wolfe, 1593), sig. Ciiiᵛ.

19. In an illuminating chapter entitled "Patriarchalism and Its Discontents," Lena Cowen Orlin discusses the competing claims of king and husband in *Edward IV*, *Arden of Faversham*, *A Warning for Fair Women*, and *Two Lamentable Tragedies*. See Orlin's *Private Matters and Public Culture in Post-Reformation England* (Ithaca: Cornell University Press, 1994), pp. 85–130.

20. *The Dramatic Works of Thomas Heywood*, ed. J. Payne Collier, 2 vols. (London: Shakespeare Society, 1851), 1.87.

21. Ibid., 1.24.

22. Ibid., 1.61.

23. In *The Drama of Landscape: Land, Property, and Social Relations on the Early Modern Stage* (Stanford: Stanford University Press, 1998), pp. 197–229, Garrett A. Sullivan, Jr., discusses the urban emphasis of Heywood's *Edward IV*, contrasting it with Shakespeare's greater attention to royal and aristocratic actors in *2 Henry VI*.

24. Heywood, *Dramatic Works*, 1.14 and 11.

25. Ibid., 1.23.

26. See Orlin's discussion of this siege imagery (*Private Matters*, pp. 119–20).

27. Heywood, *Dramatic Works*, 1.79.

28. Ibid., 1.75.

29. Daniel, *Poems*, p. 39; More, *History*, p. 56; and *Mirror for Magistrates*, p. 380.

30. Heywood, *Dramatic Works*, 1.160.

31. Ibid., 1.163.

32. Ibid., 1.125 and 170.

33. Ibid., 1.192.

34. Thomas Heywood, *An Apology for Actors* (London: Nicholas Oakes, 1612), sig. G1ᵛ.

35. Heywood, *Dramatic Works*, 1.171 and 185.

36. *Henslowe's Diary*, ed. R. A. Foakes and R. T. Rickert (Cambridge: Cambridge University Press, 1961), pp. 194 and 226.

37. *The Pepys Ballads*, ed. Hyder Edward Rollins, 8 vols. (Cambridge: Harvard University Press, 1929–32), 2.137. "The Woeful Lamentation of Mistress Jane Shore" can be found in *The Roxburghe Ballads*, ed. William Chappell, 3 vols. (London: Ballad Society, 1871), 1.483–92.

38. Christopher Brooke, *The Ghost of Richard III*, ed. J. Payne Collier (London: Shakespeare Society, 1844), p. 37. Orlin uses this passage to argue for the complexity of the original response to Jane Shore (*Private Matters*, p. 130).

39. *Mirror for Magistrates*, p. 372.

40. Judith Milhous, "The First Production of Rowe's *Jane Shore*," *Theatre Journal* 38 (1986): 318.

41. On the French reception of *Richard III* and *Jane Shore*, see Jacques Gury, "Le Monstre et la pécheresse: Richard III et Jane Shore entre Shakespeare et Rowe vus par les français de Louis XV à Louis-Philippe," *Moreana* 20 (1983): 122–33.

42. Charles Gildon, *A New Rehearsal, or Bays the Younger* (London: J. Roberts, 1714), pp. 67 and 70.

43. Irving Ribner, *The English History Play in the Age of Shakespeare* (1957; rev. ed. London: Methuen, 1965), p. 277; and Kathleen E. McLuskie, *Dekker and Heywood: Professional Dramatists* (New York: St. Martin's Press, 1994), p. 91.

44. Nicholas Rowe, *The Tragedy of Jane Shore*, ed. Harry William Pedicord (Lincoln: University of Nebraska Press, 1974), p. 75.

45. Heywood, *Dramatic Works*, 1.189.

46. Peter Szondi, "Tableau et coup de théâtre: Pour une sociologie de la tragédie domestique et bourgeoise chez Diderot et Lessing," trans. Chantal Creusot, *Poétique* 9 (1972): 1. See also Szondi's *Die Theorie des bürgerlichen Trauerspiels im 18. Jahrhundert: Der Kaufmann, der Hausvater und der Hofmeister* (Frankfurt: Suhrkamp, 1973).

47. Szondi, "Tableau," p. 14.

48. See, for example, Ann Douglas, *The Feminization of American Culture* (New York: Knopf, 1977); and Nancy Armstrong, *Desire and Domestic Fiction: A Political History of the Novel* (New York: Oxford University Press, 1987).

CHAPTER THREE

1. *Ben Jonson*, ed. C. H. Herford, Percy Simpson, and Evelyn Simpson, 11 vols. (Oxford: Clarendon Press, 1925–52), 8.94 and 97. For a fuller discussion of the relation of estate survey to country house poem, see Richard Helgerson, "Nation or Estate?: Ideological Conflict in the Early Modern Mapping of England," *Cartographica* 31 (1994): 68–74. I here paraphrase a couple of sentences from this article.

2. Three recent essays have usefully addressed the local specificities of Shakespeare's Windsor: Leah S. Marcus, "Levelling Shakespeare: Local Customs and Local Texts," *Shakespeare Quarterly* 42 (1991): 168–78; Arthur F. Kinney, "Textual Signs in *The Merry Wives of Windsor*," *Yearbook of English Studies* 23 (1993): 206–34; and Rosemary Kegl, " 'The Adoption of Abominable Terms': The Insults That Shape Windsor's Middle Class," *ELH* 61 (1994): 253–78. Marcus's essay has been reprinted in her *Unediting the Renaissance: Shakespeare, Marlowe, Milton* (New York: Routledge, 1996), pp. 68–100; and Kegl's in her *Rhetoric of Concealment: Figuring Gender and Class in Renaissance Literature* (Ithaca: Cornell University Press, 1994), pp. 77–125. Both Marcus and Kinney are much concerned with textual differences between the quarto and folio versions of *Merry Wives*. Like all modern editions, those I have used in writing this chapter are based on the 1623 folio, a text that, in the words of one recent editor, "has a close connection with the first performance of the play." See Walter Cohen's "Textual Note" on *Merry Wives* in *The Norton Shakespeare*, ed. Stephen Greenblatt et al. (New York: Norton, 1997), p. 1231.

3. Quoted by H. J. Oliver in his introduction to the Arden edition of *Merry Wives* (London: Methuen, 1971), p. xlv.

4. From Michael Drayton's *Poly-Olbion*, quoted in William Green, *Shakespeare's Merry Wives of Windsor* (Princeton: Princeton University Press, 1962), p. 7. Green develops the argument for *Merry Wives* as "Shakespeare's Garter play" that was first proposed by Leslie Hotson in *Shakespeare versus Shallow* (Boston: Little, Brown, 1931). For a further elaboration of this argument, one that adventures an implausibly grand thesis, see Giorgio Melchiori, *Shakespeare's Garter Plays: Edward III to Merry Wives of Windsor* (Newark: University of Delaware Press, 1994). The critical implications of the relation of Shakespeare's play to the Garter feast have been explored by Leslie S.

Katz, "*The Merry Wives of Windsor:* Sharing the Queen's Holiday," *Representations* 51 (1995): 77–93.

5. *Merry Wives*, 5.5.60. Act, scene, and line references are from *The Riverside Shakespeare*, ed. G. Blakemore Evans (Boston: Houghton Mifflin, 1974). In quoting from this edition, I have expanded some contractions and occasionally altered punctuation.

6. Ibid., 1.3.9–10.

7. Ibid., 3.2.73.

8. In *Shakespeare and Domestic Loss* (Cambridge: Cambridge University Press, 1999), pp. 75–76, Heather Dubrow interestingly links Falstaff's attempted sexual invasion of Windsor to the highway robbery he commits in *1 Henry IV*, to more general patterns of thievery in Shakespeare's second tetralogy of English history plays, and to fears of burglary and other invasions of the home in Elizabethan culture at large. On the broader issue of the poetics and politics of invasion, see also Jonathan Gil Harris, *Foreign Bodies and the Body Politic: Discourses of Social Pathology in Early Modern England* (Cambridge: Cambridge University Press, 1998).

9. *Merry Wives*, 5.5.231–33.

10. Ibid., 3.2.71–75 and 5.5.237.

11. Ibid., 5.5.233–34, 3.2.68–69, and 5.5.151–54.

12. Ibid., 1.4.5–6 and 3.1.77–78.

13. Ibid., 3.3.107–8 and 3.3.14–16.

14. Ibid., 3.3.157–59, 3.5.113–14, and 3.3.62–64.

15. For a description of buck-washing, see Gervase Markham, *Countrey Contentments, or the English Huswife* (London: R. Jackson, 1623), sig. Z4-Aa1. Materials collected by Lena Cowen Orlin in *Elizabethan Households: An Anthology* (Washington, DC: Folger Shakespeare Library, 1995), pp. 53–54, nicely evoke the world of Elizabethan laundering.

16. "Si dierono insieme quel piacere che l'una parte e l'altra volse." Ser Giovanni, *Il Pecorone*, ed. Enzo Esposito (Ravenna: Longo, 1974), p. 29.

17. *Merry Wives*, 4.2.104–5 and 3.5.142–43.

18. Ibid., 3.3.154–56.

19. Boccaccio's *Corbaccio*, quoted by John Hines, *The Fabliau in English* (London: Longman, 1993), p. 234.

20. *Complete Prose Works of John Milton*, ed. Don M. Wolfe et al., 8 vols. (New Haven: Yale University Press, 1953–82), 3.542. Such thinking is still current. As an example, consider Charles Murray, the conservative advocate for the abolition of welfare, who was quoted as arguing that such abolition "is needed to reverse the nation's spiraling rates of out-of-wedlock births," which, according to Murray, "portend the rise of a white underclass and an authoritarian state"—the implication being that the antidote to a strong and intrusive state is an orderly and self-sufficient citizenry, orderly and self-sufficient especially in their domestic lives (*New York Times*, April 22, 1994).

21. *Merry Wives*, 4.4.6.

22. For a reading of *Merry Wives* that emphasizes "a communal harmony not dependent on the sovereign," see Carol Thomas Neely, "Constructing Female Sexuality in the Renaissance: Stratford, London, Windsor, Vienna," in *Feminism and Psychoanalysis*, ed. Richard Feldstein and Judith Roof (Ithaca: Cornell University Press, 1989), pp. 209–29. Similarly, R. S. White argues that "just as the town is seen as a backwater under siege from the London court and Europe, so also can it be seen, in Elizabethan terms, as a bulwark of 'traditional' values which were being threatened in the late sixteenth century by the increasing dominance of London, and even by the threat posed by Queen Elizabeth marrying a foreigner in a diplomatically arranged marriage." See White's book, *The Merry Wives of Windsor* (New York: Harvester Wheatsheaf, 1991), p. 14. The dangerous enabling of virtuous women that gets represented in *Merry Wives* may have found a quick answer in Henry Porter's *The Two Angry Women of Abington* (1598), in which patriarchal order is celebrated and female unruliness exposed.

23. *Merry Wives,* 4.2.98.

24. Ibid., 3.2.14–15, 3.2.39–40, and 4.2.171–79.

25. One version of this fear has been discussed by Nancy Cotton, "Castrating (W)itches: Impotence and Magic in *The Merry Wives of Windsor,*" *Shakespeare Quarterly* 38 (1987): 320–26.

26. *Richard III,* 3.4.72.

27. The association of malignant female power with witchcraft is not confined to the early modern period. A few years ago, a Faversham agronomist assured me, on the basis of no documentary evidence that I know of, that Alice Arden was a witch and that Arden was murdered by her and her coven in a ritual sacrifice. We need not assume that the early modern witch craze was simply misogynism in action to recognize in it and its more recent echoes masculine worry about women.

28. One set of associations is suggested by the name twice used for the old woman in the 1602 quarto of *Merry Wives:* "Gillian of Brainford." The name may come from Robert Copland's *Gyl of Braintfords Testament* (c. 1560), but had considerable currency in the 1590s. In addition to allusions by Thomas Nashe and John Harington, there seems to have been a now lost play by Thomas Dowton and Samuel Rowley called *Friar Fox and Gillian of Brainford* (1598). But of still greater interest is the name's recurrence in Thomas Dekker and John Webster's *Westward Ho* (1607), where Mistress Tenterhook exclaims, "I doubt that old hag Gillian of Brainford has bewitched me." In this and other citizen comedies of the early seventeenth century, Brainford is a place where wives go to "make merry," thus suggesting the continued linking of witchcraft, Brainford, and female independence that we find in *Merry Wives.* See *The Dramatic Works of Thomas Dekker,* ed. Fredson Bowers, 4 vols. (Cambridge: Cambridge University Press, 1953–62), 2.379 and 364.

29. The first statute against witchcraft was enacted in 1542 but was repealed in 1547, along with the other newly defined felonies of Henry VIII's reign. It was revived in 1563 and remained in force throughout the Elizabethan period. Bishop John Jewel is often thought to have prompted the 1563 reenactment. Preaching before the queen in 1560, Jewel remarked that "witches and sorcerers within these few last years are marvelously increased within this your grace's realm" and argued strongly for state intervention. "Your grace's subjects pine away even unto death, their color fadeth, their flesh rotteth, their speech is benumbed, their senses are bereft. Wherefore, your poor subjects' most humble petition unto your highness is that the laws touching such malefactors may be put in due execution. For the shoal of them is great, their doings horrible, their malice intolerable, the examples most miserable. And I pray God they never practice further than upon the subject." Witchcraft menaces the monarch directly. This had long been the principal—often the only—reason royal governments had for concerning themselves with it. Jewel plays on such traditional fears to enforce his argument. But that argument has a novel emphasis. Now, in this post-Reformation and post-Marian era of radically changing social and religious values, the government must also intervene to protect subjects from the effects of their own disorderly cultural practices. Enlightened by the godly ministers of the new religion, the crown must order and control the country. See George Lyman Kittredge, *Witchcraft in Old and New England* (Cambridge: Harvard University Press, 1929), p. 252.

30. For an extraordinarily thorough and richly suggestive examination of the structures of belief that supported both allegiance to monarchy and fear of witches, see Stuart Clark, *Thinking with Demons: The Idea of Witchcraft in Early Modern Europe* (Oxford: Clarendon Press, 1997), pp. 529–682. As Clark clearly demonstrates, the monarch and the witch were thought of as competitors for much the same sort of occult power, though the ultimate source of that power was presumed to be divine in one case and diabolic in the other. In this regard, it makes sense, as Clark argues, that Jean Bodin, the great sixteenth-century French theorist of monarchic absolutism, should also have written a book on demonology. Both express the same worldview.

31. William Rowley, Thomas Dekker, and John Ford, *The Witch of Edmonton* (4.1.65–66), in *Three Jacobean Witchcraft Plays*, ed. Peter Corbin and Douglas Sedge (Manchester: Manchester University Press, 1986), p. 187.

32. Thomas Heywood and Richard Brome, *The Late Lancashire Witches*, ed. Laird H. Barber (New York: Garland Publishing, 1979), p. 213. This claim that a duly constituted officer of the state could resist witchcraft had been made earlier by no less an authority than King James himself. In his *Daemonologie* (Edinburgh: Robert Waldegrave, 1597), James argues that where a "private person," apprehending a witch, would be unable to keep her from escaping or "doing hurt," "if on the other part, their apprehending and detention be by the lawful magistrate . . . their power is then no greater than before that ever they meddled with their master [Satan]. For where God begins justly to strike by his lawful lieutenant, it is not in the Devil's power to defraud or bereave him of the office or effect of his powerful and revenging scepter" (pp. 50–51).

33. William Perkins, *A Discourse of the Damned Art of Witchcraft* (Cambridge: Cantrel Legge, 1608), sigs. L7–M1^v and Q8–R1.

34. In 1579, there was a case in Windsor itself where witches were reported to "have made away and brought to their deaths by certain pictures of wax certain persons," a matter of particular concern to the lords of the privy council because similar devices had, so it was charged, been "intended to the destruction of her majesty's person." *Acts of the Privy Council*, ed. John Roche Dasent, n.s., vol. 11 (London: HM Stationery Office, 1895), p. 22.

35. *Merry Wives*, 4.5.117–20.

36. As Jean E. Howard has shown, that other play in which Brainford figures prominently and in which Brainford's witch gets at least an allusion, Dekker and Webster's *Westward Ho*, achieves a similar reformation of wayward men by the agency of their apparently revolted wives. See her "Women, Foreigners, and the Regulation of Urban Space in *Westward Ho*," in *Material London, Circa 1600*, ed. Lena Cowen Orlin (Philadelphia: University of Pennsylvania Press, forthcoming). On this pattern in *The Wise Woman of Hogsdon*, see Howard's *The Stage and Social Struggle in Early Modern England* (London: Routledge, 1994), pp. 73–92.

37. *Merry Wives*, 4.2.221–22 and 4.4.28–29.

38. Ibid., 5.5.46 and 5.5.93–101.

39. Leah S. Marcus, *Puzzling Shakespeare: Local Reading and Its Discontents* (Berkeley: University of California Press, 1988), pp. 51–105; and Louis Adrian Montrose, " 'Shaping Fantasies': Figurations of Gender and Power in Elizabethan Culture," *Representations* 2 (1983): 61–94. Helen Hackett offers a careful discussion of these issues in *Virgin Mother, Maiden Queen: Elizabeth I and the Cult of the Virgin Mary* (New York: St. Martin's Press, 1995), pp. 163–97 and 235–41.

40. *Merry Wives*, 4.2.219.

41. Peter Erickson, "The Order of the Garter, the Cult of Elizabeth, and Class-Gender Tension in *The Merry Wives of Windsor*," in *Shakespeare Reproduced*, ed. Jean Howard and Marion O'Connor (New York: Methuen, 1987), p. 124.

42. I pursue the connection between *Merry Wives* and Shakespeare's history plays in "Language Lessons: Linguistic Colonialism, Linguistic Postcolonialism, and the Early Modern English Nation," *Yale Journal of Criticism* 11 (1998): 289–99.

CHAPTER FOUR

1. Johann Wolfgang von Goethe, *Elective Affinities*, trans. James Anthony Froude and R. Dillon Boylan (New York: Frederick Ungar, 1962), p. 166.

2. For a recent restatement of this understanding, see Tzvetan Todorov, *Éloge du quotidien: Essai sur la peinture hollandaise du XVIIe siècle* (Paris: Adam Biro, 1993).

3. The marked change in the character of Dutch painting beginning in 1650 has been well documented by Gary Schwartz in a lecture delivered at the Getty Center in 1995, "Dutch Painting in 1650: An Exercise in the Willful Suspension of Hindsight." My thanks to Gary Schwartz for sending me a copy of this lecture.

4. In a paper I saw only after this chapter was completed and that coincidentally begins with the same ter Borch painting that provides my starting point, Ann Jensen Adams suggests a reason for this enjoyment: the mercenary exchange involved in the misnamed *Paternal Admonition* "serves," as she writes, "as a psychic site for a resolution of anxieties about potential dangers of the circulation of money" (p. 251, n. 25). This seems to me a plausible understanding. As I argue elsewhere in this chapter, these paintings regularly mute the threat they may be supposed to have represented. See Ann Jensen Adams, "Money and the Regulation of Desire: The Prostitute in the Marketplace in Seventeenth-Century Holland," in *Renaissance Culture and the Everyday,* ed. Patricia Fumerton and Simon Hunt (Philadelphia: University of Pennsylvania Press, 1999), pp. 229–53.

5. Gesina ter Borch's sketchbook portrait of her brother-in-law Sijbrant Schellinger and his family, often taken to be a copy of a lost painting by her brother, provides a nice example of what happens when the householder is there. Though the scene includes many familiar genre elements—a domestically defined woman, children at rest or at play, a table and bed, a map on the back wall—the presence of the husband/father breaks the narrative absorption characteristic of genre painting, taking the familiar iconographic implication from objects like the map and the bed and replacing the anonymity of genre with the nameable particularity of a portrait. See Alison McNeil Kettering, *Drawings from the Ter Borch Studio Estate,* 2 vols. ('s-Gravenhage: Staatsuitgeverij, 1988), vol. 2, plate XXI. On the characteristic sober black clothing of Dutch burghers in this period, see Irene Groenweg, "Regenten in het zwart: Vroom en deftig?" *Nederlands kunsthistorisch jaarboek* 46 (1995): 198–251.

6. On the question of who bought seventeenth-century Dutch paintings, see John Michael Montias, *Artists and Artisans in Delft: A Socio-Economic Study of the Seventeenth Century* (Princeton, NJ: Princeton University Press, 1982); Montias, "Socio-Economic Aspects of Netherlandish Art from the Fifteenth to the Seventeenth Century: A Survey," *Art Bulletin* 72 (1990): 358–73; and Alan Chong, "The Market for Landscape Painting in Seventeenth-Century Holland," in *Masters of Seventeenth-Century Dutch Landscape Painting,* ed. Peter C. Sutton (Boston: Museum of Fine Arts, 1987), pp. 104–20. I do not, by the way, mean to suggest that such men bought these genre paintings only for their own viewing and for the viewing of other men like them. They may also have bought them for their wives and daughters, as admonitory images. That is what one might conclude from a study like Wayne E. Franits's *Paragons of Virtue: Women and Domesticity in Seventeenth-Century Dutch Art* (Cambridge: Cambridge University Press, 1993), where genre paintings are shown to illustrate the precepts of household manuals like Jacob Cats's *Houwelyck* (1625). Through the paintings men might be thought to be telling women how (and often how not) to behave. Of course, the women may have taken pleasure in the paintings in ways that had little to do with moral admonition, whatever may have been intended. But by means of these paintings, men, I would contend, were also talking to other men about men's interests, interests that are deeply implicated in the behavior of women. And it is this last possibility, the circulation of objects, images, and meanings among men, that I pursue in this chapter.

7. That soldiers do appear with remarkable frequency is clear. Fully 40 percent (thirty-eight) of the ninety-five surviving genre paintings of Gerard ter Borch include soldiers, and soldiers appear in one out of every four of the extant paintings of Jacob Ochtervelt and one out of five of Pieter de Hooch's. These numbers are no doubt unusual. Ter Borch, Ochtervelt, and de Hooch, though we may not often think of them this way, were military specialists, the successors of earlier guardroom painters like Pieter Codde, Willem Duyster, Jacob Duck, and Simon Kick. But many other genre painters of the 1650s and 1660s also included soldiers among the figures in their work. Based on Montias's calculation that 68,000 to 78,000 paintings of all sorts were produced in the Dutch Republic each year during the 1650s and 1660s ("Socio-Economic Aspects," p. 373, n. 125), Chong's determination that 5.84 percent of the paintings in Dutch inventories for these decades were genre paintings (p. 116), and my own rough but conservative estimate that soldiers

showed up in some 5 percent of all the genre paintings produced in these decades, we may suppose that between 1650 and 1670 upward of 4,000 genre paintings with soldiers were put on the market, and the number may easily have been twice that.

8. M. D. Feld, "Middle-Class Society and the Rise of Military Professionalism: The Dutch Army, 1589–1609," *Armed Forces and Society* 1 (1975): 421 and 423. Feld provides a thorough discussion of the Dutch role in the early modern military revolution. For a more general introduction, see Michael Roberts, *The Military Revolution, 1560–1660* (Belfast: M. Boyd, 1956); and Geoffrey Parker, " 'The Military Revolution, 1560–1660': A Myth?" *Journal of Modern History* 48 (1976): 195–214. On the financing of the Dutch army, see Marjolein C. 't Hart, *The Making of a Bourgeois State: War, Politics, and Finance during the Dutch Revolt* (Manchester: Manchester University Press, 1993).

9. On the political workings of this bourgeois state, see J. L. Price, *Holland and the Dutch Republic: The Politics of Particularism* (Oxford: Clarendon Press, 1994); and Jonathan Israel, *The Dutch Republic: Its Rise, Greatness, and Fall, 1477–1806* (Oxford: Clarendon Press, 1995), esp. pp. 700–795.

10. Feld, "Middle-Class Society," p. 437.

11. These books and other defenses of the "True Freedom" are discussed by Herbert H. Rowen in *John de Witt: Grand Pensionary of Holland, 1625–1672* (Princeton: Princeton University Press, 1978), pp. 380–400. See also Eco Haitsma Mulier, "The Language of Seventeenth-Century Republicanism in the United Provinces: Dutch or European?" in *The Languages of Political Theory in Early-Modern Europe*, ed. Anthony Pagden (Cambridge: Cambridge University Press, 1987), pp. 179–95.

12. Pieter de la Court, *The True Interest and Political Maxims of the Republic of Holland* (1746; reprinted New York: Arno Press, 1972), pp. viii, 316, 336, and 49. This eighteenth-century translation is based on the enlarged 1669 edition of de la Court's book, which was originally published in 1662. De la Court's rhetoric in passages like these closely resembles that of earlier political pamphlets. Consider, for example, the charge in the anonymous pamphlet *D'Onstelde Amsterdammer* (1650; Knuttel Pamfletten no. 6849) that William II's ambition is to make himself "lord and master of all the United Netherlands" and to make "us all serfs and slaves." Like de la Court, this pamphleteer is especially worried about soldiers. It is to achieve his double ambition that William "first and foremost will try to maintain the army" (sig. A3 and B2).

13. De la Court, *True Interest*, p. 7.

14. Ibid., p. 402.

15. To judge from the more than 130 surviving civic guard portraits—the kind of painting we associate with Frans Hals or with Rembrandt's *Nightwatch*—Dutch burghers had their own military identity. But few of those group portraits were commissioned after 1650, and long before that date local shooting companies had confined their activity to banqueting, guard duty, and an occasional police intervention. Not since the 1580s had a civilian militia unit met a foreign foe on the field of battle. De la Court might still argue that Dutch cities could defend themselves without a standing army, but he also had to admit that "we who are naturally merchants cannot be turned into soldiers" (p. 209), and others agreed. Sir William Temple, the English ambassador to The Hague in the late 1660s and one of the most astute foreign observers of the Dutch scene, recalled the legendary valor of the Dutch and "the desperate defenses made against the Spaniards by this people in the beginnings of their state," but he then went on to insist that such valor was a thing of the past. "Since the whole application of their natives has been turned to commerce and trade and the vein of their domestic lives so much to parsimony . . . and since the main of all their forces and body of their army has been composed and continually supplied out of their neighbor nations," the United Provinces have lost their fighting spirit. Whatever they may once have been, civic guardsmen were no longer real soldiers. See Temple's *Observations upon the United Provinces of the Netherlands*, ed. Sir George Clark (Oxford: Clarendon Press, 1972), p. 92.

16. Temple, *Observations*, pp. 92–93 and 86.

17. Israel, *The Dutch Republic*, p. 880. As Israel points out, "extolling military feats would have meant enhancing the image of the Princes of Orange," something the regents were particularly eager not to do.

18. Fredrich van Vervou quoted by J. H. Bose, *"Had de mensch met één vrou niet connen leven . . .": Prostitutie in de literatuur van de zeventiende eeuw* (Zutphen: Walburg, 1985), p. 40.

19. Quoted by Bose, *"Had de mensch,"* p. 31.

20. F. van Vervou quoted by Bose, *"Had de mensch,"* p. 32.

21. On the distinctions in dress and manner between merchants and soldiers, see Temple, *Observations*, pp. 69–71.

22. Bärbel Hedinger, *Karten in Bildern: Zur Ikonographie der Wandkarte in holländischen Interieurgemälden des siebzehnten Jahrhunderts* (Hildesheim: Georg Olms, 1986), pp. 63–70. If one were so inclined, one could extend Hedinger's allegorical reading by pointing out that in 1654, when *The Naughty Drummer* was presumably painted, the prince of Orange, William III, who was born in 1650, was about the age of the boy in this painting.

23. See, for example, William W. Robinson, "The *Eavesdroppers* and Related Paintings by Nicolaes Maes," in *Holländische Genremalerei in 17. Jahrhundert: Symposium Berlin 1984*, ed. Henning Bock and Thomas W. Gaehtgens (Berlin: Mann, 1987), pp. 283–313. For a fine discussion of Maes's domestic interiors, see Martha Hollander, "The Divided Household of Nicolaes Maes," *Word & Image* 10 (1994): 138–55.

24. E. de Jongh, "Vermommingen van Vrouw Wereld in de 17de eeuw," in *Album amicorum J. G. van Gelder*, ed. J. Bruyn et al. (The Hague: Nijhoff, 1973), pp. 198–206. For an indication of how commonplace this interpretation has become, see *Masters of Seventeenth-Century Dutch Genre Painting*, ed. Peter C. Sutton (Philadelphia: Philadelphia Museum of Art, 1984), pp. 152, 173, 241, 281, and 293.

25. Simon Schama, *The Embarrassment of Riches: An Interpretation of Dutch Culture in the Golden Age* (Berkeley: University of California Press, 1988), pp. 216–18; and Bärbel Hedinger, "Karten in Bildern: Zur politischen Ikonographie der Wandkarte bei Willem Buytewech und Jan Vermeer," in *Holländische Genremalerei*, ed. Bock and Gaehtgens, pp. 139–68.

26. Franits, *Paragons of Virtue*, p. 24.

27. Martha Hollander, "Structures of Space and Society in the Seventeenth-Century Dutch Interior" (Ph.D. diss., University of California, Berkeley, 1990), p. 77. As its English equivalent for the "popular" meaning of *naaien*, *Cassell's Dutch Dictionary* (New York: Macmillan, 1978) simply gives "fuck." It is perhaps worth noting that another of Maes's paintings, the Philadelphia *Woman Plucking a Duck*, takes a second meaning from just such a visual/verbal pun—this time on the verb *vogelen*, which meant both "to bird" and "to copulate." And in *The Woman Plucking a Duck* the erotic sense is enforced by the glimpse in a far room of a pitcher, a glass of wine, and the corner of an unidentifiable wall map. See Sutton, *Masters of Seventeenth-Century Dutch Genre Painting*, p. 240.

28. For familiar examples of needlework set aside for romance, see Vermeer's *The Love Letter* (Rijksmuseum, Amsterdam), Gabriel Metsu's *The Letter Writer Surprised* (The Wallace Collection, London), and Metsu's *Woman Reading a Letter* (National Gallery of Ireland, Dublin).

29. John Nash, *Vermeer* (London: Scala, 1991), p. 63.

30. Lawrence Gowing, *Vermeer* (New York: Beechhurst Press, 1953), p. 48. For a more recent account of these conventions, see Albert Blankert, "Vermeer's Modern Themes and Their Tradition," in *Johannes Vermeer*, ed. Frederik J. Duparc and Arthur K. Wheelock, Jr. (New Haven: Yale University Press, 1995), pp. 31–45.

31. James A. Welu, "Vermeer and Cartography" (Ph.D. diss., Boston University, 1977), p. 107.

32. Hedinger, *Karten in Bildern*, pp. 79–84.

33. On this point, see Harry Berger, Jr., *Second World and Green World: Studies in Renaissance Fiction-Making* (Berkeley: University of California Press, 1988), pp. 454–58. I differ from Berger's

fine reading only in supposing that the undecidability of Vermeer's *Soldier and the Laughing Girl* can be assigned a quite specific historical significance.

34. For reproductions of these works, see Bob Haak, *The Golden Age: Dutch Painters of the Seventeenth Century* (New York: Abrams, 1984), p. 97; Hom Bevers, Peter Schatborn, and Barbara Welzel, *Rembrandt: The Master and His Workshop/Drawings and Etchings* (New Haven: Yale University Press, 1991), p. 55; and S. J. Gudlaugsson, *The Comedians in the Work of Jan Steen and His Contemporaries* (Soest: Davaco, 1975), p. 34. Art historians sometimes cite the elbow-jutting soldier in Pieter de Hooch's Dublin *Tric-Trac Players* (c. 1652–55) as the immediate source for the posture of Vermeer's soldier, and the pose has broader associations with masculinity and militarism throughout early modern European portraiture. See Joaneath Spicer, "The Renaissance Elbow," in *A Cultural History of Gesture: From Antiquity to the Present Day*, ed. Jan Bremmer and Herman Roodenburg (Cambridge: Polity Press, 1991), pp. 84–128. Whether in this case the pose is meant to be taken as the comically stagy exaggeration of a *miles gloriosus* or as a serious indication of masculine identity is thus no more certain than any other aspect of Vermeer's painting.

35. I am here imagining Vermeer's *Soldier and the Laughing Girl* as the central panel of a triptych like Robert Campin's *Annunciation* at the Cloisters (Metropolitan Museum of Art, New York). In another of his paintings of a woman drinking with a man (or, in this case, with men) of military appearance, the Brunswick *Girl with a Wineglass*, Vermeer himself includes the displaced burgher householder in a portrait hanging behind the foreground scene.

36. *Het rechte derde deel van 't Hollands praatje* (1650; Knuttel Pamfletten number 6842), p. 26.

37. In my reading of this painting and particularly in my identification of Scipio with the House of Orange, I am following Ann Jensen Adams, *Public Faces, Private Identities: Portraiture and the Production of Community in Seventeenth-Century Holland* (forthcoming). As David Kunzle shows in his book-in-progress, "The Soldier from Criminal to Courtier in Netherlandish Art, 1550–1672," explicit identifications of the prince of Orange with Scipio became still more common after 1672, when William III was restored to his father's offices, but clearly the association was already firmly in place well before that date. My thanks to both Ann Jensen Adams and David Kunzle for letting me see their work prior to its publication.

38. Philips Angel, *Lof der Schilder-Konst* (1642; reprinted Utrecht: Davaco, 1969), pp. 49–50.

39. Ibid., p. 50.

40. Nash, *Vermeer*, pp. 79–92.

41. See Baruch D. Kirschenbaum, *The Religious and Historical Paintings of Jan Steen* (New York: Allanheld and Schram, 1977), pp. 116–17; and Ann Jensen Adams, *Dutch and Flemish Paintings from New York Private Collections* (New York: National Academy of Design, 1988), p. 112.

42. Mieke Bal, *Reading "Rembrandt": Beyond the Word-Image Opposition* (Cambridge: Cambridge University Press, 1991). See especially Bal's chapter on Rembrandt's *Bathsheba* (pp. 216–46).

43. Svetlana Alpers, *The Art of Describing: Dutch Art in the Seventeenth Century* (Chicago: University of Chicago Press, 1983). For a discussion of the earlier appreciation of Dutch painting in terms of its realism, see Peter Demetz, "Defenses of Dutch Painting and the Theory of Realism," *Comparative Literature* 15 (1963): 97–115.

44. The continuing and active engagement of the Dutch, even in the northern Netherlands, with history painting throughout the seventeenth century has been richly documented in *Gods, Saints, and Heroes: Dutch Painting in the Age of Rembrandt*, ed. Albert Blankert et al. (Washington, DC: National Gallery of Arts, 1980); and in Haak, *The Golden Age*.

45. Hoogstraten did not invent this pastiche. It comes from a painting S. J. Gudlaugsson attributes to ter Borch's student, Caspar Netscher. See Gudlaugsson, *Geraert ter Borch*, 2 vols. (The Hague: Nijhoff, 1959–60), 2.118.

CHAPTER FIVE

1. See, for example, José Antonio Maravall, *Teatro y literatura en la sociedad barroca* (1972; rev. ed. Barcelona: Editorial Crítica, 1990); and José María Díez Borque, *Sociedad y teatro en la España de Lope de Vega* (Barcelona: Antoni Bosch, 1978).

2. Because of uncertainties about words like *comendador* (should it be translated or not?) and *alcalde* (should it be "judge" or "mayor" or left as is?), there are no widely accepted English translations for these titles. Likely translations would be *Peribáñez and the Commander of Ocaña; Fuenteovejuna* (sometimes printed as two words, *Fuente Ovejuna*, and sometimes literally translated, though it is the name of a town, as *The Sheep Well*); *The Best Judge, the King;* and *The Mayor of Zalamea*. The dates I supply in the text for the composition of these plays are at best rough approximations.

3. Mitchell Greenberg, *Canonical States, Canonical Stages: Oedipus, Othering, and Seventeenth-Century Drama* (Minneapolis: University of Minnesota Press, 1994), p. 33.

4. Lope de Vega, *El arte nuevo de hacer comedias en este tiempo*, ed. Juana de José Prades (Madrid: Consejo Superior de Investigaciones Científicas, 1971), pp. 285 and 288.

5. In blaming the audience and its poor taste for the unruly form of the *comedia nueva*, Lope's "defense" repeats the attack made on the theater Lope dominated by Miguel de Cervantes, whose own, more correct plays had little of the success Lope's enjoyed. For Cervantes's attack, see *Don Quixote*, pt. 1, chap. 48.

6. Noël Salomon, *Recherches sur le thème paysan dans la "comedia" au temps de Lope de Vega* (Bordeaux: Institut d'Études Ibériques et Ibéro-Américaines de l'Université de Bordeaux, 1965), pp. 747–79; and Maravall, *Teatro y literatura*, pp. 44–60.

7. Thomas Mun, *Englands Treasure by Forraign Trade* (1664; reprinted Oxford: Economic History Society, 1928); and Pieter de la Court, *The True Interest and Political Maxims of the Republic of Holland* (1746; reprinted New York: Arno Press, 1972). For the views of such Spanish economic thinkers as Martín de González de Cellorigo, Pedro de Valencia, López de Deza, and Benito Peñalosa de Mondragon, all of whom argued for the importance of agricultural production in Spain's economy and for the respect due rich peasants, see Salomon, *Recherches*, pp. 747–79 and 808–9; and José Antonio Maravall, "Reformismo social-agrario en la crisis del siglo XVII: Tierra, trabajo y salario, según Pedro de Valencia," *Bulletin hispanique* 72 (1970): 5–55.

8. J. H. Elliott, *Spain and Its World, 1500–1700: Selected Essays* (New Haven: Yale University Press, 1989), p. 108.

9. Lope de Vega, *El mejor alcalde, el rey* (printed with *Peribáñez y el comendador de Ocaña*), ed. Teresa Ferrer (Barcelona: Planeta, 1990), p. 222 (ll. 2409–10). Further quotations from either play will be translated from this edition and will be identified by line number.

10. Helen Nader, *Liberty in Absolutist Spain: The Habsburg Sale of Towns, 1516–1700* (Baltimore: Johns Hopkins University Press, 1990), pp. 8 and 207.

11. Marcelino Menéndez y Pelayo, *Estudios sobre el teatro de Lope de Vega*, 6 vols. (Madrid: Librería General de Victoriano Suárez, 1919–27), 5.201.

12. Teresa J. Kirschner, *El protagonista colectivo en* Fuenteovejuna *de Lope de Vega* (Salamanca: Ediciones Universidad de Salamanca, 1979). Kirschner reviews twentieth-century criticism of *Fuenteovejuna* on pp. 28–41.

13. Lope de Vega, *Fuente Ovejuna*, ed. Maria Grazia Profeti (Barcelona: Planeta, 1990), p. 41 (l. 867). Quotations from this play will be translated from this edition and will be identified by line number.

14. Quoted by Richard L. Kagan, "Clio and the Crown: Writing History in Habsburg Spain," in *Spain, Europe and the Atlantic World: Essays in Honour of John H. Elliott*, ed. Kagan and Geoffrey Parker (Cambridge: Cambridge University Press, 1995), p. 73.

15. Cervantes ironically repeats the terms *gobernar* and *república* with reference to small-town, peasant government in his *Entremés de la elección de los alcaldes de Daganzo* (*Interlude of the Election of the Alcaldes of Daganzo*). See Miguel de Cervantes, *Entremeses*, ed. Nicholas Spadaccini (Madrid:

Ediciones Cátedra, 1982), p. 168. In his introduction to this edition, Spadaccini suggests that Cervantes's comic portrayal of village authorities in this interlude and in his *Entremés del retablo de las maravillas* (*Interlude of the Pageant of Wonders*) may have been in direct reaction to the more favorable treatment they were getting in plays like *Peribáñez* and *Fuenteovejuna*, both of which first appeared on stage in the years shortly preceding the 1615 publication of Cervantes's interludes (pp. 55–73). If so, this echo, which Spadaccini does not mention, may exemplify that reaction.

16.   labrador de Ocaña,
     cristiano viejo, y rico, hombre tenido
     en gran veneración de sus iguales,
     y que, si se quisiese alzar agora
     en esta villa, seguirán su nombre
     cuantos salen al campo con su arado,
     porque es, aunque villano, muy honrado. (*Peribáñez*, 824–30)

17. Fui el mejor de mis iguales,
     y en cuantas cosas trataban
     me dieron primero voto,
     y truje seis años vara. (*Peribáñez*, 3036–39)

18. CRESPO.   Vos no debéis de alcanzar,
          señor, lo que en un lugar
          es un alcalde ordinario.
   DON LOPE.   ¿Será más de un villanote?
   CRESPO.   Un villanote será,
          que si cabezudo da
          en que ha de darle garrote,
          par Dios, se salga con ello.

Pedro Calderón de la Barca, *El alcalde de Zalamea*, ed. José María Díez Borque (Madrid: Clásicos Castalia, 1976), 3.764–71. For this edition, from which all subsequent quotations from *El alcalde de Zalamea* will be taken, passages are identified by act and line.

19. Sebastián de Covarrubias Horozco, *Tesoro de la lengua castellana o española* (1611; reprinted Madrid: Ediciones Turner, 1977), p. 994.

20. Todo la justicia vuestra
     es solo un cuerpo, no más.
     Si éste tiene muchas manos,
     decid, ¿qué más se me da
     matar con aquesta un hombre
     que estotra había de matar? (*El alcalde de Zalamea*, 917–22)

21. In an effort to get Peribáñez out of the way, the commander of Ocaña names him captain of one hundred peasant soldiers and thus raises him to *hidalgo* status. This social elevation allows Peribáñez to kill the commander as an equal, but when Peribáñez appears before the king, he identifies himself as being "of peasant rank" (de villana casta).

22. This earlier version of *El alcalde de Zalamea* has been edited with Calderón's play by Juan Alcina Franch (Barcelona: Editorial Juventud, 1970). Like many before him, Franch identifies the play as Lope's. I follow S. Griswold Morley and Courtney Bruerton who "believe it evident that this play is not, at least in its present form, by Lope." See Morley and Bruerton, *The Chronology of Lope de Vega's Comedias* (New York: Modern Language Association, 1940), p. 252.

23. For these claims of *hidalgo* descent in *El mejor alcalde, el rey*, see especially ll. 417–22, 578, 1361–62, and 1389. But notice the contrasting self-characterizations as "pobres labradores" (158) or "labrador tan grosero" (1182).

24. *El mejor alcalde, el rey*, 161.

25. Menéndez y Pelayo, *Estudios*, 6.209.

26. Covarrubias, *Tesoro*, pp. 1008–9 and 72.

27. Salomon, *Recherches*, p. 92.

28. *El alcalde de Zalamea*, 1.183–84; *Fuenteovejuna*, 989, 831, and 975; and *Peribáñez*, 3105–7.

29.   el más vano
hombre del mundo, y que tiene
más pompa y más presunción
que un infante de León. (*El alcalde de Zalamea*, 1.168–71)

30. For the classic discussion of this crucial issue, see Amérigo Castro, *De la edad conflictiva: Crisis de la cultura española en el siglo XVII*, 3rd ed. (Madrid: Taurus Ediciones, 1972).

31. Kagan, "Clio and the Crown," pp. 95, 82, and 95.

32. *Peribáñez* 1925–28 (cf. 1594–97). In the earlier version, the second line reads, as Ferrer points out in his edition (p. 88): "con la su capa pardilla."

33. Villano, si os he quitado
esa mujer, soy quien soy,
y aquí reino en lo que mando,
como el rey en su Castilla.
El mejor alcalde, el rey, 1580–83. For the phrase "the image of God," see 1697.

34. *Fuenteovejuna*, 603; *Peribáñez*, 2816–17; and *El mejor alcalde, el rey*, 2203. On the phrase "soy quien soy" (I am who I am), see Leo Spitzer, "Soy quien soy," *Nueva revista de filología hispánica* 1 (1947): 113–27.

35. *Peribáñez*, 2279–80.

36. Ibid., 2350. For the currency of this legend in Spanish literature, see Ramon Menéndez Pidal, *El rey Rodrigo en la literatura española* (Madrid: La Lectura, 1924). Lope himself wrote a play based on it, his *Postrer godo de España*, also known as *El último godo* (1600; *The Last Goth of Spain*).

37. On the comic associations of the name "Crespo," see Salomon, *Recherches*, pp. 138–39.

38. Both passages are quoted by Díez Borque in his introduction to *El alcalde de Zalamea*, pp. 64–65. See also Salomon (*Recherches*, pp. 893–909) for a full discussion of this issue.

39. Walter Cohen nicely defines the radical potential of these plays: "It is hard to imagine how a fully sympathetic portrayal of the peasantry literally getting away with murder at the expense of the aristocracy, with the crown confined to ambivalent acquiescence, could have served to reinforce the social status quo." *Drama of a Nation: Public Theater in Renaissance England and Spain* (Ithaca: Cornell University Press, 1985), p. 321.

40. Menéndez y Pelayo, *Estudios*, 5.70 and 203; and Salomon, *Recherches*, pp. 431 and 888.

41. Timbre y plumas no están bien
entre el arado y la pala,
bieldo, trillo y azadón;
que en nuestras paredes blancas
no han de estar cruces de seda,
sino de espigas y pajas
con algunas amapolas,
manzanillas y retamas. (*Peribáñez*, 2046–53)

42. Ibid., 76–77.

43. James Lloyd in his edition of *Peribáñez* (Warminster: Aris and Phillips, 1980). Lloyd gives the proverb as "éste es rey que nunca vio al Rey" (p. 234).

44. Yace aquí Juan Labrador,
que nunca sirvió a señor,
ni vio la corte ni al Rey.
Lope de Vega, *El villano en su rincón*, ed. Juan María Marín (Madrid: Ediciones Cátedra, 1987), 1.735–37.

45. Ibid., 1.283–300; and *El alcalde de Zalamea*, 1.769–70.

46. *Peribáñez*, 3034–35.

47. Cohen, *Drama of a Nation*, p. 321.

48. For the text of these chronicle sources, see Menéndez y Pelayo, *Estudios*, 5.195–97 (for *Fuenteovejuna*) and 4.64–65 (for *El mejor alcalde, el rey*).

49. Los casos de la honra son mejores
    Porque mueven con fuerza a toda gente. (*El arte nuevo*, 327–28)

50. George Mariscal, "Symbolic Capital in the Spanish *Comedia*," *Renaissance Drama* n.s. 21 (1990): 145.

51. This resistance continues in some modern scholarship, most energetically in Dian Fox's *Refiguring the Hero: From Peasant to Noble in Lope de Vega and Calderón* (University Park: Pennsylvania State University Press, 1991). Convinced that Lope and Calderón cannot have meant us to admire and approve their peasant protagonists, particularly not in the bloody actions they take against their betters, Fox argues with considerable ingenuity that their behavior is villainous in every sense of the word. Needless to say, I remain unpersuaded. But I am impressed with the evidence she produces. That evidence may not prove her claim that Peribáñez, the people of Fuenteovejuna, and Pedro Crespo are the villains she wants to make them, but it does show that their actual heroic stature could be established only by reversing, as I think both Lope and Calderón do, deeply entrenched social prejudice. Socially and historically, *Peribáñez, Fuenteovejuna*, and *El alcalde de Zalamea* are as remarkable as they are theatrically.

52. *Peribáñez*:
    Soy vasallo, es mi señor,
    vivo en su amparo y defensa;
    si en quitarme el honor piensa,
    quitaréle yo la vida. (*Peribáñez*, 1750–53)
    Pedro Crespo:
    Al Rey la hacienda y la vida
    se ha de dar; pero el honor
    es patrimonio del alma,
    y el alma sólo es de Dios. (*El alcalde de Zalamea* 1.873–76)
Fuenteovejuna, 2106.

CHAPTER SIX

1. Quoted by Richard Feller, "Von der alten Eidgenossenschaft," in *Schweizerische Akademiereden*, ed. Fritz Strich (Bern: Verlag der Akademischen Buchhandlung Paul Haupt, 1945), p. 471. Thanks to Julie Carlson for help in translating this passage.

2. James H. Davis, Jr., and Ruth Lundelius, "Calderón's *El alcalde de Zalamea* in Eighteenth-Century France," *Kentucky Romance Quarterly* 23 (1976): 213–24; Martin Franzbach, *El teatro de Calderón en Europa* (Madrid: Fundación Universitaria Española, 1982), pp. 114–20; Henry W. Sullivan, "*El alcalde de Zalamea* de Calderón en el teatro europeo de la segunda mitad del siglo XVIII," *Calderón: Actas del Congreso Internacional sobre Calderón y el teatro español del Siglo de Oro*, ed. Luciano García Lorenzo, 3 vols. (Madrid: Consejo Superior de Investigaciones Científicas, 1983), 3.1471–77; and Henry Anthony Stavan, "Des adaptations françaises de L'alcalde de Zalamea à la fin du XVIIIe siècle," *Revue d'histoire du théâtre* 44 (1992): 320–29.

3. Jean-Jacques Rousseau, *Politics and the Arts: Letter to M. d'Alembert on the Theatre*, trans. Allan Bloom (Glencoe, IL: Free Press, 1960), p. 126.

4. Rousseau, *Politics and the Arts*, p. 35.

5. "Un honnête homme, sensible au deshonneur de sa maison, devient l'objet de la risée publique, parce qu'étant fort riche il avoit épousé une demoiselle qui n'avoit rien: ce qui se voit tous les jours, et ce qui est bon, politiquement, pour détruire l'horrible inégalité des fortunes"; Molière "a voulu humilier la bourgeoisie, l'ordre sans contredit le plus respectable de l'État, ou

pour mieux dire l'ordre qui fait l'État." Louis Sébastien Mercier, *Du théâtre ou nouvel essai sur l'art dramatique* (1773; reprinted Hildesheim: Georg Olms Verlag, 1973), pp. 88–89.

6. Voltaire, *Le siècle de Louis XIV*, ed. René Groos, 2 vols. (Paris: Librarie Garnier Frères, 1947), 2.322; Rousseau, *Politics and the Arts*, p. 131; and Denis Diderot, *Oeuvres complètes*, ed. Herbert Dieckmann, Jacques Proust, and Jean Varloot, 33 vols. (Paris: Hermann, 1975–), 10.395 and xvii. Unless otherwise indicated, all subsequent quotations from Diderot will be from this edition.

7. The full title of Beaumarchais's play is *L'autre Tartuffe ou la mère coupable* (*The Other Tartuffe or the Guilty Mother*). *La mère coupable* is its more familiar shortened title. I will, however, continue to refer to it as *L'autre Tartuffe* as a way of keeping attention on its connection to Molière's play.

8. "Et tel que l'on le voit, il est bien gentilhomme." Molière, *Oeuvres complètes*, ed. Georges Couton, 2 vols. (Paris: Gallimard, 1971), 1.917. Subsequent quotations from Molière will be from this Pléiade edition and will be cited by volume and page numbers.

9. "*Gentilhomme:* homme noble d'extraction, qui ne doit point sa noblesse ni à sa charge, ni aux lettres du prince." Antoine Furetière, *Essai d'un dictionnaire universel* (1690), quoted by Couton, 1.1348.

10. "Je veux avoir un gendre gentilhomme" (Molière, *Oeuvres complètes*, 2.755).

11. The play does not explicitly define Orgon's own social standing. Judging from his wealth and service to the crown, James F. Gaines has guessed that he might have been seen as an *officier de longue robe*. But even at this, Orgon would not be a *gentilhomme* and would thus be of a rank inferior to the one Tartuffe claims. As Gaines remarks, "What a treat for an *officier* to come to the rescue of a *noble de race* . . . !" See Gaines, *Social Structures in Molière's Theater* (Columbus: Ohio State University Press, 1984), pp. 201–2 and 206.

12. D'Alembert himself used *Tartuffe* to turn the question back at Rousseau: "I do not know, sir, what you think of [*Tartuffe*]; it was well made to earn your blessing." And in another response to Rousseau's *Lettre à M. d'Alembert sur les spectacles*, Jean-François Marmontel used *Tartuffe* to argue that virtue is never ridiculous in Molière: "The proof of this is that if the character who is being mocked is worthy and the wrong being done him becomes serious, the humor ends and indignation takes its place. One can see an example of this in the fifth act of *Tartuffe*, that masterpiece of comic theater, of which M. Rousseau says not a word." Quoted by Michel Delon, "Lectures de Molière au 18e siècle," *Europe* 523–24 (1972): 96.

13. According to an anonymous "relation" of 1664, quoted by Herman Prins Salomon, *Tartuffe devant l'opinion française* (Paris: Presses Universitaires de France, 1962), p. 13.

14. Hardouin, archbishop of Paris, and Pierre Roullé, curate of Saint-Barthélemy in Paris, quoted in Georges Mongrédien, *Recueil des textes et des documents du XVIIe siècle relatifs à Molière*, 2 vols. (Paris: Éditions du Centre National de la Recherche Scientifique, 1965), 1.292 and 220.

15. "Les tartuffes, sous main, ont eu l'adresse de trouver grâce auprès de Votre Majesté; et les originaux enfin ont fait supprimer la copie" (Molière, *Oeuvres complètes*, 1.890).

16. Molière's first appeal to the king begins: "Le devoir de la comédie étant de corriger les hommes en les divertissant, j'ai cru que, dans l'emploi où je me trouve, je n'avais rien de mieux à faire que d'attaquer par des peintures ridicules les vices de mon siècle" (*Oeuvres complètes*, 1.889).

17. See Salomon, *Tartuffe devant l'opinion française*, pp. 14–34.

18. See, however, Couton's argument that the secret Compagnie du Saint-Sacrement de l'Autel held a central, if not exclusive, position in the constellation of religious organizations that prompted Molière's attack (in Molière, *Oeuvres complètes*, 1.861–72).

19. ". . . usurper céans un pouvoir tyrannique" (Molière, *Oeuvres complètes*, 1.897).

20. "L'esprit de tout cet acte et son seul effet et but jusqu'ici n'a été que de représenter les affaires de cette pauvre famille dans la dernière désolation. . . . Il me semble que si, dans tout le reste de la pièce, l'auteur a égalé tous les anciens et surpassé tous les modernes, on peut dire que dans ce dénouement il s'est surpassé lui-même, n'y ayant rien de plus grand, de plus magnifique

et de plus merveilleux, et cependant rien de plus naturel, de plus heureux et de plus juste, puisqu'on peut dire que s'il était permis d'oser faire le caractère de l'âme de notre grand monarque, ce serait sans doute dans cette plénitude de lumière, cette prodigieuse pénétration d'esprit, et ce discernement merveilleux de toutes choses qu'on le ferait consister" (Georges Couton in Molière, *Oeuvres complètes*, 1.1168).

21. Quoted in Mongrédien, *Recueil*, 1.334–35. For Boileau's defense of *Tartuffe*, see 1.225. It is worth noting that Boileau's rewrite of *Tartuffe* would produce a play much more like *The Merry Wives of Windsor*, where the community unites to expose and punish the sexually predatory invader. Even if that exposure and punishment occur in Windsor Park and at the hands of a queen of fairies, the actual queen of England is not made its agent.

22. As Mercier acknowledges, the source of his play *La maison de Molière* is *Il Moliere* of Carlo Goldoni. On Goldoni's own relation to the bourgeois drama of Diderot, Mercier, and their contemporaries, see Michel Olsen, *Goldoni et le drame bourgeois* (Rome: "L'Erma" di Bretschneider, 1995).

23. Louis Sébastien Mercier, *Théâtre complet* (Geneva: Slatkine Reprints, 1970), p. 300. In this facsimile reprint of the 1778 Amsterdam edition of Mercier's *Théâtre complet*, the play is simply called *Molière*. The title appears as *La maison de Molière* on the Paris edition of 1788.

24. "Notre théâtre touche à une révolution nécessaire et inévitable"; "on se servira de mon nom même, pour arrêter les progrès de l'art, et barrer ceux qui viendront après moi" (Mercier, *Théâre complet*, pp. 272 and 315).

25. Quoted by Norbert Elias, *The Court Society*, trans. Edmund Jephcott (Oxford: Basil Blackwell, 1983), p. 54.

26. Robert Darnton, *What Was Revolutionary about the French Revolution?* (Waco, TX: Markham Press Fund, 1990), p. 21.

27. "Un incident imprévu qui se passe en action et qui change subitement l'état des personnages, est un coup de théâtre. Une disposition de ces personnages sur la scène, si naturelle et si vraie, que rendue fidèlement par un peintre, elle me plairait sur la toile, est un tableau" (Diderot, *Oeuvres complètes*, 10.92).

28. On Wille's friendship with Diderot, see Else Marie Bukdahl, *Diderot, critique d'art*, trans. Jean-Paul Faucher, 2 vols. (Copenhagen: Rosenkilde and Bagger, 1980), 1.248, 1.283, 1.377, 2.116, 2.286. As Wille reports in his *Mémoires*, he and Diderot, when both were in their twenties, had rooms in the same house in Paris. See Johann Georg Wille, *Mémoires et journal*, 2 vols. (Paris: Jules Renouard, 1857), 1.91.

29. "Justine approche un métier à tapisserie. Rosalie est tristement appuyée sur ce métier. Justine est assise d'un autre côté. Elles travaillent. Rosalie n'interrompt son ouvrage que pour essuyer des larmes qui tombent de ses yeux. Elle le reprend ensuite. Le silence dure un moment, pendant lequel Justine laisse l'ouvrage et considère sa maîtresse" (Diderot, *Oeuvres complètes*, 10.29).

30. For the importance of this "quiet intensity and absorption" in eighteenth-century French painting and for Diderot's appreciation of these qualities, see Michael Fried, *Absorption and Theatricality: Painting and the Beholder in the Age of Diderot* (Berkeley: University of California Press, 1980). On the more specific meaning of Chardin's genre paintings and still lifes, see Jack Undank, "Chardin and the Domestic Sublime," *Studies in Eighteenth-Century Culture* 19 (1989): 3–22.

31. "Elles sont occupées à des petits ouvrages de broderie ou de filets; elles se regardent plusieurs fois comme voulant se parler et ne le font pas; enfin. . . ." Jean Marie Collot d'Herbois, *Il y a bonne justice ou le paysan magistrat* (Marsailles: Sube et Laporte, 1778), p. 7.

32. Diderot's comments on Chardin are collected in Marianne Roland Michel's *Chardin*, trans. Eithne McCarthy (New York: Harry N. Abrams, 1996), pp. 264–67.

33. "C'est vraiment là mon homme que ce Greuze. Oubliant pour un moment ses petites compositions qui me fourniront des choses agréables à lui dire, j'en viens tout de suite à son tableau de la *Piété filiale*, qu'on intitulerait mieux: *De la récompense de la bonne éducation donnée*.

D'abord le genre me plaît. C'est la peinture morale. Quoi donc, le pinceau n'a-t-il pas été assez et trop longtemps consacré à la débauche et au vice? Ne devons-nous pas être satisfaits de le voir concourir enfin avec la poésie dramatique à nous toucher, à nous instruire, à nous corriger et à nous inviter à la vertu? Courage, mon ami Greuze! Fais de la morale en peinture, et fais-en toujours comme cela. Lorsque tu sera au moment de quitter la vie, il n'y aura aucune de tes compositions que tu ne puisses te rappeler avec plaisir. Que n'étais-tu à côté de cette jeune fille qui regardant la tête de ton *Paralytique*, s'écria avec une vivacité charmante: 'Ah, mon Dieu, comme il me touche; mais si je le regarde encore, je crois que je vais pleurer'; et que cette jeune fille n'était-elle la mienne! Je l'aurais reconnue à ce mouvement. Lorsque je vis ce vieillard éloquent et pathétique, je sentis, comme elle, mon âme s'attendrir et des pleurs prêts à tomber de mes yeux" (Diderot, *Oeuvres complètes*, 13.393–94).

34. "Le principal personnage, celui qui occupe le milieu de la scène, et qui fixe l'attention" (Diderot, *Oeuvres complètes*, 13.394).

35. Much of what I say here and in the following pages about Diderot and the bourgeois drama would apply equally well to Rousseau and especially his *Julie ou la nouvelle Héloïse* (1761; *Julie or the New Heloise*). Though by the time he had completed *La nouvelle Héloïse*, Rousseau had broken with Diderot, had attacked bourgeois drama (including especially Diderot's *Père de famille*), and was claiming to consider *les philosophes* as little a part of his fit audience as any denizen of the old regime's fashionable *monde*, his literary values, aims, and means closely resembled theirs. On Rousseau and *La nouvelle Héloïse*, see Tony Tanner, *Adultery in the Novel: Contract and Transgression* (Baltimore: Johns Hopkins University Press, 1979), pp. 113–78; Robert Darnton, *The Great Cat Massacre and Other Episodes in French Cultural History* (New York: Basic Books, 1984), pp. 214–56; and Elizabeth J. MacArthur, *Extravagant Narratives: Closure and Dynamics in the Epistolary Form* (Princeton: Princeton University Press, 1990), pp. 186–270.

36. "Qui est-ce qui a lu les ouvrages de Richardson sans désirer de connaître cet homme, de l'avoir pour frère ou pour ami? Qui est-ce qui ne lui a pas souhaité toutes sortes de bénédictions?" (Diderot, *Oeuvres complètes*, 13.196). Compare the response to Greuze by the abbé de la Porte: "This artist is only 29 years old. Here are works that can gain a man glory. They do honor to his mind; they sing the praise of his heart. One believes that he has a delicate and sensitive soul. One would like to come to know him." But de la Porte then goes on to add this suggestive comment: "He is the Molière of our painters." Molière stands both for a kind of work, familiar and domestic, and for a sensitivity of soul. De la Porte quoted and translated by Thomas E. Crow, *Painters and Public Life in Eighteenth-Century Paris* (New Haven: Yale University Press, 1985), p. 140.

37. "[L]es années du travail et de la moisson des lauriers se passent, et je m'avance vers le dernier terme, sans rien tenter qui puisse me recommander aussi aux temps à venir" (Diderot, *Oeuvres complètes*, 13.208).

38. Mercier, *Du théâtre*, pp. v–vi, 45, and 152. Compare the significant but nevertheless far more limited sense Voltaire gave the term in applying it to Molière, whom he called "a legislator of good manners [*des bienséances*]" (*Le siècle de Louis XIV*, 2.125). Needless to say, Mercier's poet-legislator would not limit his edicts to matters of *bienséance*.

39. "Tombez, tombez, murailles, qui séparez les genres!" (Mercier, *Du théâtre*, p. 105n).

40. *Lettre sur le drame, à M. P. . .* (1774), quoted by Julie Candler Hayes, *Identity and Ideology: Diderot, Sade, and the Serious Genre* (Amsterdam: John Benjamins Publishing House, 1991), p. 86. The full quotation, which I have abridged and paraphrased in the text, reads: "Il est admis et démontré depuis longtemps par le bon goût, qu'il existe entre le tragique et le comique: *nec ultrà, nec infrà*. . . . Expliquez donc vos vues et vos prétentions. Ou vous entendez par votre intermédiaire, un genre nouveau découvert entre le tragique et le comique, et vous flottez dans le vuide; ou vous entendez un composé des deux seuls genres qui puissent réellement exister; et ce composé n'est autre chose que l'ancienne Tragi-comédie, vieux monstre proscrit depuis si longtemps; alors vous devenez monstreux."

41. *Seconde lettre de M. le comte D**** (1777), quoted by Edgar Munhall, *Jean-Baptiste Greuze, 1725–1805* (Hartford: Wadsworth Atheneum, 1976), p. 171.

42. "Cependant je proteste que le Père qui fait la lecture à sa famille, le Fils ingrat et les Fiançailles de Greuze . . . sont autant pour moi des tableaux d'histoire que les Sept Sacrements du Poussin, la Famille de Darius de le Brun, ou la Susanne de Vanloo" (Diderot, *Oeuvres complètes*, 14.398–99). See also the discussion of Greuze's ambitions as a history painter in Munhall, *Greuze*, pp. 12–13 and 170–81. The Salons themselves and Greuze's place in them have been brilliantly investigated by Thomas E. Crow in *Painters and Public Life in Eighteenth-Century Paris*. Crow quotes, in particular, an anonymous eighteenth-century critic who clearly reverses Diderot's position, arguing that Greuze's "invalid grandfather" and the figures from his other genre paintings are specifically unfit for history (p. 17). Diderot's own inconsistencies with regard to Greuze and the hierarchy of painting are suggested by Jean Seznec, "Diderot et l'affaire Greuze," *Gazette des Beaux-Arts*, 6th ser., 67 (1966): 339–56.

43. "Sous ce point de vue j'oserai dire que souvent l'histoire est un mauvais roman, et que le roman, comme tu l'as fait, est une bonne histoire" (Diderot, *Oeuvres complètes*, 13.202). As the surrounding paragraph makes clear, Diderot means *histoire* in the sense of *history* not of *story*. It is Richardson's superior truthfulness that lifts his work into the realm of history, that makes it more historical than most history.

44. It should perhaps be added that the separation between the arts—between drama, painting, and prose narrative—proves equally porous in Diderot's work. Not only does drama make itself over as a kind of painting, but it also finds at least one model for its new gestural language in neither theater nor painting but rather in the novels of Richardson, though once again Diderot's language characteristically runs the kinds together: "It is the painting of movement that enchants, especially in domestic novels" (Diderot, *Oeuvres complètes*, 10.411). With similar generic synesthesia, he calls *Pamela, Clarissa*, and *Sir Charles Grandison* "three great dramas," suggests that it would be easy to write a novel based on Greuze's paintings, and constructs his own plays as a series of affecting *tableaux* (13.196 and 14.177). Indeed, it is difficult when reading *Le fils naturel* and its accompanying *Entretiens* to know whether Diderot means to give us a play, a picture gallery, a novel, an autobiographical sketch, a treatise, or a strange hybrid drawn from all five.

45. "Si la mère d'Iphigénie se montrait un moment reine d'Argos et femme du général des Grecs, elle ne me paraîtrait que la dernière des créatures. La véritable dignité, celle qui me frappe, qui me renverse; c'est le tableau de l'amour maternel dans toute sa vérité" (Diderot, *Oeuvres complètes*, 10.93). "Croyez vous qu'une femme d'un autre rang aurait été plus pathétique? Non. La même situation lui eût inspiré le même discours" (10.100).

46. "Est-il possible qu'on ne sentira point que l'effet du malheur est de rapprocher les hommes?" (Diderot, *Oeuvres complètes*, 10.92).

47. "Tout ce qui mêle les différens états de la société, et tend à rompre l'excessive inégalité des conditions, source de tous nos maux, est bon politiquement parlant. Tout ce qui rapproche les citoyens est le ciment sacré qui unit les nombreuses familles d'un vaste Etat, qui doit les voir d'un oeil égal" (Mercier, *Théâtre complet*, p. 243).

48. Scott S. Bryson, *The Chastened Stage: Bourgeois Drama and the Exercise of Power* (Saratoga, CA: Anma Libri, 1991), p. 117 (italics Bryson's). For an extended account of the relation of the family scenes in bourgeois drama and genre painting to revolutionary ideology, see Lynn Hunt, *The Family Romance of the French Revolution* (Berkeley: University of California Press, 1992), pp. 17–52.

49. "Le dirai-je? . . . J'ai vu de la diversité des jugements, naître des haines secrètes, des mépris cachés, en un mot, les mêmes divisions entre des personnes unies, que s'il eût été question de l'affaire la plus sérieuse. Alors je comparais l'ouvrage de Richardson à un livre plus sacré encore, à un Évangile apporté sur la terre pour séparer l'époux de l'épouse, le père du fils, la fille de la mère, le frère de la soeur; et son travail rentrait ainsi dans la condition des êtres les plus parfaits de la nature" (Diderot, *Oeuvres complètes*, 13.200; ellipsis in original).

50. "On pourroit juger de l'ame de chaque homme par le degré d'émotion qu'il manifeste au Théâtre: si son visage reste indifférent, si son oeil n'est point humide . . . c'est un méchant, à coup sûr"; "le Poëte doit sçavoir aussi que les orages civils sont le garant de la santé des peuples" (Mercier, *Du théâtre*, pp. 12–13 and 225). Elsewhere in this *Essai sur l'art dramatique*, as the book is subtitled, Mercier talks of the theater as "a sovereign court" and compares its action to that of a "poor and virtuous" cobbler of Messina, who decided to solve the corruption of his native city by murdering anyone he judged guilty (pp. 62–65).

51. Peter Szondi, "Tableau et coup de théâtre: Pour une sociologie de la tragédie domestique et bourgeoise chez Diderot et Lessing," *Poétique* 9 (1972): 1–14.

52. Robert Mauzi, *L'idée du bonheur au XVIIIe siècle* (Paris: Librairie Armand Colin, 1960), p. 175 (Mauzi's italics). See also Mauzi's chapter "Le bonheur bourgeois" (pp. 269–89).

53. The classic expression of this new vision is to be found in Emmanuel Joseph Sieyès (Abbé Sieyès), *Qu'est-ce que le tiers état?* (1789).

54. Raymond Williams, *Marxism and Literature* (Oxford: Oxford University Press, 1977), pp. 180–81.

55. Hayes, *Identity and Ideology*, p. 10. The charge of despotism was lodged against the "characters" of Molière's kind of comedy by Mercier, who makes it clear that he considers this theatrical despotism a close relation of the political despotism of absolute monarchs (*Du théâtre*, pp. 106–7 and passim).

56. Diderot (*Oeuvres complètes*, 10.144); and Beaumarchais, *Théâtre complet*, ed. Maurice Allem and Paul Courant (Paris: Éditions Gallimard, 1957), pp. 5–21. Subsequent quotations from Beaumarchais's dramatic writings will be taken from this Pléiade edition. Julie Carlson discusses identification in bourgeois and domestic drama in "Like Me: An Introduction to Domestic/Tragedy," *South Atlantic Quarterly* 98 (1999): 331–53. The pun in Carlson's title points toward what she calls "the genre's founding joint imperatives to 'like' and to 'be like'"—i.e., to feel affection for and to sense an identification with the bourgeois and domestic world the plays represent.

57. The element of moral coercion in bourgeois drama is central to the argument of Scott S. Bryson's *The Chastened Stage*. As Bryson summarizes his thesis, "the drama's utopian aspirations to a democracy of sentiment and virtue disclose another, less sanguine democracy, that of universal submission and docility to a system of representational and disciplinary power. Behind the somewhat saccharine moral virtue of the bourgeois stage and genre painting is, literally, virtue ('virtus'): *force, power*" (p. 5).

58. I have borrowed these quotations from Julie Candler Hayes's excellent discussion of the critical response to eighteenth-century bourgeois drama (*Identity and Ideology*, pp. 85–87). For a comprehensive documentary record of the contemporary response to Diderot's two bourgeois dramas, see Anne-Marie Chouillet, "Dossier du *Fils naturel* et du *Père de famille*," *Studies on Voltaire and the Eighteenth Century* 208 (1982): 73–166.

59. I am here summarizing in a single sentence arguments developed with great richness and complexity in Michael Fried's *Absorption and Theatricality* and in David Marshall's *The Surprising Effects of Sympathy: Marivaux, Diderot, Rousseau, and Mary Shelley* (Chicago: University of Chicago Press, 1988). Marshall interestingly notes in passing that Molière's attack on hypocrisy in *Tartuffe* made that play especially attractive to Diderot in his own attack on theatricality (p. 111).

60. "Spectacle domestique et réel." See Marshall's discussion of this phrase from Diderot's *Paradoxe sur le comédien* (*The Surprising Effects of Sympathy*, pp. 118–19). Though Diderot refers here to an actual, rather than a theatrical, deathbed scene, the phrase captures the effect he was trying to achieve in his bourgeois dramas.

61. "Heureux, cent fois heureux . . . , M. Baliveau capitoul de Toulouse! C'est M. Baliveau qui boit bien, qui mange bien, qui digère bien, qui dort bien. C'est lui qui prend son café le matin; qui fait la police au marché, qui pérore dans sa petite famille, qui arrondit sa fortune, qui prêche à ses enfants la fortune, qui vend à temps son avoine et son blé, qui garde dans son cellier ses vins, jusqu'à ce que la gelée des vignes en ait amené la cherté, qui sait placer sûrement ses fonds,

qui se vante de n'avoir jamais été enveloppé dans aucune faillite, qui vit ignoré et pour qui le bonheur inutilement envié d'Horace, le bonheur de mourir ignoré fut fait" (Diderot, *Oeuvres complètes*, 16.208). M. Baliveau is a character in Alexis Piron's popular play *La métromanie* (1738), where he is contrasted with his poet nephew.

62. ". . . rares et divins insensés [qui] font de la poésie dans la vie. De là leur malheur" (Diderot, *Oeuvres complètes*, 16.207). The full passage from which the reference to Clarissa's lost honor is taken reads as follows: "Et quel est le moment où Clémentine [in *Sir Charles Grandison*] et Clarisse deviennent deux créatures sublimes? Le moment où l'une a perdu l'honneur et l'autre la raison" (13.207).

63. "Le poëte est l'interprète des malheureux, l'orateur public des opprimés" (Mercier, *Du théâtre*, p. 135).

64. "Ce tableau offert à la patrie, pourroit l'éclairer par sentiment, lui donner des idées plus saines de politique et de législation"; "nourrir le génie républicain, et rendre la Monarchie odieuse" (Mercier, *Théâtre complet*, p. 10).

65. In the preface to *Jenneval*, Mercier raises the question that faced all the French eighteenth-century writers of bourgeois drama: "Mais comment aussi conserver toute la force théâtrale, et ménager la délicatesse Françoise qui, dans ce point, me parait juste et respectable? Comment exposer la passion dans toute son énergie, et ne point perdre le but moral; faire frémir et ne point faire horreur?" (*Théâtre complet*, p. 9).

66. Adherence to one of the three unities, the unity of place, did, however, serve to intensify the domestic focus of eighteenth-century French bourgeois drama. Virtually without exception, these plays begin in a bourgeois (or bourgeoislike) home and never leave it.

67. We might recall here the many images of needlework or of needlework set aside for romance in Dutch genre painting, the account of Casilda sewing under the commander's arms in *Peribáñez*, or the scene of Jane Shore at her work as the disguised King Edward enters her husband's shop in Heywood's *Edward IV*. Throughout early modern European drama and painting, sewing figures as the opposite of illicit desire. For a valuable discussion of this motif in English Renaissance drama, see Lena Cowen Orlin, "Three Ways to be Invisible in the Renaissance: Sex, Reputation, and Stitchery," in *Renaissance Culture and the Everyday*, ed. Patricia Fumerton and Simon Hunt (Philadelphia: University of Pennsylvania Press, 1999), pp. 183–203.

68. *Le Mercure de France* (December 1740): 2711. For the strict moral lesson some contemporary viewers read into this painting and the engraving based on it, see Anne L. Schroder, "Genre Prints in Eighteenth-Century France: Production, Market, and Audience," in *Intimate Encounters: Love and Domesticity in Eighteenth-Century France*, ed. Richard Rand (Princeton: Princeton University Press, 1997), pp. 72–75.

69. See Edgar Munhall, "Greuze and the Protestant Spirit," *Art Quarterly* 27 (1961): 1–23.

70. "Les Protestants en France, sont soumis à un intolérable despotisme. Quoi qu'il n'y ait pas à présent de persécution ouverte, ils dépendent d'un caprice du roi, de la reine, du parlement ou d'un ministre. Leurs mariages ne sont pas légaux; leurs testaments n'ont aucune force devant la loi; leurs enfants sont considérés comme bâtards; leurs personnes comme pendables." Marie Joseph Yves Gilbert du Motier, marquis de Lafayette, quoted by Munhall, "Greuze and the Protestant Spirit," p. 4.

71. "Sottises de toutes espèce: la liberté de penser, l'attraction, l'électricité, le tolérantisme, l'inoculation, le quinquina, l'Encyclopédie et les drames" (Beaumarchais, *Théâtre complet*, p. 176).

72. Beaumarchais's characterizations of his various plays and of his theatrical career as a whole can be found in his preface to *Le mariage de Figaro* (*Théâtre complet*, pp. 233–58).

73. "C'est détestable, cela ne sera jamais joué, il faudrait détruire la Bastille pour que la représentation de cette pièce ne fût pas une inconséquence dangereuse." From the report of Madame Campan, quoted by Félix Gaiffe, *Le mariage de Figaro* (Paris: Librarie Nizet, 1956), p. 52.

74. "Quel calculateur peut évaluer la force et la longueur du levier qu'il faudrait, de nos jours,

pour élever jusqu'au Théâtre l'oeuvre sublime de *Tartuffe?*" (Beaumarchais, *Théâtre complet*, p. 234).

75. Elizabeth J. MacArthur, "Embodying the Public Sphere: Censorship and the Reading Subject in Beaumarchais's *Mariage de Figaro*," *Representations* 61 (1998): 58.

76. "Cette défense du Roi parut une atteinte à la liberté publique. Toutes les espérances déçues excitèrent le mécontentement à tel point que les mots d'oppression et de tyrannie ne furent jamais prononcés, dans les jours qui précédèrent la chute du trone, avec plus de passion et de véhémence" (quoted by Gaiffe, *Le mariage de Figaro*, p. 63).

77. "On n'obtient ni grand pathétique, ni profonde moralité, ni bon et vrai comique, au Théâtre, sans des situations fortes et qui naissent toujours d'une disconvenance sociale" (Beaumarchais, *Théâtre complet*, p. 234).

78. Alain Bourreau, *Le droit de cuissage: La fabrication d'un mythe (XIIIe–XXe siècle)* (Paris: Éditions Alban Michel, 1995).

79. Noël Salomon, *Recherches sur le thème paysan dans la "comedia" au temps de Lope de Vega* (Bordeaux: Institut d'études Ibériques et Ibéro-Américaines de l'Université de Bordeaux, 1965), pp. 883–88.

80. This attenuation—the avoidance of abduction, rape, or even successful seduction, notable in *Le mariage de Figaro*, as in French bourgeois drama generally—was due to the French "delicacy" Mercier mentioned (*Théâtre complet*, p. 9). For unattenuated versions, one must look outside France, to such works as Richardson's *Clarissa*, Lessing's two bourgeois dramas, *Miss Sara Sampson* (1755) and *Emilia Galotti* (1772), or Friedrich Schiller's *Kabale und Liebe* (1783; *Intrigue and Love*). Yet what Erich Auerbach (following H. A. Korff) says of Schiller's play, that it was "a dagger thrust to the heart of absolutism," is true as well of French bourgeois drama, despite the attenuation of its plots. The "connection of sentimental middle-class realism with idealistic politics and concern for human rights" that in Auerbach's view is not finally made "until the *Sturm und Drang* period" is, I would contend, already well established in the work of Diderot, Mercier, and Beaumarchais and is clearly adumbrated, with no dramatic attenuation at all, though without a conscious revolutionary intent, as early as Heywood's *Edward IV* and the Spanish peasant drama of Lope and Calderón. See Auerbach, *Mimesis: The Representation of Reality in Western Literature*, trans. Willard R. Trask (Princeton: Princeton University Press, 1953), pp. 438–40. On the similar political effect of Richardson's *Clarissa*, see Terry Eagleton, *The Rape of Clarissa: Writing, Sexuality, and Class Struggle in Samuel Richardson* (Minneapolis: University of Minnesota Press, 1982).

81. "[U]n malheur domestique," "l'humanité souffrante," "[le] malheur d'un honnête homme," "un événement malheureux, arrivé parmi nous," and "celui dont on enlève la femme, la fille, l'honneur ou le bien" (Beaumarchais, *Théâtre complet*, pp. 8, 10, 12, 15, and 16).

82. Gustave Flaubert, quoted by MacArthur ("Embodying the Public Sphere," p. 57). This view was shared by others closer to the Revolution. Danton is reported to have said that "Figaro killed the nobility" (Figaro a tué la noblesse) and Napoleon that "*Le mariage de Figaro* is already the revolution in action" (*Le mariage de Figaro*, c'est déjà la révolution en action). Danton and Napoleon are quoted in Frédéric Grendel, *Beaumarchais ou la calomnie* (Paris: Flammarion, 1973), p. 413. For a careful assessment of the relation of Beaumarchais's play to the Revolution, see Claude Petitfrère, *Le scandale du 'Mariage de Figaro': Prélude à la Révolution française?* (Brussels: Éditions Complexe, 1989).

83. The full quotation from which the charges against both *Le barbier de Seville* and *Le mariage de Figaro* are taken reads as follows: "Ainsi dans *le Barbier de Seville* je n'avais qu'ébranlé l'État; dans ce nouvel essai, plus infâme et plus séditieux, je le renverserais de fond en comble" (Beaumarchais, *Théâtre complet*, p. 238).

84. Robert Darnton, *The Forbidden Best-Sellers of Pre-Revolutionary France* (New York: W. W. Norton, 1995), p. 122.

85. Though it includes neither a libertine nor a tyrant, Michel Sedaine's *Philosophe sans le savoir* nicely turns on an implicit condemnation of the old regime's prejudice against the bourgeois

and the Protestant. The "philosopher" of its title, Monsieur Vanderk, though by birth a member of the ancient French nobility of the sword, adopts both the name and the profession of a Dutch merchant, and he shows his enlightened views by honoring the credit of a Protestant officer others had disdained.

86. The sentences—or rather sentence fragments—from which these phrases are taken read as follows in *Le fils naturel:* "Mais s'il paraissait aujourd'hui . . . parmis nous . . . un monstre, tel qu'il en a produit dans les temps de ténèbres, où sa fureur et ses illusions arrosaient de sang cette terre . . . qu'on vît ce monstre s'avancer au plus grand de ses crimes, en invoquant le secours du Ciel, . . . et tenant la loi de son Dieu d'une main, et de l'autre un poignard, préparer aux peuples de longs regrets . . . ." (Diderot, *Oeuvres complètes*, 10.65; ellipses in the original). Constance, the character who speaks these lines, points to Enlightenment books and plays as the great force that has kept this monster at bay.

87. J. H. Elliott, *Spain and Its World, 1500–1700: Selected Essays* (New Haven: Yale University Press, 1989), p. 108.

88. See, for example, Mercier, *Du théâtre*, pp. 8, 29, and 226.

89. Simon Schama, *Citizens: A Chronicle of the French Revolution* (New York: Vintage Books, 1989), pp. 123–82.

90. "Je suis un citoyen, c'est-à-dire je ne suis ni un courtisan, ni un abbé, ni un gentilhomme, ni un financier, ni un favori, ni rien de ce qu'on appelle puissance aujourd'hui. Je suis un citoyen, c'est-à-dire quelque chose de tout nouveau, quelque chose d'inconnu, d'inouï en France. Je suis un citoyen, c'est-à-dire ce que vous devriez être depuis deux cents ans, ce que vous serez dans vingt ans peut-être!" Quoted by Roger Caratini, *Dictionnaire des personnages de la Révolution* (Paris: Le Pré aux Clercs, 1988), p. 76.

91. In a letter dated August 4, 1789, Beaumarchais signs himself "Caron de Beaumarchais, soldat citoyen de la garde bourgeoise de Paris" (Grendel, *Beaumarchais ou la calomnie*, p. 468).

92. Albert Soboul, *Dictionnaire historique de la Révolution française* (Paris: Presses Universitaires de France, 1989), p. 735; and Darnton, *Forbidden Best-Sellers*, p. 63.

93. ". . . tendante . . . à détuire l'autorité royale, à établir l'esprit d'indépendance et de révolte et . . . à élever les fondements de l'erreur, de la corruption des moeurs, de l'irréligion et de l'incrédulité." Quoted by Robert Darnton, *The Business of Enlightenment: A Publishing History of the Encyclopédie, 1775–1800* (Cambridge: Harvard University Press, 1979), p. 10.

94. On Linguet, see Stavan, "Des adaptations françaises de *L'alcalde de Zalamea*," p. 322; on Restif de la Bretonne, see Bryson, *The Chastened Stage*, pp. 80–90; and on Sade, see Hayes, *Identity and Ideology*, pp. 105–40.

EPILOGUE

1. Nancy Armstrong, *Desire and Domestic Fiction: A Political History of the Novel* (New York: Oxford University Press, 1987), p. 3. Armstrong presents her own account of the prehistory of modern domesticity and the novel in a book coauthored by Leonard Tennenhouse, *The Imaginary Puritan: Literature, Intellectual Labor, and the Origins of Personal Life* (Berkeley: University of California Press, 1992). In the work of defining the representational sphere of bourgeois domesticity, Armstrong and Tennenhouse's master narrative, the North American story of Indian captivity, interestingly supplements the Old World story of aristocratic oppression central to this book.

2. Louis Sébastien Mercier, *Du théâtre ou nouvel essai sur l'art dramatique* (1773; reprinted Hildesheim: Georg Olms Verlag, 1973), p. 10.

3. Armstrong, *Desire and Domestic Fiction*, p. 3.

4. Jean-Jacques Rousseau, *Politics and the Arts: Letter to M. D'Alembert on the Theatre*, trans. Allan Bloom (Glencoe, IL: Free Press, 1960), pp. 47 and 49. I have changed Bloom's "maid" to "governess" in the last sentence. This seems closer to what Rousseau means here by *bonne*—that is, *une bonne d'enfants*. Thanks to Elizabeth MacArthur for alerting me to this distinction.

5. On Mercier's authoritarian and patriarchal misogynism, see Julie C. Hayes, "Changing the

System: Mercier's Ideological Appropriations of Diderot," *Studies in Eighteenth-Century Culture* 18 (1988): 343–57. In *The Republic of Letters: A Cultural History of the French Enlightenment* (Ithaca: Cornell University Press, 1994), Dena Goodman describes the importance of women in the salon culture of eighteenth-century Paris but also the attacks on that culture, and especially on the place of women in it, by Rousseau and his followers.

6. Jane Tompkins, "Me and My Shadow," in *The Intimate Critique: Autobiographical Literary Criticism,* ed. Diane P. Freedman, Olivia Frey, and Frances Murphy Zauhar (Durham: Duke University Press, 1993), p. 25. The italics are Tompkins's. For an account of the pre-Revolutionary moment in France—and its long aftermath—that stresses the continuing exclusion of women, see Juliet Flower MacCannell, *The Regime of the Brother: After the Patriarchy* (London: Routledge, 1991).

7. Tony Tanner, *Adultery in the Novel: Contract and Transgression* (Baltimore: Johns Hopkins Press, 1979). Like Armstrong's, Tanner's book begins in the mid-eighteenth century, just about where my book leaves off. Armstrong's starting point is Richardson; Tanner's is Rousseau.

8. For a witty and wonderfully suggestive review of the multiple meanings of *home*—including George Bernard Shaw's definition of it as "the girl's workhouse and the woman's prison"—see John Hollander's "What You Mean by Home," in his collection of essays, *The Work of Poetry* (New York: Columbia University Press, 1997), pp. 64–77. Thanks to Heather Dubrow for drawing my attention to this essay.

9. Jürgen Habermas provides a brief but trenchant account of these issues in *The Structural Transformation of the Public Sphere: An Inquiry into a Category of Bourgeois Society,* trans. Thomas Burger (Cambridge: MIT Press, 1991), pp. 43–51. It is precisely as an element in what Habermas calls "the bourgeois public sphere" that the plays and paintings we have been examining had their effect. As a subject of representation, the "private," nonaristocratic home was made actively public and even political. In the terms I have been using, the home was, as a result of its prominent inclusion in the public sphere, made part of the "history" from which it had been so ignominiously expelled.

10. *The Tragedy of Master Arden of Faversham,* ed. M. L. Wine (London: Methuen, 1973), p. 11.

11. Set in early fourteenth-century Scotland, *Braveheart* makes the medieval Scots, including its central character, the Scottish rebel William Wallace, victims of an English "revival" of the *jus primae noctis.* Reports that Gibson's film have fed Scottish nationalist fervor seem to be confirmed by a photograph that ran in my local newspaper the day after the election for a Scottish parliament, the first in nearly three hundred years. It showed a Scots nationalist garbed and painted like Gibson's Wallace.

12. *The Best Revenge,* shown at the Santa Barbara International Film Festival (March 1997). This film begins by alerting its audience to issues of power and sexuality with a conspicuous allusion to David and Bathsheba, and it gives a nice twist to the usual plot by having the Salvadoran victim invade the home of his American oppressor and steal away the oppressor's wife, who years earlier, as the victim's fiancée, had been abducted by the oppressor from the victim's home. *Braveheart* does something similar when it has William Wallace, whose wife had been sexually attacked and then murdered by English soldiers, make love with the daughter-in-law of his ultimate oppressor, King Edward I. If one follows the implications of Mel Gibson's history, William Wallace fathered the future Edward III. For both films, sexual payback is "the best revenge."